# An Introduction to the
# Old Testament Poetic Books

### Revised and Expanded

# AN
# INTRODUCTION
## TO THE
# OLD TESTAMENT
# POETIC
# BOOKS

### REVISED AND EXPANDED

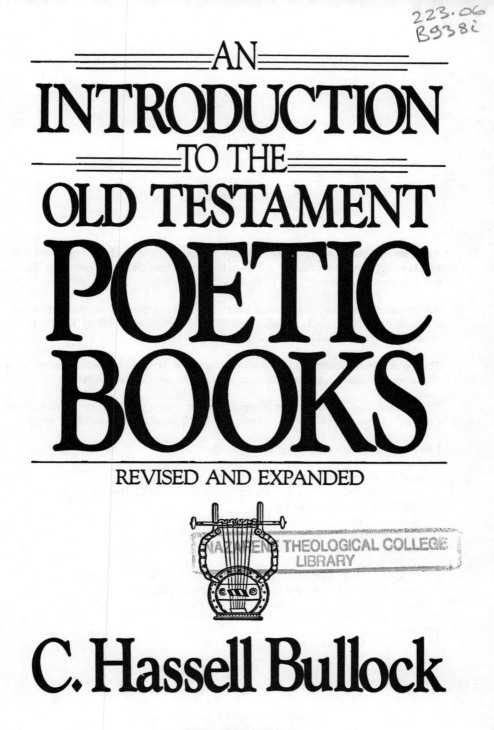

# C. Hassell Bullock

**MOODY PRESS**
**CHICAGO**

© 1988 by
THE MOODY BIBLE INSTITUTE
OF CHICAGO

All Scripture quotations, unless noted otherwise, are from the *New American Standard Bible,* © 1960, 1962, 1963, 1968, 1971, 1972, 1973, 1975, and 1977 by The Lockman Foundation, and are used by permission.

The use of selected references from various versions of the Bible in this publication does not necessarily imply publisher endorsement of the versions in their entirety.

The standard used for Hebrew transliteration is the system presented by J. Weingreen, *Practical Grammar for Classical Hebrew*, 2d. ed. (Oxford: Clarendon, 1959), pp. 1, 4.

**Library of Congress Cataloging in Publication**

Bullock, C. Hassell.
    An introduction to the Old Testament poetic books / by C. Hassell
Bullock. — Rev. and expanded.
      p.    cm.
    Bibliography: p.
    Includes indexes.
    ISBN 0-8024-4141-6
    1. Bible. O.T.—Criticism, interpretation, etc. 2. Hebrew
poetry, Biblical—History and criticism. 3. Wisdom literature-
-History and criticism. I. Title.
BS1405.2.B84   1988
223'.061—dc19                                88-15300
                                                        CIP

1 2 3 4 5 6 Printing/BC/Year 92 91 90 89 88

*Printed in the United States of America*

*To Rhonda*
*". . . her worth is far above jewels."*
(Prov. 31:10)

# CONTENTS

# PREFACE TO THE
# SECOND EDITION

To all of those who have used the first edition of this book I express my sincere appreciation. Learning is progressive, and the intervening years since the book's publication have been a time of thinking and rethinking the contents of this work. While I have not made substantive changes in the format, except for the two introductory chapters, nor have I substantially altered many of the ideas contained in it, I have attempted to sharpen some of them as a result of my ongoing experience in the setting of a college classroom and of an active life in the world and the church. A sense of the power of this literature has continued to grow in me, and I am more convinced than ever that if studied and applied seriously to modern life, its effect will be no less than transforming. That remains the goal of this book, even though its purpose is largely academic. My discussion of wisdom and the Psalms in Chapter 2 is an attempt to apply the theology of this material to modern life.

In all honesty, I would like to acknowledge that my thinking on a few matters has not yet matured to the point that I can say, "Here I stand." I am not hesitant to call attention to the Song of Songs, where I have allowed the literal interpretation (including my satirical interpretation) to stand. Yet, while I have on the one hand tried to take into account the recent studies of the Egyptian love songs and their importance for the Song, I have opened the door wider to the allegorical method in deference to two thousand years of interpretation, including its significance for the canonization of that book.

Books are never really finished, I suppose, and that is a good reason to issue a revised edition. Those who have studied the Talmud know that every new tractate begins on page two. An old explanation of this practice is that it reminds us from the beginning that no one will ever know it all. If the midrashic method can still be permitted (how impoverished we would be without it!), I might suggest that the frequent practice of publishers to bind blank pages at the end of a book can be a reminder, quite unintended of course, that there is no end of knowledge. Much yet remains to be learned and written. I submit this revised edition as another stage in that process.

I wish to thank Moody Press, particularly Messrs. Garry Knussman and Dana Gould, for permitting and encouraging this revised edition, as well as the editorial staff who have worked so congenially with me in the past. Special thanks is due to Mr. Robert Ramey whose conscientious editing of this revised edition has contributed many improvements to it. Appreciation is also appropriate to Miss Valori Hughes, my teacher's assistant, who has helped me complete this task. Finally, I offer thanks to Mr. Don Patrick who, as loyal friend and expert bibliographer, has assisted my research and collected the bibliography for this volume.

And to God be the glory!

# PREFACE TO THE
# FIRST EDITION

The teacher and student share a mutual and complementary relationship quite unlike any other. Qoheleth expressed it well—the teacher's words are like "goads," whereas the students who master them are like "well-driven nails" (Eccles. 12:11). If the astute teacher seeks to prick the conscience and pry open the mind of his students, it is only in the interest of producing a more stable and productive life. A more stable individual ultimately means a more stable society. The wisdom teachers, therefore, began with the smallest social unit, the individual, and sought to transmit their thought to the wider spectrum of the social order. Motivated by the "fear of the Lord," and driven by the desire to understand human life and live in harmony with the world, the wisdom sages engaged both mind and heart in the effort to comprehend.

This special teacher-student relationship, exemplified so beautifully in the ancient wisdom schools, has both motivated and nurtured the effort here represented. Sharing, it is hoped, the motivation and compulsion of the wisdom teachers, I undertook the task of writing a volume that would both introduce the five poetic books, only three of which are technically wisdom literature (Job, Prov., Eccles.), and also provide significant guidelines for interpretation. Therefore, in addition to the standard introductory matters, I have devoted several pages to hermeneutical issues on each book and provided an analysis of the book itself to guide the student through the material. This analysis in no way is intended to substitute for the commentary and broader treatment of each book. Rather it is designed to provide the reader with an ingress to the biblical books and the secondary literature on them. Further, the introduction to this volume includes an extended discussion of the cognate literature in the ancient Near East in order to set the biblical material in its literary context. If the nonoriented student at first finds that section laborious, he should come to a greater appreciation as the study takes shape.

So much energy and time have had to be devoted to this task that I find at the end of the process that, rather than indebting others to me for this effort, I have become a great debtor to those who have aided, encouraged, and tolerated the undertaking. My gratitude is hereby expressed to the Wheaton College Alumni Association for a summer stipend to support this project. Deserved appreciation goes also to Marian Filkin, Jane Marston, Karen Mason, and Judy Klopfenstein, all of whom have graciously typed portions of the manuscript in its various stages. Special gratitude is extended to Donna Kozarski who sympathetically read, reread, organized, and typed the entire manuscript, and to John Rollwitz, Bruce Schut, and Ken Hawley, teacher's assistants, for their help in research and proofreading. I must not fail to remember also the many students, all of whom must necessarily remain nameless, though well remembered in my own mind and heart, who have passed through my classes and helped me to understand. My sympathy goes to Scott and Rebecca, my dear children, who have played around my typewriter while I worked instead of having their father on an adventure more exciting to them. And to my wife, Rhonda, who has been more on the side of tolerating my neglect of family and home, but whose tolerating is indistinguishable from the love that motivates it, I lovingly dedicate this book. Finally to the God and Father of our Lord Jesus Christ, I submit the words of petition and praise:

*Open my eyes, that I may behold*
*Wonderful things from Thy law.*
(Ps. 119:18)

# ABBREVIATIONS

| | |
|---|---|
| AJSL | *American Journal of Semitic Languages and Literature* |
| ANET | *Ancient Near Eastern Texts Relating to the Old Testament* |
| ANET Supp. | *Ancient Near East: Supplementary Texts and Pictures Relating to the Old Testament* |
| ASTI | *Annual of the Swedish Theological Institute* |
| BASOR | *Bulletin of the American Society of Oriental Research* |
| Bib | *Biblica* |
| CanJTh | *Canadian Journal of Theology* |
| CBQ | *Catholic Biblical Quarterly* |
| ChQ | *Church Quarterly* |
| EQ | *Evangelical Quarterly* |
| ExT | *Expository Times* |
| HTR | *Harvard Theological Review* |
| HUCA | *Hebrew Union College Annual* |
| Int | *Interpretation* |
| JAAR | *Journal of the American Academy of Religion* |
| JBL | *Journal of Biblical Literature* |
| JSS | *Journal of Semitic Studies* |
| Jud | *Judaism* |
| KJV | *King James Version* |
| LXX | *Septuagint* |
| NASB | *New American Standard Bible* |
| NIV | *New International Version* |
| NovTest | *Novum Testamentum* |
| NTS | *New Testament Studies* |
| PTR | *Princeton Theological Review* |
| RSV | *Revised Standard Version* |
| SEAJT | *Southeast Asia Journal of Theology* |
| SJT | *Scottish Journal of Theology* |
| TGUOS | *Transactions of the Glasgow University Oriental Society* |

| | |
|---|---|
| **VT** | *Vetus Testamentum* |
| **WIANE** | *Wisdom in Israel and in the Ancient Near East* |
| **WJT** | *Westminster Journal of Theology* |
| **ZAW** | *Zeitschrift für die alttestamentliche Wissenschaft* |

# 1

# INTRODUCTION

The Old Testament books considered in this volume contain some of the most potent literature of human history, and the ideas they treat are among the most cogent that the human heart has entertained.

These books are not historically oriented. In fact, with the exception of the Psalms, they are relatively devoid of historical allusions. But while they do not reflect upon historical events, they are alive with the spirit of history. They grasp for and grapple with those essential concepts that set the Hebrew faith apart from that of its neighbors and insure its survival in a pantheistic, power-greedy world.

Reflecting the essential theology of the Pentateuch, these books in general do not seek to convey directly God's word to man, as do the Prophets (e.g., "thus says the Lord"), but they entertain the questions that arise in the presence of the divine imperative. In part, the spokesmen in these five books speak for man to God (esp. in Job and many of the psalms), in contrast to the Prophets, who normally speak for God to man. Yet the book of Ecclesiastes is more a human monologue than a dialogue between man and God, whereas the Song of Songs is even more anthropocentric.

Moreover, they breathe a certain universality. The problem of suffering, the conscience marred by sin, the transience of human life, and the passionate love of woman and man, to mention only a few of the matters dealt with in these books, cut across national and ethnic lines to include all of the human race. The spokesmen in these books formulate questions that have lain in man's subconscious mind, often without his having had courage to bring them to the surface.

The courageous spirit of Job, Ecclesiastes, and many of the psalms, therefore, is another characteristic of this literature. It is marked frequently by a mood of challenge and skepticism, saying things that are rooted deeply in man's being. These books focus on man's reflections on God and His response rather than on God's search for man.

Yet the divine Spirit hovers over man's effort to understand, to figure out his world, to fathom the meaning of his relationship to God. The theological orientation toward creation in wisdom literature is not coincidental. For to unravel the meaning of human life will lead one all the way back to its beginning. The individual and personal nature of the books that we undertake to study is evidence of the attention given in the Old Testament to the importance of the individual to God. He began the race with an individual, and His love continues to be applied personally as well as corporately. One might read the Pentateuch and see only a faint shadow of himself reflected there. The historical books may overwhelm him with facts and events. The Prophets, by some mere chance, may pass him by with their deep convictions and concerns about their own societies and world. But the poetic books will find him wherever he is.

## THE POETIC BOOKS

The five books known as the Poetic Books are found in the third division of the Hebrew Bible, which is called the "Writings," or *Kethubim*.[1] The Greek language has given this division the title *Hagiographa* (sacred writings). The term "Poetic Books" obviously points to the poetic nature of the contents, even though Ecclesiastes is included and is written in an elevated prosaic style that only at times has a metrical pattern (e.g., 11:7–12:8).

The Masoretes of the Medieval Age grouped Job, Proverbs, and Psalms together by giving a special system of poetic accentuation to these three books, mnemonically called "The Book of Truth" because in Hebrew the first letter of each of these books taken together spelled *'emeth* (truth). The other two books of the five, Ecclesiastes and the Song of Songs, were included in a special subgroup of the Writings called the *Five Megilloth* ("scrolls"), namely, Song of Songs, Ruth, Lamentations, Ecclesiastes, and Esther. The purpose of this grouping was liturgical, for each book was read at an important Jewish festival, a practice that continues to this day.

The order of the Five Megilloth follows the order of the festivals to which they are assigned: Song of Songs (Passover), Ruth (Pentecost), Lamentations (Fast of the Ninth of Ab, commemorating the destruction of both Temples), Ecclesiastes (Feast of Tabernacles), and Esther (Purim). The reading of the Song of Songs during the Passover celebration alludes to the spiritual interpretation of the book that was normative in ancient Judaism, and that emphasized the love between the Lord and Israel. Since the Passover commemorated the formalization of that special relationship, the Song seemed appropriate. The reading of the

---

1. The Hebrew Bible has these three divisions:
   I. Torah (Pentateuch)
   II. Prophets
      A. Former Prophets (Joshua, Judges, Samuel, Kings)
      B. Latter Prophets (Isaiah, Jeremiah, Ezekiel, and the Book of the Twelve Prophets)
   III. Writings

book of Ecclesiastes on the Festival of Tabernacles, however, seems inconsistent with the great joy of that feast. On this matter Victor Reichert remarks:

> The juxtaposition of piety and scepticism, irreconcilable as they may appear, seems to belong to the whole paradox of the Jewish mind. Faith and Reason write one upon the other in the palimpsest of our past. Perhaps it was to strike the balance of sanity that the Fathers of the Synagogue chose the recital of Ecclesiastes, with its melancholy refrain *Vanity of vanities, all is vanity*, on the Festival of Tabernacles when the Jew is commanded to rejoice. At all events, it is hard to escape the judgment that the major emphasis of Jewish thinking has indeed been that of setting our shoulders joyously to the world's wheel. That we have spared ourselves some unhappiness by, beforehand, slipping the Book of Ecclesiastes beneath our arm, seems likewise true.[2]

The Greek Septuagint placed all the poetic books after the historical writings and before the Prophets in the following order: Psalms, Proverbs, Ecclesiastes, Song of Songs, and Job. The Latin Vulgate set Job at the head of the list rather than at the end, thus giving an order that the English versions have followed. This order evidently was dictated by chronological considerations. Since Job was considered to have lived in the patriarchal times, the book of Job would precede Psalms, which was written largely by David several centuries after the Patriarchal Age. The last three books follow the Psalms by virtue of their association with David's son Solomon. Thus Proverbs, Ecclesiastes, and the Song of Songs have been grouped together as a Solomonic collection.

We must keep in mind as we approach the study of these books that the present order of the biblical books does not necessarily carry the authority of divine inspiration. Divine inspiration applies to content only. Rather, the order is the work of various editors in the history of transmission, as the varying arrangements of the versions and manuscripts testify.

Three of the five Poetic Books constitute the wisdom literature of the Old Testament: Job, Proverbs, and Ecclesiastes. While most of the book of Psalms and possibly the Song of Songs cannot be strictly classified as "wisdom" in the technical sense, they certainly have affinities with it. As our subsequent discussion will show, several of the psalms may be classified as wisdom psalms, and the Song of Songs shares the didactic nature of wisdom literature as well as its literary form (i.e., a song). Therefore, we are no more inaccurate referring to this collection of five books as "wisdom literature" than we are by attributing to it the title "Poetic Books." Indeed the bulk of the material truly belongs in the category of wisdom. Thus we may better understand all these books in the context of the wisdom movement and literature in ancient Israel and the Near East.

2. Victor E. Reichert and A. Cohen, "Ecclesiastes," *The Five Megilloth*, p. 105.

## WISDOM AS A PERSONAL DYNAMIC

Biblical wisdom was a dynamic in ancient Israel that operated in three dimensions: the personal, universal, and literary. The personal dimension was characterized by both theological and practical categories. The universal dimension dealt with the ultimate categories of theology, explaining wisdom as an attribute of God Himself. The literary dimension was merely the vehicle of the wisdom movement, inscripturating the propositions and precepts of wisdom for posterity. We shall further explain this three-dimensional nature of wisdom.

### IN PERSONAL SKILLS

An examination of those passages in the Old Testament that use the noun "wisdom" (*hochmāh*) and the adjective "wise" (*hāchām*) reveals that they were used even in reference to practical arts and skills. These terms were applied to those artisans who designed and constructed the Tabernacle: Bezalel, the architect of the Tabernacle (Ex. 35:30–36:1), the craftsmen who made Aaron's priestly garments (Ex. 28:3), and the women weavers (Ex. 35:25-26). Of Bezalel and Oholiab it is said that the Lord "filled them with skill [lit., *hochmah* of heart] to perform every work of an engraver and of a designer and of an embroiderer" (Ex. 35:35). The application of these terms to the practical arts is even broader than the Tabernacle narrative. Goldsmiths (Jer. 10:9), sailors (Ps. 107:27; Ezek. 27:8), women skilled in lamentation (Jer. 9:17), magicians and soothsayers (Gen. 41:8; Isa. 44:25), and military strategists and statesmen (Isa. 10:13; 29:14; Jer. 49:7) share these terms to designate their particular skills. Moreover, wisdom is closely associated with the musical arts in 1 Kings 4:32, for the product of God's gift of wisdom to Solomon included songs as well as proverbs.

### IN PERSONAL PHILOSOPHY

Yet this use of the terms "wisdom" and "wise" does not get to the heart of the personal dimension of wisdom. The nature of language is to develop a broad spectrum of meaning for a single word, and the above examples illustrate the use of our terms for the technical arts and skills without actually opening up the essential meaning of wisdom as it is used in the wisdom literature of the Bible. As one reads through that material, one quickly recognizes that wisdom was a *personal life dynamic* that enabled one to assimilate, sort, and categorize the elements and issues of life so as to provide a meaningful synthesis. Its wide span encompasses the struggle of a righteous man to understand his suffering and the limp efforts of a lazy man to overcome his sloth. We might begin with examples out of Proverbs regarding the basic relationships within the family unit, which are frequently the subject of this literature, both from the standpoint of the parents' responsibility to their children (Prov. 13:22, 24; 22:6) and the children's to their parents (1:8-9; 15:5). The stability of the family is further assured by admonitions that highly esteem marriage (12:4; 19:14; 31:10-31) and warn against adultery and sexual promiscuity (5:1-14).

Yet the scope of wisdom reaches outside the family unit to regulate personal and social behavior that builds a stable and productive community. Moral virtues such as self-discipline (10:17; 13:13), temperate speech (10:19; 11:12), and honesty (15:27; 16:11), and vices such as slander (10:18; 19:5), envy (23:17-18), and gluttony (23:1-3), are subjects of wisdom's regulatory function. The scope broadens to include advice for the people's relationship to the king (25:6-7) and the king's to the people (14:28; 25:4-5), and justice in the courts (24:23). This list could be greatly extended.

While these principles and regulations describe the horizontal scale of ancient Israelite life, wisdom admonished her patrons on the vertical aspect of their lives as well. The Lord's sovereign will was uppermost in the world, and the individual was the object of His careful guidance:

> The mind of man plans his way,
> But the Lord directs his steps.
> > (Prov. 16:9)

> Many are the plans in a man's heart,
> But the counsel of the Lord, it will stand.
> > (Prov. 19:21)

Human ingenuity has its place, but only God can assure success in life:

> Commit your works to the Lord,
> And your plans will be established.
> > (Prov. 16:3)

> Trust in the Lord with all your heart,
> And do not lean on your own understanding.
> In all your ways acknowledge Him,
> And He will make your paths straight.
> > (Prov. 3:5-6)

Indeed, the undergirding notion of the wisdom-controlled life is the "fear of the Lord." It is a phrase that has layers of meaning. The ground layer may be understood as a *personal attitude* or *disposition* toward the Lord, illustrated by the analogy of one's fear of the king:

> My son, fear the Lord and the king;
> Do not associate with those who are given to change;
> For their calamity will rise suddenly,
> And who knows the ruin that comes from both of them?
>                                                   (Prov. 24:21-22)

At the risk of confusing the issue by modern use (or abuse) of theological terminology, the "fear of the Lord" denotes piety in the most positive sense of the word, a spiritual disposition that may be described as a proper relationship to God and one's neighbor. It is wisdom's comprehensive term for religion.[3]

A second layer, not unrelated to the first, is that of moral virtue or appropriate behavior. Job is described in these terms as one who was "blameless, upright, fearing God, and *turning away from evil*" (Job 1:1, emphasis added; cf. also Prov. 8:13). "Fearing God" and "turning away from evil" are parallel expressions, the second expanding on the first. The book of Proverbs, as seen above, provides ample proof that moral virtues are an important part of the personal portrait of one who feared the Lord. Admittedly the revelation at Sinai is not consciously wisdom's mode of communicating the will of God, but the theological/moral principles of the books of Proverbs and Job are those of the Decalogue, which calls for sexual purity, honor of parents, integrity toward one's neighbor, and so on.[4]

A third layer intermeshes with the second. The knowledge of human frailty and divine strength is endemic to the fear of the Lord (Prov. 3:5-7). It is a balanced perspective on God and man.

It would not be inaccurate to say that comprehensively the fear of the Lord is a world view that attempts to synthesize the elements of human life and work. It is an "educational standard" (compare our objective standard of research) that gives balance to the individual as he relates both to his world and God.

Henri Blocher contends that all three wisdom books as they have come to us are a witness to the theological premise that the fear of the Lord is the principle of wisdom. The "fear of the Lord" forms a literary *inclusion* in Proverbs, for the book opens with the statement that "the fear of the Lord is the beginning of knowledge" (1:7a), and concludes with the portrait of the virtuous woman who personifies the fear of the Lord (31:30). Moreover, the author of Job begins the book by describing his hero as the paragon of wisdom in terms of his fear of the Lord (1:1) and underscores that character portrait with God's affirmation at the end of the poem on wisdom (chap. 28, note v. 28). Likewise Ecclesiastes'

---

3. Bernard Bamberger, "Fear and Love of God in the Old Testament," HUCA 6 (1929):43-47.
4. Brevard S. Childs, *Old Testament Theology in a Canonical Context* (Philadelphia: Fortress, 1985), p. 64.

assessment of human responsibility is to "fear God and keep His commandments" (Eccles. 12:13).[5]

## WISDOM AS A UNIVERSAL DYNAMIC

In addition to being a personal dynamic, wisdom is also a universal dynamic. This second dimension of wisdom is readily seen in Proverbs 8:22-31. Some scholars believe that this passage presents wisdom as an hypostasis, having an existence distinct from God though expressing His nature, much like wisdom in the apocryphal *Wisdom of Solomon* (Wisd. of Sol. 1:6-7; 6:12-24; 7:1–8:18) or the Logos in John's gospel. The critical word is *qānāh* (Prov. 8:22), which generally means "to acquire," or "to possess," but in fewer instances has the sense of "create" (Deut. 32:6; Ps. 139:13). The sense of "possess" is preferable in the context because the Lord is the Creator and wisdom is merely present with Him prior to and during His work of creation.[6]

It is my opinion that Solomon seeks to personify a divine attribute. Yet, in this way he asserts that wisdom is an emanation of the divine life, much as one would understand love to be an emanation of the life of God. Whereas law and prophecy admonished Israel to turn to *God* for life, wisdom personified admonished individuals to turn to *her* and receive life. This further supports the view that wisdom was a symbol of a divine attribute. The Hebrew mind would not entertain a dualism between *God* as source-of-life versus *wisdom* as source-of-life. The effect of this argument is to connect wisdom both to God and to the created world in a way that unites God, people, and the world in an inseverable bond.

God addressed Israel through the law by commandment and precept, through the prophets by His word, and through the sages by wisdom. As a principle of revelation, wisdom was the "rationale of the cosmos,"[7] imparting understanding to mankind. Without it the world and human life would be devoid of meaning. Wisdom is the all-pervasive presence of God that permeates the physical universe and human social order (Prov. 2:1-15; 8:22). It is God's communicative word written in nature and human experience.

While redemptive history is not a conscious rubric of wisdom literature in the Bible, the sovereign control of God in the universe nevertheless lies behind the literature, and this inevitably involves history, for God is the originator of the dynamic force that moves history and nature (Job 9:4; 11:6; 12:13; 32:8;

---

5. Henri Blocher, "The Fear of the Lord as the 'Principle' of Wisdom," *The Tyndale Bulletin* 28 (1977):3-4.
6. R. B. Y. Scott, *Proverbs and Ecclesiastes*, pp. 71-72.
7. Walther Eichrodt, *Theology of the Old Testament*, 2:89.

37:16; Prov. 2:6; 8:22-31). This implicit concept came to fruition in the Wisdom of Solomon where wisdom is depicted as the driving force of history (Wisd. of Sol. 10-19). So critical is God's revelation through wisdom that the individual's posture toward her determines his destiny (Prov. 8:32-36). Just as in the Pentateuch one's response to the law, or in the Prophets one's response to the prophetic word, so in wisdom literature one's response to wisdom, the medium of divine revelation, determines one's happiness and well-being.

## WISDOM AS A LITERARY DYNAMIC

The three wisdom books of the Old Testament (Job, Proverbs, and Ecclesiastes), the wisdom elements of the Psalms,[8] and other wisdom fragments distributed throughout the Old Testament testify to the importance of the wisdom movement in ancient Israel. The literary legacy is as rich in its variety of genres as prophetic literature. In the Old Testament the term *māshāl* is used rather broadly to include a proverb, riddle, or longer composition involving comparisons and analogies. The term itself comes from the verb that means "to be like, compare."

### WISDOM GENRES

More specifically the literary form of the *proverb* was a favorite genre of wisdom literature. It was short and pithy, its effectiveness depending in part upon the concise, witty manner of expressing an idea or truth. It provided the mind with an easily accessible entry into the truth expressed. With only a few words one might recall a truth that could effervesce and effect a change of mind or attitude in a given situation:

> A good name is to be more desired than great riches,
> Favor is better than silver and gold.
> 
> (Prov. 22:1)

This proverb might raise to a level of consciousness a truth that could otherwise be smothered in circumstances where one's action easily endangered one's reputation. Thus one would be diverted from a wrong course. Moreover, the terms of comparison—great riches, silver and gold—further highlight the precious value of one's reputation. Thus both mental accessibility and the impact of the literary form contribute to the effectiveness of the proverb.

The *riddle* was the more enigmatic form of wisdom literature. Its method was to disguise an idea so that the hearers might be confused or challenged to search for its meaning. Samson used this form with the Philistines (Judg. 14:14),

---

8. See p. 136 (on wisdom psalms).

and the Queen of Sheba came to investigate the degree of Solomon's wisdom by testing him with riddles (1 Kings 10:1). Proverbs 1:6 equates riddle and proverb, but no riddle of the classical type found in Judges 14:14 has survived in biblical wisdom literature. Yet Crenshaw makes the interesting suggestion that disintegrated riddles lie behind some of the proverbs.[9]

One clear example of *allegory* can be seen in Ecclesiastes 12:1-7, where old age is described, at least in part, as a deteriorating estate. Elsewhere in the Old Testament the allegory is found in Judges 9:8-15 and Ezekiel 17:2-10.

The *dialogue* is represented *par excellence* by the book of Job. Elsewhere in canonical wisdom literature, however, dialogue is not prominent.

Ecclesiastes 1:12–2:16 takes the form of an *autobiographical narrative* in which the narrator relates his own personal experience.

The *prophetic address* twice becomes the literary form of wisdom's message in Proverbs (1:20-33; 8:1-36). She speaks through the lips of the prophetess. As already suggested, this implies that wisdom and prophecy were not basically antagonistic.

THE ADDRESSEES OF WISDOM

Since wisdom literature was addressed to the individual rather than to corporate society, national interests fell into the background. In this respect the literature is quite different from the Law and the Prophets. Because of this aspect of wisdom, history was not one of the foci of the canonical wisdom writers, although we should not assume that they had no interest in history. Their concern for the past was more philosophical than historical—how does one view the past? They had little concern for writing about historical events. Thus, while the corporate concern of wisdom was in no way primary, it was nevertheless served by pointing the individual in the direction of the good life, which in the long run contributed to the good society.

One of the purposes of wisdom literature was to instruct the young on how to achieve the good life and serve the social order well. In Proverbs the addressees were often the upper-class youth who were potential future leaders. Ecclesiastes addressed itself to the issues that were of concern to the upper class as well—the futility of wealth and pleasure, yet their proper use for life's enjoyment. So the teachers had the responsibility of transferring to their students the moral and cultured life, which involved manners before royalty, personal honor, morality, and many other matters. They sought to equip them for decision making and a life of responsible leadership.

9. In this regard, James L. Crenshaw, "Wisdom," *Old Testament Wisdom*, ed. John H. Hayes (San Antonio: Trinity Univ., 1974), p. 242, draws attention to Proverbs 5:1-6, 15-23; 6:23-24; 16:15; 20:27; 23:27, 29-35; 25:2-3; 27:20. See his helpful discussion of wisdom genres on pp. 229-62.

Yet wisdom was not limited to the upper class. The book of Job, whose main character is wealthy and a leader in his community, nevertheless deals with timeless issues that cut across social structures. Injustice knows no class boundaries. Unmerited suffering is nondiscriminatory.

Ecclesiastes lamented the social oppression of that age, a matter that anyone, indiscriminate of social boundaries, could identify with. The book of Proverbs issued folk proverbs and moral instruction that encompassed the shared experience and concern of people in general. The practicality of wisdom literature in the Old Testament leads us to believe that the common people were attracted to it, even though the wisdom activities of the royal court may have had an elite character not accessible to the commoner. We are left with the impression that Solomon's court was buzzing with wisdom activity (1 Kings 4:29-34). In fact, his reputation for wisdom was the one thing that attracted the Queen of Sheba to make her state visit (1 Kings 10:1-9). Her reaction to what she observed prompted her to speak of the privilege of those who were permanent members of the court: "How blessed are your men, how blessed are these your servants who stand before you continually and hear your wisdom" (1 Kings 10:8).

During the time of Hezekiah, the Judean court was quite alive with wisdom activity as well, for this king was the benefactor who gave inducement to his "men" (evidently a technical term that refers to scholastics; cf. "your men" in the above passage) to collect and edit the Solomonic proverbs (Prov. 25:1).

In view of the emphasis upon marriage, the home, child rearing, and domestic stability and responsibility, it is quite conceivable that wisdom was popularly employed in the family as part of the home educational process.

LIFE SETTING OF WISDOM

With the development of form criticism in the last century came an interest in the real-life situation out of which certain genres of literature arose. This method provided both a way to understand the literature better and to peer through literary peepholes into the sociological structure of the society. From our discussion above, it would naturally follow that the life situation of wisdom was diverse. Granted that the court was at times the place where wisdom thought was sustained and nurtured, wisdom was still not limited to royal circles. We would infer from the down-to-earth nature of wisdom and its interest in the family that the home was one of the life situations where proverbial wisdom was born and nurtured.

THE SCRIBE

It is believed by some scholars that in the monarchical period the "scribe" was an official in the king's court. That he was a very important person is verified by the following texts: 2 Samuel 8:17; 20:25; 2 Kings 12:10; 18:18; 1 Chronicles 27:32; Jeremiah 36:12; 37:15. Quite obviously in a world where the art of writing was not generally shared by all, those who could read and write had vistas of opportunity open to them that were not available to those without those skills. Thus in the monarchical period it is quite possible that scribes and wise men were very closely associated and were sometimes identical. During the postexilic era the scribes were definitely the teachers of wisdom.

## Wisdom, Law, and Prophecy

As a religious phenomenon, wisdom belonged, along with law and prophecy, to the mainstream of religious life. And while the three constituted, for the most part, the total religious experience of ancient Israel, wisdom nevertheless distinguished itself in ways that were not characteristic of law and prophecy.

Prophecy, despite its prominent differences to the law, was not basically a countermovement to law, but rather it reawakened Israel's consciousness to God's covenant demands laid out in the law of Moses. Its impact on Israel is incalculable, and ironically its greatest failure, that is, to turn Israel and Judah away from idolatry and thus avert the historical disasters of 722 and 586 B.C., became its greatest success, especially in regards to Judah. The prophets were there to reassure and comfort the devastated and dispersed people, and the unparalleled return to Palestine in the late sixth century was underwritten by Judah's spiritual return to the Lord. A repentant people recognized at last that the prophets were right. But as for the great historical success, witnessed by the restoration of Judah, prophecy did not last to see Judah's political independence restored. As that era approached,[10] the prophetic voice was no longer heard (1 Macc. 4:46). Yet after the disquieting lull, the momentum that the prophets had imparted to religious experience revived in the form of apocalyptic messages.

The role of wisdom as compared to prophecy has been much discussed. Some scholars infer from Jeremiah 8:8-9 that the prophets came into conflict with wisdom when it attempted to supersede the word of the Lord.[11] They certainly had strong words of condemnation for the sacrificial system when people and priest insisted that sacrifice possessed an intrinsic redemptive value (cf. Isa. 1:10-15; 28:7; Jer. 2:8; 7:22; Hos. 4:4-6; 5:1; Amos 7:10-11; Mic. 6:6-8; Mal. 1:6–2:17). Yet the fact that the prophets attributed wisdom to the Lord (Isa.

---

10. After the return to Judah, which was made possible by the decree of Cyrus in 538 B.C. (Ezra 1:1-4), Palestine was controlled by the Persians, Greeks, and Seleucids in succession, and only in 142 B.C. did the Maccabees succeed in restoring the country to an independent state. That brief period of independence terminated when the Romans took control in 63 B.C.

11. Johannes Lindblom, "Wisdom in the Old Testament Prophets," WIANE, pp. 195-96. McKane takes strong exception to the opinion that the prophets and wise men lived in accord. Rather he urges that their basic presuppositions were so different as to arouse stiff antagonism between the two groups. See esp. pp. 126-30.

28:23-29; Jer. 10:12) and shared its stylistic features (such as the use of the proverb—Isa. 49:24; Jer. 13:12; 15:12; 23:28; 31:29; Ezek. 16:44; 18:2—and common vocabulary[12]) would sustain the position that the prophets did not wholly reject wisdom.

The congenial spirit of wisdom toward prophecy can be seen in Proverbs 8 where wisdom is personified as a prophetess who calls out her message in the city gates. The poem blends the functions of wisdom and prophecy,[13] federating their concerns for truth, justice, and righteousness, and depicts them jointly authorizing kings to reign. Having established the joint function of prophecy and wisdom in the providential maintenance of the world (vv. 4-21), the poem then turns to creation and, by virtue of wisdom's assumption of the prophetic role, associates prophecy, like wisdom, with creation.

Law, which had its institutional structure interrupted by the destruction of the Temple in 586 B.C., was a more pervasive phenomenon than prophecy, for it regulated every facet of Israelite life. Even a temporary cessation of priestly functions could not break its hold on the religious life of the ancient Israelites. Most likely the oral law had already begun to take shape prior to 586,[14] and its ongoing development made room for the establishment of the synagogue in the exilic period. The oral law had the effect of extending the influence of the written law in that it regulated the minute details of daily life. Wisdom moved in a similar direction. While it provided broad theological/philosophical categories for understanding life and its issues (sometimes called *higher wisdom*), it also offered advice for the development of personal behavior, social protocol, and ethical standards (sometimes called *lower wisdom*).

Without imposing a wisdom character upon the creation narrative of Genesis 1, we can see the triune paradigm of wisdom spelled out in Genesis 1:26-27. First, it is *theological*, relating mankind to His Creator: "Let us make man in Our image, according to Our likeness." So we should not be surprised that the "fear of the Lord" is the theological cornerstone of biblical wisdom. Second, it is *ecological*, involving the human race in an inseverable relationship to the natural order: "and let them rule over the fish of the sea and over the birds of the sky and over the cattle and over all the earth, and over every creeping thing that creeps on the earth." Third, it is *sociological*, for it commits human beings to

12. Ibid., pp. 197-204. Cf. these passages where the Lord is presented as the originator of wisdom: Job 9:4; 11:6; 12:13; 32:8; 37:16; Proverbs 2:6; 8:22-31.
13. Compare this joint function with Hosea 12:13 where Israel's existence is attributed to the work of prophecy.
14. See Deuteronomy 1:5, "Moses undertook to expound this law," which may establish the interpretative precedent. Thus the Levitical interpretation of the law, which accompanied Ezra's reading of it in 444 B.C., although sometimes considered the beginning of the oral law, would likely be only evidence that such a function was normative. Ezra's implicit endorsement of this interpretative tradition may have lent greater authority to the oral law.

interpersonal relationships: "male and female He created them." In effect, wisdom, like law but unlike prophecy, sought to develop a comprehensive system of thought and behavior, reaching into every facet of life. We should not think, however, that the two operated on parallel tracks without intersecting (cf. Prov. 6:21-22 and 7:3 to Deut. 6:4-9). Wisdom drew from law, and quite likely law drew from wisdom. They were not mutually exclusive. Perhaps their kindred spirits are best illustrated by the fact that by the time of Jesus ben Sirach the two had become companions.

In a sense, wisdom supplemented the law and cultic practice. It sought to do what the cult could not do—to instruct in those ways with which the Temple and priests were not greatly concerned. Some scholars have described the earliest form of Israelite wisdom, or "old wisdom" as it is sometimes called, as purely secular. William McKane, representing this position, has argued that the wise man was a statesman, or official, and that his "counsel" was not religious at all. He viewed the life situation as the court and old wisdom as entirely secular.[15] Although the sphere of operation of wisdom may seem noncultic, we must agree with von Rad that the basic element of wisdom even in preexilic times was the "fear of God." A purely secular character for wisdom would seem out of keeping with a society where the secular and the sacred were so closely intertwined. Even though the Temple and priestly order did not likely spawn the wisdom movement, it is not very likely either that they were opposed to it. The emphasis within the wisdom books upon keeping the commandments and faithfulness to God and the law would suggest a supportive role for wisdom in relation to the religious institution.[16]

It is doubtful that wisdom as a religious phenomenon was ever intended to stand alone. It undergirded the law, supporting its ethical and juridical principles, while it shared the concerns of the prophets for truth, justice, and righteousness. That is not to suggest, however, that there were no creative tensions or diversity of emphases between wisdom and its religious counterparts.

## Hebrew Poetry

The Hebrew language has an intrinsic musical quality that naturally supports poetic expression. It is basically a language of verbs and nouns, and these are the building blocks for Hebrew poetry. Although there are no strict rules of

15. William McKane, *Prophets and Wise Men*, p. 53. See also Claus Westermann, *What Does the Old Testament Say About God?* pp. 99-100, n. 33; *Genesis* 1:436-67; Walter Zimmerli, *Old Testament Theology in Outline*, pp. 155-66.
16. Gerhard von Rad, *Old Testament Theology*, 1:433-34. Cf. also R. B. Y. Scott, "Priesthood, Prophecy, Wisdom, and the Knowledge of God," JBL 80 (1961):1-15, who proposes that there is evidence for a certain mingling of the functions of prophet, priest, and sage, and that there was a common element in their teaching.

rhyme and meter,[17] the language depends largely upon stress or accent for its rhythmic quality. Theodore H. Robinson has observed:

> The immense strength of its accent gives it a rhythmic movement which we miss in languages which have a slighter stress. The paucity of adjectives adds to the dignity and impressiveness of the style, and the absence of a large stock of abstract terms leads the poet to use imagery and metaphor in its place.[18]

Since the discovery of the Ugaritic texts in 1929 and subsequent years, lively discussion of the poetry of Ugarit and of the Old Testament has taken place. The landmark lectures of Bishop Robert Lowth on Hebrew poetry in 1753 showed *parallelism* to be the primary feature of Hebrew poetry. Lowth identified three types of parallelism: *synonymous, antithetic,* and *synthetic.*[19] In recent years, based in part upon Ugaritic studies, there seems to be developing a scholarly consensus that this scheme was too simplistic. We must speak in terms of both *syntactic* (word order) and *semantic* (word meaning) parallelism. Syntactic parallelism is more difficult to represent in English because the word order is often difficult to render in translation in an intelligible way. Semantic parallelism is easier to illustrate.

In his recent work Robert Alter presents a stimulating discussion of Hebrew poetry and emphasizes the idea that language tends to avoid true synonymity. He speaks in terms of *focusing*, by which the poet introduces a term in one line and then focuses more specifically on it in the next. Sometimes the effect is an intensification of meaning.[20]

We may speak of "units" or "terms" in Hebrew poetry, rather than of metrical feet. Each unit has one major stress, which normally falls on a verb, noun, or adjective, or some other major word in the thought structure that is to be emphasized. Whereas the major words will generally be obvious in English translation, that will not always be the case, nor will a smooth translation always permit placing the accented terms in the order of the Hebrew text (syntactic parallelism). Thus the units have to be determined on the basis of the Hebrew. In the translations below we indicate each thought-unit in hyphenated form. The end of a line (some prefer the term *verset* instead of line) is represented by the single diagonal and the end of a verse by the double diagonal.

Units combine to form a verse-member (sometimes called a "stich," from Greek *stichos*, "line") or a line (or verset), two units being the minimum number for constituting a line, and generally no more than three.[21] The lines then

---

17. There is presently no scholarly consensus on the prominence of strict meter in Hebrew poetry.
18. Theodore H. Robinson, *The Poetry of the Old Testament*, p. 25.
19. Robert Lowth, *Lectures on the Sacred Poetry of the Hebrews*, vol. 1, lect. 3, pp. 68-69.
20. Robert Alter, *The Art of Biblical Poetry* (New York: Basic Books, 1985), pp. 3-26, 62-84.
21. Theodore H. Robinson, *The Poetry of the Old Testament*, p. 25.

combine to form the larger component of Hebrew verse, called a *distich* if two lines are involved, and a *tristich* if three. Psalm 19:1-2 will illustrate this:

| | | |
|---|---|---|
| 1. The-heavens | are relating | the-glory-of-God;/ |
| and-the-firmament | is telling | the-work-of-his-hands.// |
| 2. Day-by-day | pours-out | speech,/ |
| and-night-by-night | declares | knowledge.// |

(author's trans.)

The individual units in the first line (stich) number three, with three corresponding units in the second line. The first unit, "the heavens," has a corresponding unit, "and the firmament," in the second line, as does each of the other units in line one. Further, since each of the units or terms in line one has a corresponding term in the second line, this parallelism is considered *complete*.[22] In addition, the parallelism operates within the same verse, or distich, and is termed *internal* parallelism. When the parallel thought set up in one distich has its corresponding components in a successive distich, it is called *external*. Since the larger verse is composed of two lines, it is called a distich. The three units of the two lines of verse 1 may be diagrammed as:

| | | |
|---|---|---|
| a | b | c |
| a´ | b´ | c´ |

However, this parallelism does not entirely do justice to the Hebrew parallelism, since in verse 1 "the-work-of-his-hands" comes first in Hebrew (i.e., "The work-of-his-hands is telling the firmament," which is ambiguous because "the firmament," not "the work-of-his-hands," is the subject of the verb in the Hebrew line). While verse 2 more exactly renders the syntactic parallelism of the Hebrew line, verse 1b as rendered within the parenthesis shows the difficulty of reproducing the exact Hebrew order in translation, since following that order produces an ambiguous sentence.

Yet semantic parallelism is another matter. "The heavens" is a more general term (Gen. 1:1), whereas the parallel unit, "the firmament," is a more specific term for the expanse above the earth (Gen. 1:6-8). Similarly, "the glory of God" is a more general term, and "the work of his hands" a more specific one for the same idea. Although they are parallel, they are not strictly synonymous. Thus the parallelism has moved from the general to the specific (what Alter calls "focusing").

Within each unit of the above lines there is one stress (accent) that falls on the main idea, producing a rhythmical pattern of 3:3.

22. George Buchanan Gray, *The Forms of Hebrew Poetry*, p. 59.

Our example from Psalm 19 has three units in each line, but the simplest kind of synonymous parallelism has two units in each. Jacob's blessing in Genesis 49 provides a good illustration:

I-will-divide-them                                     in-Jacob,/
and-I-will-scatter-them                                in-Israel.//
                                          (v. 7*b*, author's trans.)

This would be diagrammed as:

a                                                      b
a′                                                     b′

The rhythmical pattern would be 2:2, which is also the simplest metrical pattern in Hebrew verse.

The semantic parallelism moves from the idea of "divide" in the first line and intensifies to "scatter" in the second. The parallel second terms ("in Jacob" and "in Israel") suggest different thoughts and associations. So semantic parallelism is not exact.

Gray has also pointed out that frequently synonymous parallelism is syntactically *incomplete*.[23] That is, not every unit in the first line has a corresponding unit in the parallel line. For example:

The-earth          is-the-Lord's,          and-the-fulness-thereof;/
the-world,                                  and-they-that-dwell-therein.//
                                          (Ps. 24:1, KJV)

The first and third terms of the first line have corresponding terms in the second line, but the second term ("is the Lord's") does not, which means that the parallelism is *incomplete* (even though the idea of "is the Lord's" is implicitly carried over into the second line). Although the sense of the Lord's possessing the earth is implied, formally it is not expressed in the second line. We would diagram this verse thus:

a                            b                            c
a′                                                        c′

The rhythmical pattern is 3:2 (three terms in the first line and two in the second), and the larger member itself is a distich.

To demonstrate how important, yet how ambiguous, rhythm is in Hebrew poetry, we may take the distinctive rhythm of the lament, called *qinah* ("la-

23. Ibid.

ment''), identified by both Lowth[24] and Karl Budde.[25] The book of Lamentations is a classical illustration of this rhythmical pattern, which has three stresses in the first line and two in the second (3:2). The falling pattern from three to two seemed appropriate for the tone of lamentation and mourning. Amos's dirge over Israel may illustrate:

| She-has-fallen, | she-will-not-rise | again—/ | | The-virgin | Israel.// |
| She-lies-neglected | on | her-land;/ | There-is-none | | to-raise-her-up.// |
| | | | | | (Amos 5:2) |

While this verse illustrates the 3:2 rhythm in the first distich, it also illustrates the difficulty with this rhythmical pattern. In order to get the three stresses in the second distich, we have to allow a stress upon the preposition "on." Actually the second distich may be 2:2 rather than 3:2, although the first is clearly 3:2. There are even instances when the 3:2 rhythmical pattern is used to express joy and trust:

| The-Lord-is | my-light | and-my-salvation;/ | | |
| | | | whom | shall-I-fear?// |
| The-Lord-is | the-strength-of | my-life;/ | | |
| | | | of-whom | shall-I-be-afraid?// |
| | | | | (Ps. 27:1, KJV) |

The difficulty of forcing Hebrew poetry into a strict metrical system is hereby illustrated, and the strict identification of one rhythmical pattern with one emotional mood should be apparent as well.

The second type of parallelism that Lowth identified was *antithetic*. This means that the terms of the second part of the parallelism express the opposite, or contrary, idea:

| For-the-Lord | knoweth | the-way-of | the-righteous:/ | |
| | | but-the-way-of | the-ungodly | shall-perish// |
| | | | | (Ps. 1:6, KJV) |

It will be noted that the life of the righteous is put in contrast with that of the wicked. The effect of this type of parallelism is contrast. The diagram would be:

| a | b | c | | d |
| | | c´ | b´ | d´ |

24. Lowth, vol. 2, lect. 22, pp. 121-39.
25. Karl Budde, "Poetry [Hebrew]," *A Dictionary of the Bible*, ed. James Hastings, 4:2-13.

The terms of the second line do not always follow the same order as those of the first. Here the second term of line one (''knoweth'') has its corresponding term (''shall perish'') at the end of line two (the English order does not, as here, always represent the Hebrew order of the terms).

The third type of parallelism that Lowth identified was *synthetic*. This has been the most disputed of the three. Some have claimed that this is simply a category into which all the examples that are not synonymous and antithetic can be grouped. The idea of synthetic parallelism, however, is that the thought of the first verse-member is extended by an additional term or terms in the second member. Psalm 1:2-3 may illustrate:

| | | |
|---|---|---|
| But-his-delight-is | in-the-law-of-the-Lord;/ | |
| and-in-his-law | doth-he-meditate | day-and-night.// |
| | | |
| And-he-shall-be-like-a-tree | planted-by-the-rivers-of-water,/ | |
| that-bringeth-forth | his-fruit | in-his-season.// |
| | | (KJV) |

In the first verse the idea of line one is extended in line two to describe the extent of his meditation (''day and night''), an idea not contained in the first line. In the second verse the description of the ''tree'' of the first line is given in the second line (''that bringeth forth his fruit in his season''), thus expanding the thought of line one.

One of the basic methods of deriving greater impact from the terms used is varying their position in the line. One such method is called *chiasm* (because when diagrammed it forms the points of the Greek ''x,'' which is called *chi*). Proverbs 2:4 supplies a good example. We will need to restore the English terms to the Hebrew order.

| | |
|---|---|
| If-thou-seekest-her | as-silver,/ |
| and-as-for-hid-treasures | searchest-for-her// |
| | (KJV) |

Our diagram will be

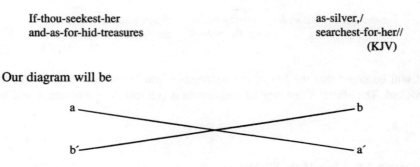

The variation of position in the second line highlights the great value of wisdom, which is spoken of here, by inverting the corresponding terms.

The line is the basic component of Hebrew verse (above the level of the individual units or terms), but there is evidence in some instances of a larger component, which may be called *stanza* or *strophe*. In the case of the alphabetic acrostic discussed below, each new letter suggests a new strophe. Sometimes a refrain may mark the end of one strophe and signal the beginning of a new. An example may be found in Psalms 42-43 where the same couplet punctuates the poem (42:5, 11; 43:5). Another illustration is Isaiah 9:7–10:4, where the recurring refrain points toward a strophic structure. Sometimes in the Psalms the term *selah* seems to break the poem into stanzas (e.g., Ps. 46), but this must not be taken too rigidly, for in other instances it does not seem to function like that. We can often appeal, moreover, to thought content, which sometimes provides the clue for dividing the psalm into stophes. Psalm 91, to illustrate, may fall into eight two-line stanzas, each being somewhat independent of its neighbors.[26]

Besides these features of Hebrew poetry, certain sound techniques are used to enhance the beauty and the impact of the words used. It is usually impossible to imitate these in an English translation, so we lose the beauty in the transfer from Hebrew to the receptor language. One such technique is *alliteration*, which is the use of the same or similar sounds at the beginning of words or syllables and in stressed positions. When the sound is consonantal, it is called *consonance*. Psalm 126:6, for example, uses the Hebrew letter *kaph* (similar to the German *ch*) in the first three terms of the line and three different sibilants in the next three terms (*s*, *sh*, and *z*).

*Assonance*, the other alliterative technique, employs the same or similar vowel (rather than consonant) sounds in accented positions. This may be seen, for example, in Ezekiel 27:27 as Ezekiel celebrates the fall of Tyre. The emotional tone of the verse is intensified by the repetition of the *ê* and *ai* sounds.

A favorite technique of the prophets was *paronomasia*, a play upon the sound and meaning of words (a pun). It was a way of concentrating much meaning in a word or two. In Amos 8:2 the prophet sees a basket of summer fruit (*kelûb qayiṣ*), whereupon the Lord took the consonants (*q*, *ṣ*) and pronounced the "end" (*qēṣ*) upon Israel.[27]

Aside from the internal features of Hebrew poetry, there is one external form we should take account of, the *alphabet acrostic* poem. This entails the repetition of the same Hebrew letter at the beginning of verses, half-verses, or stanzas in the order of the letters of the alphabet. Among the poetic books, several acrostic poems occur in the Psalms: 9-10, 25, 34, 37, 111, 112, 119, and 145. One complete acrostic is to be found in Proverbs 31:10-31, the praise of the

26. Robinson, p. 45.
27. See N. K. Gottwald, "Hebrew Poetry," *The Interpreter's Dictionary of the Bible*, ed. George A. Buttrick, 3:829-38, from whose article I have received much help in a concise form. Also R. K. Harrison, "Hebrew Poetry," *The Zondervan Pictorial Encyclopedia of the Bible*, ed. Merrill C. Tenney, 3:76-87.

faithful wife and mother. Nahum 1:1-10 seems to have been intended as an acrostic, but the order and position of the letters are not regular. The book of Lamentations exhibits the acrostic form in the first four chapters, each verse beginning with a new letter of the alphabet. In the case of chapter 3, the same letter begins three verses in succession, and that pattern is followed throughout the alphabet. While all the letters of the alphabet are used in these four acrostics, the *ayin* is not in its usual position in chapters 2, 3, and 4. The Psalms, however, provide us with an adequate view of the variations of this type of formal structure. Psalms 9 and 10 show the acrostic scheme irregularly carried through both psalms, with only eighteen letters used. Psalm 25 begins each new verse with a new letter, but the *waw* and the *qoph* are missing. Psalm 37 starts every alternate verse with a new letter, and the *ayin* is missing (but in v. 28 the letter may be hidden). Psalms 111 and 112 begin each half-verse with a new letter, and both acrostics are complete. Psalm 119 is an acrostic masterpiece, each letter of the alphabet heading up eight successive lines before a new letter is introduced. Psalm 145 begins each new verse with a different letter, but the *nun* is missing.

The alphabetic acrostic formed such a formalized structure that it did not lend itself very well to logical development, but it did facilitate memory. The device was also found in other literatures. Lambert has noted that five acrostics have been recovered from Akkadian literature.[28]

In regards to syntactic parallelism, the English reader is at a disadvantage when he approaches Hebrew poetry. However, the availablity of good English translations along with commentaries and Bible word dictionaries will greatly help him to understand and appreciate syntactic parallelism. Hopefully also, an increased knowledge of the nature of Hebrew poetry will enhance his appreciation for it and sensitize him to its basic features.

## WISDOM IN THE ANCIENT NEAR EAST

Although we cannot accept the hypothesis that Israelite religion was the result of an evolutionary process or that it was the eclectic best drawn from the neighboring religious cultures, we must acknowledge the intercultural influences upon Hebrew faith and literature. Lying at the crossroads of commercial and cultural interchange between Mesopotamia and Egypt, Israel was both the beneficiary and the victim of cross-cultural currents. A recognition of the commonality of literary genres and concepts between Israel and the cognate literatures of the ancient Near East is less likely to result in a depreciation of the Old Testament faith than in enhanced appreciation.

In terms of mass, the extant texts that fall within the general category of wisdom literature are most numerous in Egypt. Two periods of Egyptian history

28. Lambert, p. 67.

yield the bulk of these texts, the Old Kingdom (c. 3000-2500 B.C.) and the New Kingdom (c. 1555-945 B.C.). The Mesopotamian texts may be divided into the Sumerian and the Babylonian, neither of which is as numerous as the Egyptian.

The Sumerian documents likely originated in the third millennium B.C., although our extant texts, mostly from Nippur, date mainly from the eighteenth century B.C. The Sumerians were a non-Semitic people who inhabited lower Mesopotamia. They established the first great civilization there. They did not, like the Babylonians, build an empire; rather, their major sphere of influence was culture.

The Babylonians were in many respects the beneficiaries of Sumerian culture, although they were Semitic in origin. The literature from Babylonia that will occupy our concern dates largely from the second millennium B.C. In the west, the last half of the second millennium witnessed the flourishing culture and state whose remains have been discovered at Ugarit (modern Ras Shamra). Although Ugarit has not as yet yielded a didactic literature, the poetry and language bear marked affinities with biblical Hebrew. Thus in lexicography and literary form the Ugarit texts have shed much light in which Old Testament wisdom studies can take place. Also the El Amarna Letters (c. fourteenth century B.C.), composing a group of correspondences between the Egyptian kings and their nominal vassals in Syria-Palestine and neighboring countries, offer some linguistic enlightenment.

All these texts contribute to an understanding of the world and literature of ancient Israel. However, they are not the key to understanding, only an aid. The master key to unlocking the meaning of the poetic books is a thorough knowledge of the Old Testament in general and Hebrew wisdom literature in particular. To use the cognate literatures as our major informant can be misleading indeed. Methodologically, since the Old Testament faith is divinely revealed, our starting point and stopping point must be that faith itself in its revealed form. However, to bypass the additional dimension and the aid to understanding that the cognate languages and literature can provide for us would be a tragedy in itself. Procedurally we shall look at the following types: instructions, hymns, proverbs, and dialogues/monologues.

INSTRUCTIONS

Egyptian society was perceived as mirroring the order of the universe.[29] To the end that such a society might be achieved, a literary form called *instructions* developed to offer moral guidance. Very popular in Egypt, they also appear in Mesopotamia and Asia Minor. Extant texts span the biblical period, reaching

29. Miriam Lichtheim, *Ancient Egyptian Literature: A Book of Readings*, 3 vols. (Berkeley, Calif.: U. of California, 1973), 1:5.

from the third millennium B.C. to Greco-Roman times.[30] K. A. Kitchen identifies two types, *Type A*, which has a formal title followed immediately by the text, and *Type B*, which begins with a formal title, followed by a prologue, and then the main text. Based on the extant texts, both types exist side by side throughout this period, except for the absence of Type A in the early second millennium B.C. in Egypt and western Asia.[31]

Among biblical wisdom books, these instructions have most affinities with the book of Proverbs. Like Proverbs, they are filled with proverbs and moral insights, often given by a prince or king to his son. Kitchen identifies the Solomonic materials of Proverbs 25-29, the words of Agur (chap. 30), and the words of Lemuel (chap. 31) as Type A, while Proverbs 1-24 is Type B.[32] One should not be surprised to discover that Solomon's work shared literary resemblances to Near Eastern literature, for the writer of Kings saw the comparison and observed that "Solomon's wisdom surpassed the wisdom of all the sons of the east and all the wisdom of Egypt" (1 Kings 4:30). Some examples from Egypt are "The Instruction of Duauf,"[33] which appears only on exercise tablets of schoolboys (c. 1300 B.C.). A father on his way to enroll his son in school commends the life of student pursuits to the boy. Yet other texts, such as "The Instruction of King Amen-em-het"[34] and "The Instruction of Amen-em-opet,"[35] were not limited to scholastic use. In the former, King Amen-em-het I (c. 1995-1965 B.C.) made his son, Sen-Usert I, coregent and informed his son about the events that led him to that decision. In the Instruction of Amen-em-opet, closely akin to Proverbs 22:17–24:22, are the admonitions of a father to his son. It contains many items of advice as to how the son should conduct his life and affairs. One example will have to suffice:

> Do not associate to thyself the heated man,
> Nor visit him for conversation.
>
> (chap. 9)

Attention has been drawn to the similarity of this saying to Proverbs 22:24:

> Do not associate with a man *given* to anger;
> Or go with a hot-tempered man.

---

30. Kenneth A. Kitchen, "The Basic Literary Forms and Formulations of Ancient Instructional Writings in Egypt and Western Asia," *Orbis Biblicus et Orientalis*, vol. 28 of *Separatum aus Studien zu Altaegyptischen Lebenslehren*, ed. Erik Hornung and Othmar Keel (Fribourg, 1979), pp. 235-82, esp. p. 241.
31. Kenneth A. Kitchen, "Proverbs and Wisdom Books of the Ancient Near East: The Factual History of a Literary Form," *The Tyndale Bulletin* 28 (1977):69-114, esp. p. 73.
32. Ibid., pp. 100-101.
33. Adolf Erman, *The Literature of the Ancient Egyptians*, pp. 67-72.
34. Ibid., pp. 72-74; ANET, pp. 418-19.
35. ANET, pp. 421-24.

HYMNS

Although this literary genre is not distinctive to wisdom literature, we will find a consideration of the *hymn* in other literature helpful when we approach the book of Psalms. Our knowledge of hymnody in the cognate literature derives largely from Sumerian, Babylonian, and Egyptian writings. One interesting hymn from Sumer, "Hymn to Enlil, the All-Beneficent,"[36] reveals the level of piety one may have found in some echelons of Sumerian society. This hymn glorifies the patron god of Nippur, his temple, and his wife, Ninlil. Among other things, Enlil is called "the shepherd of the teeming multitudes" (lines 84, 93; cf. Ps. 23). The laudatory nature of the hymn is similar to the praise of the Lord in the biblical psalms. Another hymn, "Hymn to Ninurta as a God of Wrath,"[37] celebrates this god's vengeful nature. Composed in two-line stophes, each new line begins alternately with "my king" and "Lord Ninurta":

> My king who vanquishes the houses of the rebellious lands,
>> great lord of Enlil,
> You, with power you are endowed.
> Lord Ninurta who vanquishes the houses of the rebellious lands,
>> great lord of Enlil,
> You, with power you are endowed.

> (lines 5-6)

In both form and content this hymn brings to mind the recognition of Israel's God as the great Judge of the earth, as frequently articulated in the Psalms, for example, Psalm 9:

> But the Lord abides forever;
> He has established His throne for judgment,
> And He will judge the world in righteousness;
> He will execute judgment for the peoples with equity.

> (vv. 7-8)

A prayer addressed to the Babylonian gods in general is found in the well-furnished library of the Assyrian king Ashurbanipal (668-633 B.C.). In it the worshiper appealed to all the gods and goddesses for relief from his sickness, which he believed to have been caused by transgression against one of them about whose identity he was uncertain:

> May the fury of my lord's heart be quieted toward me.
> May the god who is not known be quieted toward me;
> May the goddess who is not known be quieted toward me. . . .

36. James B. Pritchard, ed., ANET Supp., pp. 573-76.
37. Ibid, p. 577.

> When the goddess was angry with me, she made me become ill.
> The god whom I know or do not know has oppressed me;
> The goddess whom I know or do not know has placed suffering
>     upon me.
>
> (lines 1-3, 32-34)[38]

In Egypt we also have examples that help to paint the fuller picture of hymnody in the world of ancient Israel. In "A Prayer to Re-Har-akhti"[39] (manuscript from about 1230 B.C.) the worshiper appeals to Atum Re-Har-akhti, the sun-god, and confesses numerous sins that he has committed, pleading for Atum's mercy:

> Do not punish me for my numerous sins, [for] I am one who knows not his own self, I am a man without sense. I spend the day following after my [own] mouth, like a cow after grass.

The common spirit of these hymns from Babylonia and Egypt and the biblical penitential psalms (Pss. 6, 32, 38, 51, 102, 130, 143) is evident. David, after his adultery with Bathsheba, prayed with a kindred spirit of penitence:

> Wash me thoroughly from my iniquity,
> And cleanse me from my sin.
> For I know my transgressions,
> And my sin is ever before me.
>
> (Ps. 51:2-3)

In the same vein of penitence, another Egyptian devotee to the goddess Meresger celebrates humbly his deliverance from illness brought about by transgression against the goddess. In the prayer the worshiper, Nefer-abet, prays:

> I knew not good or evil. When I did the deed of transgression against the Peak,[40] she punished me, and I was in her hand by night as well as day.[41]

The suffering penitent of Psalm 38 likewise believed that his illness was a result of his sin against the Lord:

> O Lord, rebuke me not in Thy wrath;
> And chasten me not in Thy burning anger.
> For Thine arrows have sunk deep into me,
> And Thy hand has pressed down on me.

38. ANET, pp. 391-92.
39. Ibid., p. 379.
40. "Peak" may have been the location of the goddess.
41. ANET, p. 381.

There is no soundness in my flesh because of Thine indignation;
There is no health in my bones because of my sin.

(vv. 1-3)

In another Egyptian hymn[42] the worshiper appeals to his god for help in the court of law, while still another religious devotee thanks Amon-Re for recovery of his son from an illness.[43]

Syria-Palestine has not been so generous in the way of hymnodic material. The primary archaeological site for cognate literature, ancient Ugarit (modern Ras Shamra), on the north Syrian coast, has thus far yielded no hymns as such. However, Mitchell Dahood has drawn heavily upon the lexicography and philology of the Ugaritic texts in his extensive commentary on the Psalms.[44] Thus, the language of Ugarit, which is widely believed to be close to biblical Hebrew, has provided a context for the study of the Psalms that is even closer home than Babylonia and Egypt. We should, however, be careful that we do not permit these materials to become dictatorial in our study of psalmic literature. The further presence of hymnodic literature in Syria-Palestine is suggested by the frequent reference to Canaanite hymns in the El Amarna Letters[45] (c. fourteenth century B.C.), a body of correspondence between the Egyptian kings and their nominal vassal states in Syria-Palestine and neighboring countries.

That hymnody was a generalized literary form of religious expression is obvious. Further, the hymns in the cognate literatures demonstrate form and content that are often similar to that in the book of Psalms. However, the polytheism of these cultures never permitted the high level of theological attainment and expression represented by the biblical psalms. Monotheism was perhaps the greatest legacy of ancient Israel and the strongest impetus for a highly developed religious literature.

## PROVERBS

As the content of the book of Proverbs attests, the *proverb* takes a form that varies in length from a single line (in the Old Testament some one-line proverbs are found outside the book of Proverbs, e.g., 1 Sam. 10:12, but the basic length of the biblical proverb is two lines) to a multiline form.

In addition to the proverbs found in the Egyptian instructions,[46] the Sumerian literature has provided evidence of the popularity of proverbs among the Sumerians. W. G. Lambert discusses the nature of these, some of which occur in

---

42. "A Prayer for Help in the Law Court," ANET, p. 380. The translator dates the manuscript from about 1230 B.C.
43. ANET, pp. 380-81. About the same date as preceding hymn.
44. Mitchell Dahood, *Psalms.*
45. Ibid., 1:xxxii.
46. See the discussions of "Instructions" above, and of the proverb on pp. 149-52.

bilingual texts, and observes that they constitute not only short, pungent sayings, but also brief fables and anecdotes.[47] Unfortunately, however, they are often not only obscure linguistically, but their meaning is uncertain.[48] To grasp the sense of the following one, however, is not difficult:

> Seeing you have done evil to your friend, what will you do to your enemy?[49]

Strangely, however, very few Babylonian proverbs have survived. Lambert is of the opinion that the proverb was not a popular genre in the literature of the Babylonians and Assyrians, although there is evidence that it was popularly used in oral discourse.[50]

While Ugarit has not as yet brought forth any didactic material, C. I. K. Story has demonstrated that the poetic form of Proverbs is often the same as that in the Ugaritic epics.[51] Further, Proverbs contains many words and word-parallels that also appear in the Ugarit texts.[52] Despite the paucity of didactic material from Ugarit, however, Albright has drawn attention to the evidence of aphorisms furnished by the El Amarna Letters (c. fourteenth century B.C.). One such proverb in a letter from Lab'ayu of Shechem is quoted by Albright:

> If ants are smitten, they do not accept (the smiting) quietly,
> but they bite the hand of the man who smites them.[53]

Two biblical proverbs use the ant as their subject (Prov. 6:6; 30:25). Albright further advances the position that Proverbs 8-9 contain many Canaanite words and expressions.[54] Thus the general literary form of the proverb and proverbial literature is well attested in the major cultures of the world of ancient Israel.

DIALOGUE/MONOLOGUE

The concerns of this genre of literature move beyond the day-to-day conduct of life to deal with the issue of divine justice in a broader theological frame-

---

47. W. G. Lambert, *Babylonian Wisdom Literature*, p. 222. Although extant copies from Nippur date from about the eighteenth century B.C., W. F. Albright proposes that they were composed in the third millennium B.C., which would make them as early as the oldest didactic material from Egypt. See W. F. Albright, "Some Canaanite-Phoenician Sources of Hebrew Wisdom," WIANE, pp. 1-15, esp. pp. 3-4.
48. Lambert, p. 224.
49. Ibid., p. 232, from the so-called Assyrian Collection, although it did not originate in Assyria.
50. Ibid., pp. 275-76.
51. Cullen I. K. Story, "The Book of Proverbs and Northwest-Semitic Literature," JBL 64 (1945): 319-37.
52. Albright, pp. 6-7.
53. Ibid., p. 7.
54. Ibid., pp. 7-9.

work. The literary form is that of a *monologue* or a *dialogue*. Job and Ecclesiastes fall into this category. Job is the supreme example of dialogue in the ancient Near Eastern literature. Egypt has not yet yielded any texts of such consequence from this genre as those in Babylonia. First, we will look at those compositions that remind us of Job and the questions raised there. In fact, the reflective literature of Babylonia seems preoccupied with the question of justice. "The Poem on the Righteous Sufferer" (or "I will praise the lord of wisdom")[55] tells how a devotee of the god Marduk believed himself deserted by his god and goddess. In the midst of the suffering and humiliation that followed, he was unable to divine the will of Marduk. Although compatriots took advantage of his suffering, he did not enter into dialogue with them, as did Job. Rather his speech took the form of a monologue in which he recounted his problem and suffering. As he reflected upon the problem of injustice, he concluded that the moral standard of the gods took an inverted form as compared to man's standard of justice:

> What is proper to oneself is an offence to one's god,
> What in one's own heart seems despicable is proper to one's god.
>
> (lines 34-35)

Some scholars connect a fourth tablet with this document, although Lambert points out the difficulties of making this association.[56] If it belongs to the composition, then the worshiper is restored by his god, Marduk. Whether or not Tablet IV belongs to this particular composition, it certainly provides us with the theme of divine justice vindicated.

Job too was preoccupied with the problem of divine justice. And he too entertained the possibility that the human standard of morality was quite different from God's:

> I am guiltless;
> I do not take notice of myself;
> I despise my life.
> It is all one; therefore I say,
> "He destroys the guiltless and the wicked."
> If the scourge kills suddenly,
> He mocks the despair of the innocent.
> The earth is given into the hand of the wicked;
> He covers the faces of its judges.
> If it is not He, then who is it?
>
> (Job 9:21-24)

---

55. Lambert, pp. 30-62, includes a transliteration and translation of the text. His introduction to the composition (pp. 21-27) is also very helpful. Quotations are from this work.
56. Ibid., pp. 24-46.

Yet Job transcended the materialism of this Babylonian poem because the God speeches revealed to him that divine justice has more dimensions than the well-being of the righteous man. It extends to all parts of God's creation, and if it had been as mechanical as Job had alleged, then there was really no problem at all. Although the epilogue of the book of Job recognized justice as one valid and important part of God's multifarious relationship to His world, that relationship could not be reduced to the common denominator of justice.

A second piece of literature, called "The Babylonian Theodicy," and dated by Lambert at around 1000 B.C., was composed as an acrostic poem of twenty-seven stanzas of eleven lines each. Each of the eleven lines, like Psalm 119, began with the same cuneiform sign.[57] Whereas "The Poem of the Righteous Sufferer" virtually ignored the friends who took advantage of the hero's ill-fortune, this poem was a dialogue between the sufferer and a friend. The sufferer raised the question of social injustice to which his friend responded with "orthodox" answers. Much like Job, the victim recalled how he had devoted himself to his god:

> In my youth I sought the will of my god;
> With prostration and prayer I followed my goddess.
> But I was bearing a profitless corvée as a yoke.
> My god decreed instead of wealth destitution.
> A cripple is my superior, a lunatic outstrips me,
> The rogue has been promoted, but I have been brought low.
>
> (VII. 72-77)

And much like Job's friend, the friend responded that the sufferer had transgressed against his god:

> My reliable fellow, holder of knowledge, your thoughts are perverse.
> You have forsaken right and blaspheme against your god's designs.
> In your mind you have an urge to disregard the divine ordinances.
>
> (VIII. 78-80)

The friend's "orthodox" position, like that of Job's friends, was that piety is rewarded with the god's favor:

> The godless cheat who has wealth,
> A death-dealing weapon pursues him.
> Unless you seek the will of the god, what luck have you?
> He that bears his god's yoke never lacks food, though it be sparse.

57. Ibid., pp. 63-91. Quotations are from Lambert.

Seek the kindly wind of the god,
What you have lost over a year you will make up in a moment.

(XXII. 237-42)

Yet, like Job, the sufferer had not found that always to be true in experience:

I have looked around society, but the evidence is contrary.
The god does not impede the way of a devil. . . .
How have I profited that I have bowed down to my god?
I have to bow beneath the base fellow that meets me;
The dregs of humanity, like the rich and opulent, treat me with contempt.

(XXIII. 243-44, 251-53)

The final solution proffered by the friend was that the gods had built human perversity and injustice into the human race:

Narru, king of the gods, who created mankind,
And majestic Zulummar, who dug out their clay,
And mistress Mami, the queen who fashioned them,
Gave perverse speech to the human race.
With lies, and not truth, they endowed them for ever.
Solemnly they speak in favor of a rich man,
"He is a king," they say, "riches go at his side."
But they harm a poor man like a thief,
They lavish slander upon him and plot his murder,
Making him suffer every evil like a criminal, because he has no
    protection.
Terrifyingly they bring him to his end, and extinguish him like a
    flame.

(XXVI. 276-86)

The sufferer, apparently accepting that solution, ended the poem by appealing to the god for mercy (XXVII).

The presupposition that the universe was not founded upon the principle of justice was one that Job was tempted to embrace but could not. His friends definitely did not believe that. Nor did Job and his friends conclude that God had built moral corruption into the human race. Although this poem has some striking affinities with Job, it is basically very different in its presuppositions and conclusion.

S. N. Kramer has identified another poem among the Sumerian texts from Nippur as containing the motif of the suffering, righteous individual.[58] Dated

58. S. N. Kramer, "Man and His God, A Sumerian Variation on the 'Job' Motif," WIANE, pp. 170-82. Also ANET Supp., pp. 589-91.

about 1700 B.C., but likely composed as early as 2000 B.C.,[59] the poet set forth
the thesis that in cases of suffering and adversity, no matter how unjustified they
may seem, the only recourse the victim has is to continue to glorify his god and
keep wailing and lamenting before him until the god intervenes in his situation.
As a result of the devotee's persistence, his personal god was moved and delivered him.

Thus the motif of the suffering of the righteous individual is attested in both
Mesopotamian and Hebrew literature. The motif, however, is a universal one;
the basic difference is not in the motif, but in how it is formulated and particularly in what solution is offered.

The second reflective book among the poetic books is Ecclesiastes. It too
has its literary cousins among the Babylonian compositions. One is "The Dialogue of Pessimism"[60] in which a master and servant entered into a dialogue
about the profit of various human endeavors. Lambert calls it a satire,[61] although
opinions have varied. The pattern is that the master's statement of an activity he
intended to undertake was followed by a counterstatement by the servant. This
counterstatement was probably not so much intended as a contradiction as it was
a suggestion of the futility of the undertaking:

> Slave, listen to me. "Here I am, sir, here I am."
> I am going to love a woman. "So love, sir, love.
> The man who loves a woman forgets sorrow and fear."
> No, slave, I will by no means love a woman.
> "(Do not) love, sir, do not love.
> Woman is a pitfall—a pitfall, a hole, a ditch.
> Woman is a sharp iron dagger that cuts a man's throat."
>
> (lines 46-52)

Finally the master called upon the servant to tell him what is the good activity,
whereupon the slave replied that death is the only good in life (lines 79-86).

Although the book of Ecclesiastes entertains death as an alternative to life
(Eccles. 4:2) and nonexistence as even more desirable (4:3), that is not Qoheleth's final conclusion. For life is a gift of God, and man's responsibility is to
get the most out of it (5:18). The nihilistic note, therefore, is certainly sounded
in Ecclesiastes, but its dissonance is resolved into the more realistic philosophy
of pleasure. Death is not the greatest good, even though it is the common lot of
all mankind.

59. Ibid., p. 170.
60. Lambert, pp. 139-49. Also ANET Supp., pp. 600-601. Quotations are from Lambert.
61. Ibid., p. 139.

A fragmentary composition called "Counsels of a Pessimist"[62] presents a skeptical view of life, but it is not nihilistic. Rather, somewhat as Ecclesiastes, this writer recommends the pursuit of religion and agriculture despite the transitory nature of man:

> Mankind and their achievements alike come to an end. . . .
> Let your free-will offering be constantly before the god who created you,
> Bow down to your city goddess that she may grant you offspring,
> Take thought for your livestock, remember the planting.
>
> (lines 10, 12-14)

Yet even with these samples of literature, we still have not risen to the level of uniformity of faith and profundity of thought that we find in the reflective literature of the Old Testament. Although the biblical literature has a vital diversity about it, the fundamental monotheism permeates the literature, and the basic covenantal morality underlies its concepts and precepts.

## WISDOM IN THE APOCRYPHA

Among those books not included for various reasons in the Jewish canon, two very nobly carry forth the content and style of canonical wisdom. They are Ecclesiasticus (or the Wisdom of Jesus ben Sirach) and the Wisdom of Solomon.

After the exile and the eventual cessation of prophecy, Hebrew wisdom became increasingly important as a mode of religious expression. Whereas the prophetic urging of the word of the Lord upon Israel and the counsel of the wise had existed side by side in preexilic times (Jer. 18:18, even though they were not always, as this passage attests, in accord), the postexilic era witnessed the demise of prophetic activity. When we recognize that Israel had depended upon the prophetic word for several centuries, then the vacuum left by its cessation appears serious. Of course, even before prophecy ceased, wisdom had already developed certain strengths that could in part compensate for the loss. It was instructive, just as the prophets' words had been, even though it lacked the prophetic imperative that called for repentance and radical change. One of the points at which postexilic wisdom offered the most compensation was its emphasis upon the law, which had also been an element of prophetic emphasis (Isa. 24:5; Jer. 7:9; 9:13; Hos. 4:2; 8:12).

The book of Ecclesiasticus, written in Hebrew about 190 B.C. and translated into Greek in the late second century B.C.,[63] is distinctive by its attention to

---

62. Lambert, pp. 107-9. Quotation from Lambert.
63. Otto Eissfeldt, *The Old Testament, An Introduction*, p. 597, dates the translation after 117 B.C.

the law. Already wisdom was recognized as an attribute of God and personified (Prov. 8). Jesus ben Sirach identified law and wisdom and thus gave law the same high status wisdom had come to enjoy. In 15:1 he declared that keeping the commandments is wisdom:

> If thou wilt, thou canst keep the commandments—
> And it is wisdom to do his good pleasure.

Following the legacy of Ecclesiastes, he associated the fear of the Lord with keeping His commandments, affirming that they constitute wisdom:

> He that keepeth the law becometh master of the intent thereof;
> And the end of the fear of the Lord is wisdom.
>
> (21:11)

Wisdom and law are inseparable. In a superb passage, ben Sirach avowed that the law produces wisdom:

> All these things are the book of the covenant of the Most High
>     God,
> The law which Moses commanded as an heritage for the
>     assemblies of Jacob,
> Which maketh wisdom abundant as Pishon,
> And as Tigris in the days of new fruits;
> Which maketh understanding full as Euphrates,
> And as Jordan in the days of harvest;
> Which maketh instruction to flow down as the Nile,
> And as Gihon in the days of vintage,
> The first man knew her not perfectly;
> And in like manner the last will not trace her out.
> For her thoughts are fuller than the sea,
> And her counsels than the great deep.
> And I came out as a stream from the river,
> And as a conduit into a garden.
> I said, "I will water my garden,
> And will water abundantly my garden bed";
> And, lo, my stream became a river,
>
> And my river became a sea.
> I will yet pour out doctrine as prophecy,
> And leave it unto generations of eternity.
>
> (24:23-33)

In regard to wisdom, ben Sirach believed that it was a direct emanation from God (24:3-5), created before the world, and eternal (1:4; 24:9). Oesterley has pointed out that ben Sirach based his teaching on Proverbs, but that his work was a transitional stage between Proverbs and the Wisdom of Solomon.[64] By the time of ben Sirach, therefore, the personification of wisdom in Proverbs 1-9 was moving toward an hypostatization, that is, wisdom having an existence distinct from, though dependent upon, God and possessing consciousness and personality.

The wisdom movement, however, reached its zenith in the Wisdom of Solomon. In part or in whole it probably dates from the first century B.C. Plumptre put forth the hypothesis, subsequently accepted by many scholars, that the writer of this book had as one of his purposes the refutation and correction of the teaching of Ecclesiastes, which he believed was incorrect.[65] Barton has laid out the parallelism between the books for us:

### PARALLELS BETWEEN *WISDOM OF SOLOMON* AND ECCLESIASTES

| *Wisdom* | *Ecclesiastes* |
| --- | --- |
| 2:1 | 2:23; 5:18 |
| 2:2 | 3:19 |
| 2:3 | 12:7 |
| 2:4 | 1:11; 2:16; 9:5; 2:11 |
| 2:5 | 6:12; 8:8 |
| 2:6 | 2:24 |
| 2:7 | 9:7 |
| 2:8 | 9:8 |
| 2:9 | 3:22; 5:18; 9:8.[66] |

Troubled by the suffering to which the righteous had been subjected, the writer resisted the temptation to abandon his faith as others had done. He probed the mysteries of the universe (chaps. 1-10), as did the writers of Job, Ecclesiastes, and Psalms 37, 49, and 73, in an effort to explain the suffering of the righteous. His greatest comfort was the hope of immortality (3:1-9; 5:15-23).

64. W. O. E. Oesterley, *The Wisdom of Jesus, the Son of Sirach, or Ecclesiasticus*, pp. 46-48.
65. E. H. Plumptre, *Ecclesiastes; or, the Preacher*, pp. 70-75.
66. George Aaron Barton, *A Critical and Exegetical Commentary on the Book of Ecclesiastes*, pp. 57-58.

Impersonating King Solomon, the author delivered a beautiful oration (6:9–11:1) in which he depicted wisdom as a heavenly being endowed with the divine glory:

> For Wisdom is more mobile than any motion,
> Yes, she pervadeth and penetrateth all things by reason of her
>     pureness.
> For she is a vapour of the power of God,
> And a clear effluence of the glory of the Almighty;
> Therefore nothing defiled findeth entrance into her.
> For she is a reflection from (the) everlasting light,
> And an unspotted mirror of the working of God,
> And the image of His goodness.
>
> (7:24-26)

Moreover, wisdom was the all-pervasive force that entered into Israel and became her life-giving force, propelling history ever since creation (10:1-21).

Much has been made of the influence of this book upon New Testament thought, particularly on Pauline thought and the doctrine of the Logos in John's gospel. Gregg observed the vital difference between wisdom in this book and John's Logos—John declares, "The Word was God."[67]

The wisdom movement in noncanonical literature is far broader than these two books. Along with the apocalyptic movement, it provided a spiritual impetus and a mode of expression that has left its indelible imprint upon both Jewish and Christian life and faith.

67. R. A. F. Gregg, *The Wisdom of Solomon*, p. 54.

# 2

# THE THEOLOGY OF WISDOM

The broad and comprehensive nature of the wisdom books makes it difficult to bring together their theology in only a few pages. Yet, if we can see their general theological contours, we may approach the wide scope of wisdom with keener perception.

Procedurally, we will here confine our attention largely to the wisdom books, except in the section on immortality where the related material from Psalms is included. Certain other theological emphases in the book of Psalms are discussed in a later chapter. The Song of Songs may be conveniently omitted from this present discussion because of the peculiar complexities of that book. It may be noted that any theology of the Song will be greatly shaped by the particular hermeneutic applied to the book (e.g., allegorical or literal). The reader will find these matters discussed in the introduction to the Song in this volume.

Since biblical theology, in our view, must explain what the text *meant* to its ancient hearers and what it *means* to us today, we shall in turn address ourselves to both questions.

## WHAT WISDOM THEOLOGY MEANT THEN

### A SOVEREIGN GOD

The wisdom books exhibit a marvelously varied doctrine of God. In Job, for example, we move, through that man's experience, from the view of God as an omnipotent yet amoral being to the view of God as One who is both omnipotent and mysteriously benevolent. The variety of views in biblical wisdom literature, however, seems to yield some common denominators. Since biblical wisdom provides us with the record of man's search for God and for those cohering elements in the universe, it logically follows that the view of God most often given will be in terms of those elements as wisdom defined them, that is, in terms of divine justice, moral values, human happiness, the wonders of the physical world, and the like.

In pursuit of social and personal stability, wisdom concentrated primarily upon the personal and social dimensions of human life and secondarily upon the physical world to which man was related and with which he sought to live in harmony. This ancient religious "humanism" avoided the inflation of man's importance and abilities by its emphatic affirmation of the Creator God. Belief in the supernatural was a qualifier of this mode of thought and life.

Although some scholars have urged that the older strata of Hebrew wisdom was purely secular,[1] it is difficult to conceive that a movement so broadly based in Hebrew society and so penetrating of the meaning of life could be purely secular, even in its most pragmatic form. The religious and the secular in the ancient Near East had an inseparable relationship. Even in the older strands of Egyptian wisdom the religious element penetrated such documents as Ptah-hotep (c. 2450 B.C.)[2] and the Instruction for King Meri-Kar-Re (c. twenty-second century B.C.).[3] The vertical perspective (God and man) permeated and dominated the horizontal perspective (man and man).

Therefore, the doctrine of God is a key issue in wisdom literature. In general, however, God does not communicate in wisdom literature quite so intimately as He does through the prophets. Rather His mode of self-revelation assumes the medium of human reason and nature. It falls within the broad range of what we now call "natural revelation." Yet we should not erroneously conclude that "special revelation" is not involved, since it definitely stands as the backdrop for human reason and natural observation. That is, man is not left aloof to figure out the universe apart from God. The law undergirds the process. On rare occasions we even receive a more direct word from God, as in Job's poem on wisdom (28:28) and the God speeches in Job (38:1–42:6).

The "humanism" of biblical wisdom does not make the assumption that all man has to work with is human reason and the natural order. Basic to the system of thought represented in these books is the assumption that God is working through the human mind and the world of nature. Upon that assumption, wisdom begins with the natural order and launches upon a search for deeper understanding of the God who created and controls the world and human existence.

One of the basic attributes of God as we see Him in biblical wisdom is His creative power and activity (Job 28:23; 25-27; 38:4–39:30; Prov. 3:19-20; 8:22-34). As we have explained elsewhere, this follows logically from the fact that wisdom seeks to answer the existential question, How did the world and human life come about in the first place? In other words, wisdom is more concerned with why we are here than where we are going. Eschatology is not one of the focal points of this literature. In that respect, as well as many others, it is quite different from the prophets. Rankin has perceptively observed that the ethical

---

1. See p. 31.
2. James B. Pritchard, ed., ANET, pp. 412-14.
3. Ibid., pp. 414-18.

content of wisdom rests securely upon the doctrine that God is the world Creator.[4] It is that precept that requires that man consider what is right behavior toward his fellow human beings, since all are alike created by God.

The Old Testament doctrine of creation, moreover, mandated a universal perspective on God, for He created the whole world and all mankind. The low profile of the doctrine of redemption in this literature does not imply that redemption was unimportant to the wisdom sages. Rather wisdom accentuates God's creative role in relation to the universe and thereby ties man's relationship to God to the beginning of all things. It is truly the canonical emphasis as we see it set forth in the first book of the Bible. One hardly needs to say that the doctrine of redemption can only be comprehended in its universal proportions if one recognizes that the Redeemer is at the same time the Creator. Although canonical wisdom literature does not delineate that phase of thought for us, it does provide a theological component in Old Testament theology that complements the redemptive content of the law and the prophets.[5]

A RESPONSIBLE HUMANITY

*Individually considered.* Wisdom literature took the lowest common denominator of the social order, the individual, and addressed the matter of how he could contribute to social stability. The wisdom teachers, though concerned with the larger social order, recognized the truth that social change sometimes is best brought about by effecting change in the basic unit of society. The potential of man was explored and to a great extent recognized by the wisdom writers. For them, man was a marvelous creature endowed with reason and will and fully responsible for his actions in the world. He was called to personal responsibility, and how he accepted that challenge determined his destiny in life. Therefore, human weaknesses such as laziness, greed, and dissipation of resources had no valid place in the individual's disposition, for they denied personal responsibility to use fully all human endowments. Wisdom literature called upon man to live up to his potential. It gave him no room to escape responsibility.

Some scholars believe that individual responsibility was a late development in Israel, coming to maturity only in the time of Jeremiah (Jer. 31:29-30; Ezek. 18). However, it probably did not develop so monolithically as has been held.[6]

4. O. S. Rankin, *Israel's Wisdom Literature: Its Bearing on Theology and the History of Religion*, pp. 9-10.
5. In the noncanonical *Wisdom of Solomon*, the two doctrines, creation and redemption, are brought together by that sage, depicting wisdom as the dynamic force in history.
6. Rankin, p. 70, observes: "Since both outside the Wisdom literature of Israel and within it the idea of God as Guarantor of reward and of the individual as personally responsible to the deity for his conduct is current in pre-prophetic times, the view, which has done service as a principle of literary criticism, that Jeremiah and Ezekiel are the first exponents of personal religion and personal responsibility, must be abandoned."

Emphatic instances may be identified. For example, the Ten Commandments (Ex. 20; Deut. 5) are phrased in the second person singular ("You shall not"). Further, the upper limit of the Old Testament ethic recorded in Leviticus 19:17-18, 33-34 is phrased also in the second person singular: "But you shall love your neighbor as yourself."

Yet, though individual moral responsibility was not a novel emphasis in wisdom literature, it was raised to a prominent level of consciousness by the wisdom teachers. Their emphasis was on individual rather than on corporate responsibility. It was largely a matter of emphasis. Moreover, it is doubtful that the wisdom sages underscored individualism to the exclusion of corporate responsibility. Since they were working from the smallest social unit upward, their emphasis fell there. It would have been self-defeating to accentuate the corporate role in morality when they sought to heighten the role of the individual in establishing social and moral stability.

*Collectively considered.* Though biblical wisdom is primarily individualistic, the totality of the human race does not by any means fall out of attention. In fact, the book of Job provides a good illustration of this. Job moved from a self-contemplative mood (esp. Job 3, and this is the dominant tone of the first two exchanges of Cycle One—chaps. 6-7, 9-10) to a disposition in which he began to apply the implications of his personal dilemma to the whole of mankind (Job 14:1-22):

> Man, who is born of woman,
> Is short-lived and full of turmoil.
> Like a flower he comes forth and withers.
> He also flees like a shadow and does not remain.
> (vv. 1-2)

In 7:1-2 he had briefly compared the life of man to the hard service of a hired laborer and then applied that metaphor to his own life (7:3-10). Admittedly this hero of faith began with his individual tragedy and subsequently saw that it had wider implications for the whole race.

Likewise the book of Ecclesiastes has the wider dilemma of man in view as the author contemplated that situation through his own personal experience. He began his inquiry by engaging the generic term "man" (*ādām*):

> What advantage does man have in all his work
> Which he does under the sun?
> (Eccles. 1:3)

The fate of the race was still in his mind when he closed his investigation: "For man goes to his eternal home while mourners go about in the street" (12:5c). Of course, as may already be obvious, this application of the individual's dilemma to the race as a whole was more characteristic of reflective wisdom (Job and Eccles.) than of practical (Prov.). The balance between these two emphases in biblical wisdom is worthy of any age.

In conclusion, we may observe that biblical wisdom looks at man, both individually and corporately, in the light of the biblical injunction: "Be fruitful and multiply, and fill the earth, and subdue it; and rule over the fish of the sea and over the birds of the sky, and over every living thing that moves on the earth" (Gen. 1:28). How he accepts and executes that responsibility is determinative of his destiny.

## AN ORDERLY UNIVERSE

The basic universal principle in biblical wisdom is that the physical and moral universe operates by the law of cause-effect. This means that in the realm of human actions, good deeds are rewarded, and evil deeds are punished. This is clearly illustrated in Proverbs 10:30:

> The righteous will never be shaken,
> But the wicked will not dwell in the land.

Gelin has divided the theoretical development of divine retribution into three stages: (1) collective and temporal, (2) individual and temporal, and (3) individual and otherworldly. He further sees their development along a chronological continuum.[7] Although the three models can all be identified in wisdom literature, the attempt to reconstruct the history of ideas is a risky task. More probably these three stages have wide overlaps in Old Testament thought. Yet the three models will serve our discussion purpose very well.

The first model is not very common in wisdom literature because of wisdom's predominant emphasis upon the individual. It is illustrated very well, however, in the Pentateuch. For example, Exodus 20:5-6 states the position clearly:

> For I, the Lord your God, am a jealous God, visiting the iniquity of the fathers on the children, on the third and the fourth generations of those who hate Me, but showing lovingkindness to thousands, to those who love Me and keep My commandments.

The second model, individual and temporal, is the most repeated model in biblical wisdom. It takes several different forms, the simplest of which is represented by Job's friend, Bildad:

7. Albert Gelin, *The Key Concepts of the Old Testament*, p. 73.

> If your sons sinned against Him,
> Then He delivered them into the power of their transgression.
>                                                    (Job 8:4)

Sin is penalized, and the judgment is *punitive*. Job's friends in general shared this model. However, Eliphaz suggested (Job 5:17-26) and Elihu developed (Job 36:8-12) the idea that suffering or punishment was *disciplinary* or *instructive*. It was designed to put one back on the right road to moral wholeness.

Job himself could not accept the first form, and even though he did not reply to Elihu's speeches, he probably did not accept his thesis either. He maintained that suffering is not necessarily a result of sin for he had not committed any wrong. Eventually he came to the admission that there might, however, be some rationale for suffering. If there was, it was *probationary*, God's way of testing man's loyalty:[8]

> But He knows the way I take;
> When He has tried me, I shall come forth as gold.
>                              (Job 23:10; see also v. 14)

Viewed from the perspective of good deeds, righteousness also has its reward. The simplest form of this doctrine may be seen in numerous instances in the book of Proverbs, especially chapters 10-18. Though righteousness may include both the perspective of man's relationship to God and that of his relationship to his neighbor, in Proverbs the latter is the predominant idea. It is measured in terms of good deeds and rewarded in terms of temporal blessings:

> Blessings are on the head of the righteous,
> But the mouth of the wicked conceals violence.
>                                     (Prov. 10:6)

Yet this form of the doctrine did not occupy the entire field of wisdom thought. Job found that this doctrine did not apply in his situation, for he had lived a righteous life and still suffered (cf. Job 31:5-40). The only resolution he could discover was one that was enshrouded in the mystery of God's own being. He did a commendable job controlling the world of nature, and even if man could not see clearly, he could at least extrapolate that He also performed His job well in the moral order (Job 38-39). The psalmist arrived at a slightly different conclusion, but one just as noble and worthy—to be near God is the reward of righteousness:

8.  J. Coert Rylaarsdam, *Revelation in Jewish Wisdom Literature*, p. 53.

> But as for me, the nearness of God is my good;
> I have made the Lord God my refuge,
> That I may tell of all Thy works.
> (Ps. 73:28)

The third model, individual and otherworldly, is illustrated in Psalm 49. The psalmist affirmed that God would redeem him out of the power of Sheol (v. 15). Job also momentarily entertained the idea:

> Even after my skin is destroyed,
> Yet from my flesh I shall see God.
> (Job 19:26)

The doctrine was further affirmed and developed in the Wisdom of Solomon (3:8, 9, 14; 4:7-18; 5:16; 9:15). This exalted and worthy notion in time took its place at the head of the system of retributive justice and became the predominant model in the New Testament.

*Universalism.* We have already referred to the universal nature of wisdom literature. This probably stems in part from the method of wisdom, which began with the smallest unit of society and worked upward. It did not begin with Israel and work down to the individual, as did the prophets. That would likely have given wisdom a national rather than a universal character. To begin with the individual, however, was to open a wide range of possibilities. In this manner wisdom did not aim toward national concerns as such but toward human concerns. Rankin finds the explanation for this phenomenon partly in the fact that wisdom writings were dependent upon international traditions and sources.[9] That indeed may help to explain the universal perspective. However, the universal element was already present in Israelite religion. Yehezkel Kaufmann, in fact, asserts that the individual and universal emphasis was the earlier, and the societal and national the later development.[10] Wisdom preserved those individual and universal elements that were basic to early Israelite religion (Gen. 12:3; Ex. 9:29).

*Law.* The Law, or Torah, does not enter prominently into the biblical wisdom books, except in an indirect way. It stands behind their teaching, even though it is not a recurring term. It does take a place of prominence, however, in Psalms 1, 19, 111, and 119. Its visibility and significance are most obvious in the apocryphal books of Ben Sirach and the Wisdom of Solomon.

## A RECOGNIZABLE IMMORTALITY

The question of whether or not the Old Testament before the postexilic era taught the doctrine of life after death has long been a matter of discussion. A. F.

9. Rankin, p. 12.
10. Yehezkel Kaufmann, *The Religion of Israel,* p. 326.

Kirkpatrick in his commentary on the Psalms was willing to admit that Psalms 16, 17, 49, and 73 contained the germ and principle of the doctrine of eternal life.[11] So widely held was the view that no such doctrine existed in preexilic Israel that many scholars would rule out potential textual candidates for this doctrine simply because they had already concluded that it was nonexistent.

In recent times, however, the question has been reopened by several scholars. Notable among them is Mitchell Dahood. Bringing his knowledge of Ugaritic poetry and mythology to bear upon the Psalms, he has identified thirty-three passages in the Psalter where he sees the doctrine of the future life. In addition, he cites eight passages in Proverbs along with one each in Numbers, Ecclesiasticus, Isaiah, and Daniel.[12] Another intriguing study on the subject has been done by H. C. Brichto[13] in which he draws the conclusion:

> We believe that the evidence deduced from earliest Israelite sources through texts as late as the exilic prophets testifies overwhelmingly to a belief on the part of biblical Israel in an afterlife, an afterlife in which the dead, though apparently deprived of material substance, retain such personality characteristics as form, memory, consciousness, and even knowledge of what happens to their descendants in the land of the living.[14]

He further observes that the basic difference between the concept as we find it in Israel and that in the pagan religions of the ancient Near East is that the idea of reward and punishment in the afterlife was of the essence of the basic Hebrew concept.[15] Whatever may be the criticisms of these two studies, we must acknowledge the new vistas they have opened up for us.

The doctrine of Sheol in the Old Testament is one that has a strange kind of fascination about it. The term occurs sixteen times in the Psalms and forty-nine times elsewhere in the Old Testament. When it refers to a place, it is a place of shadows and darkness where the dead go and from which they do not return (e.g., Job 10:21; 17:13-16; Ps. 88:5-12). Sometimes it refers not so much to a place as to the state of death (e.g., Ps. 49:14-15). G. S. Gunn is of the opinion that Psalms 16 and 17 go beyond the doctrine of Sheol and rise to the summit of eternal hope.[16]

11. A. F. Kirkpatrick, *The Book of Psalms*, p. xcv.
12. Mitchell Dahood, *Psalms*, 3:xlvi-li.
13. Herbert C. Brichto, "Kin, Cult, Land and Afterlife—A Biblical Complex," HUCA 44 (1973): 1-54.
14. Ibid, p. 48.
15. Ibid, pp. 49-50.
16. George S. Gunn, *Singers of Israel: The Book of Psalms*, p. 82.

For Thou wilt not abandon my soul to Sheol;
Neither wilt Thou allow Thy Holy One to undergo decay.
Thou wilt make known to me the path of life;
In Thy presence is fulness of joy;
In Thy right hand there are pleasures forever.

(Ps. 16:10-11)

As for me, I shall behold Thy face in righteousness;
I will be satisfied with Thy likeness when I awake.

(Ps. 17:15)

Peter understood Psalm 16 to predict the resurrection of Christ, and he stated this in his Pentecost sermon (Acts 2:24-28). Gunn further locates the rationale for the afterlife in the concept of personal communication with God, referring to Jesus' statement in Matthew 22:32 and concluding: "These words mean that, because God graciously entered a personal relationship with these men in their lifetime, they are alive still, for such a relationship cannot be broken by death."[17] Rankin essentially agrees, adding to that the "deepening conception of the unconditional righteousness of God."[18]

Three other passages may be considered (the reader may refer to Dahood's long list for others). The first is Job 19:25-27. The writer of Job does not seem to have readily accepted the view of the afterlife, for earlier Job had declared that death would be final for him:

Would He not let my few days alone?
Withdraw from me that I may have a little cheer
Before I go—and I shall not return—
To the land of darkness and deep shadow;
The land of utter gloom as darkness itself,
Of deep shadow without order,
And which shines as the darkness.

(Job 10:20-22)

When, however, Job climbed to his spiritual Mount Nebo, he seemed to be far more confident that vindication would come even after death, and that he personally would witness it. The text of 19:26 is admittedly difficult, but the allusion is certainly to some kind of postdeath experience, whether in his body or outside it. The concept of afterlife is there even though it is not defined. We may suggest, therefore, that the author of Job was struggling with the concept and wanted desperately to embrace it. When he could attain the summit, he still resisted the temptation to resolve Job's dilemma by merely relegating it to the next

17. Ibid., p. 83.
18. Rankin, p. 147.

world. That is obvious because he did not refer to the concept in the God speeches or in the epilogue.

Both Psalms 49:15 and 73:24 employ the word "take" (*lāqaḥ*), which some commentators have understood as a technical word with the sense of "take" up into heaven as it is used in Genesis 5:24 and 2 Kings 2:3,5,9,10 of the assumptions of Enoch and Elijah.[19] Rankin, on the other side, disqualifies the technical term and disassociates it from the Genesis and Kings texts. His conclusion is that the idea of immortality is tantamount to communion with God.[20] It would appear, however, as mentioned above, that communion with God leans in the direction of immortality and is the starting point for understanding the concept. But they are not equivalents. The psalmist expected God to redeem him from the power of death:

> But God will redeem my soul from the power of Sheol;
> For He will receive me. Selah.
>
> (Ps. 49:15)

In 73:24 the psalmist, already conscious of his continuous communion with God, enunciates his belief that God will afterward receive him into glory:

> With Thy counsel Thou wilt guide me,
> And afterward receive me to glory.

Dahood reinforces the technical meaning of "receive" ("take") by his observation that the parallel verb *nāḥāh* in the first part of the verse also bears a technical meaning, "to lead into Paradise."[21] The term occurs further in Psalms 23:3 and 139:24.

Although we may exercise some caution in following all of Dahood's suggestions, it is significant that he has begun to cast some light into some of the obscure tunnels of the Psalms. If it turns out that one tunnel leads nowhere, then we will still be better off by virtue of having explored it and made that discovery. Yet the very idea that Israel should have had no hope of an afterlife in a world where that hope loomed so large in neighboring cultures seems strange indeed.

That is not to suggest at all that Israel borrowed the dominant feature of her faith from her neighbors. Rather the superiority of Israel's monotheism over the polytheism of the ancient Near East and the high regard in which human life was held in Hebrew religion seem to demand more on the side of potential afterlife than on the side of extinction. Furthermore, even death and Sheol could hardly

19. E.g., Dahood, *Psalms*, 3:li; 1:301-2; 2:195.
20. Rankin, pp. 154-62.
21. Dahood, *Psalms*, 2:195.

have escaped the comprehensive power of redemption, which is so predominant in Old Testament theology.

The denial of this doctrine by modern scholarship is in part due to the pervasive methodology that insists that Hebrew religion resulted from an evolutionary line of development and that the more lofty concepts stand at the end of the process. Even biblical scholarship, though not generally abandoning this critical method, continues to amass evidence to the contrary. Standing on this side of the incarnation and the resurrection of Christ, the temptation is strong to read our Christian hope into the Old Testament. But in resisting the temptation, we ought not overrule the evidence.

## What Wisdom Theology Means Now

Recent interest in biblical wisdom is a vindication of a powerful literature that has been greatly neglected in the past. However, it goes beyond that. The declining faith of biblical critics in the historical content of the Old Testament has left a void that wisdom can fill. Apart from the desperation left by negative criticism of the Bible, there is a strong role for wisdom in biblical theology and modern life. Fortunately evangelical theology has never agonized over whether the proper role of biblical theology was to explain what the Bible *meant* or what it *means*. It has assumed that both are demanded. Thus it seems both necessary and appropriate to discuss the significance of wisdom for modern men and women.

### BIBLICAL HUMANISM

Old Testament theology has both an inner and outer circle. The inner circle is found in the revelation of God in history, both in word and event, recorded basically in the Torah and the Prophets of the Old Testament. The outer circle is to be identified in Old Testament wisdom.

The wisdom literature outlines and defines one of the first themes of the Bible, the awakening self-consciousness of mankind. At the prompting of the serpent he contemplated his potential: "For God knows that in the day you eat from it your eyes will be opened, and you will be like God, knowing good and evil" (Gen. 3:5). And when Satan had infected Adam and Eve with his autonomous spirit, man's rude awakening of self-consciousness came: "Then the eyes of both of them were opened, and they knew that they were naked; and they sewed fig leaves together and made themselves loin coverings" (Gen. 3:7). This self-consciousness that might have become a blessing had become a bane. He was doomed to live under its burden.

Wisdom literature, probably more than any other biblical genre, deals with that human self-consciousness. It is an exposition of the words, "Then the eyes of both of them were opened . . ." (Gen. 3:7). They were opened to the world and to themselves. Unfortunately the distorted view demanded that man do something to change his circumstances. So he did two things: he sewed fig leaves to make aprons that could cover his nakedness, and he hid from God. These two acts revealed the mental confusion about himself and about his God. The rest of the biblical narrative might in simplistic terms be described as a reflection on and a corrective of this distorted perspective. Wisdom literature falls within the scope of both, even though the first is its preoccupation. It is the literature of human self-consciousness.

Humanism as a philosophy falls within the first category, that of human self-contemplation. In its most elementary form it is as ancient as Adam, while in its modern configuration it traces its history back to the Greeks of the fifth century B.C. The ancient Greeks were concerned with reconciling the life of man with the world in which he lived. Their gods became the media of this harmonization. Little more than superhuman beings, the gods and man met at the juncture of nature and there found common ground. From the time of the Sophists who likely gave the first expression to this spirit, the Greeks sought to harmonize the spirit of man with the spirit of nature. Protagoras, the most eminent of the Sophists, articulated their dictum, "Man is the measure of all things; of the being of things that are and of the non-being of things that are not." The meaning of his statement seems to be that "there is no objective standard of appeal."[22] The Stoics, however, gave ancient humanism its most mature form. "Salvation, for the Stoic, meant self-realization by self-reliance and self-discipline. Their whole ethical system centered itself in man."[23]

No less man-centered were the Epicureans. They taught that man should look to himself to achieve whatever he believed was good. "Pleasure was the one true good, intellectual rather than the physical or sensual pleasures."[24]

The Romans amassed a great empire and mastered social organization, but, as Elias Andrews observes, they accomplished the marvelous feat of maintaining a unity of life without suppressing individuality.[25]

When the Renaissance spirit began to take shape in the fifteenth century, it was essentially a revival of the Greek spirit of humanism, and the individual again assumed proportions of utmost importance in the world. The medieval idea of the world as evil was set aside as man undertook his renewed search for beauty and truth. Renaissance humanism, for all its trust in man, did not repudiate God, but took for granted the significant place religion had held in life.[26]

Modern humanism has taken a turn away from Renaissance humanism in that man has been elevated to the level where he is both man and god. And that

22. *The Cambridge Ancient History*, 5:278.
23. Elias Andrews, *Modern Humanism and Christian Theism*, p. 29.
24. Ibid., pp. 31-32.
25. Ibid., p. 35.
26. Ibid., pp. 38-39.

is its congenital defect. It has no god but man. F. R. Barry has pointed out the intrinsic problem this poses: "There seems to be a law in the moral order that what is natural tends to become unnatural unless redeemed by what is supernatural."[27]

I do not intend to suggest that the Bible has a humanism that has a one-to-one correspondence to the kind of humanism that the Greeks and modern man have embraced. Yet wisdom literature does aim in a similar direction, and its thrust has similarities. The following are some of the characteristics of biblical humanism.

1. It focuses on *human life, morality,* and *the natural order.* Like modern humanism, the individual comes clearly in view. As a result, the social concerns of this literature are prominent. The social units of the family, community, and state are centers of attention. The stability of these social units is an aim of the wisdom movement.

2. Biblical humanism recognizes *the worth of man* and contemplates the formidable problems of his existence—death, injustice, immorality, and so forth. The fact that man stands at the center of the world only serves to deepen the trauma created by the fundamental problems of human life. When Job observed that a tree was more enduring than man (14:7-17), he formulated the acute statement,

> Man, who is born of woman,
> Is short-lived and full of turmoil.
> (Job 14:1)

3. Biblical humanism *speaks for man.* It is his charter of self-consciousness. The book of Job speaks to God about man, while Proverbs and Ecclesiastes in large part speak to man about man. But we must acknowledge that this talk about mankind takes place within a devoutly theistic context and is not devoid of admonitions that turn the attention of the human creature toward God.

4. Biblical humanism is *theistic* in its foundation. While wisdom literature observes the natural order, the rationale is to see God in it, to learn what He would say to man about life in the world He has made. God is behind nature, speaking through it. It is one of His media of communication. He is the Artist, the Master Designer, the Creator. To understand the Artist one must study His works.

In contrast modern humanism does not seek God in the natural order. It has sealed the mouth of the created world so that the voice of God cannot be heard through it.

On the other side, the fear of the Lord is the cohesive force in biblical humanism. It is the appointment that God and man have together. Only in relation

27. F. R. Barry, *The Relevance of Christianity,* p. 59.

to God can man achieve the kind of self-consciousness that will not lead him into a blind alley of moral ambiguity.

5. Biblical humanism has a *telos*. Different from modern humanism that seeks a new order within mankind, wisdom literature seeks a new order for all the human species. It would come only by attention to the disciplined life of wisdom, which was the distillation of the divine will for man. Thus man would not and could not produce the new social order, but God could bring it about through obedient, self-disciplined persons who feared Him and kept His commandments (Eccles. 12:13). Wisdom, while emphasizing the need for man to know himself, taught that ultimate satisfaction is only achieved in relationship to God.

Yet biblical wisdom has a built-in deficiency that cries out for God to break into man's world and dismantle his vital questions with answers that are clear and forthright, immediate and personal. Therefore, without being disparaging, we may speak of the failure of biblical humanism. That is not to imply that the Word of God has in the least fallen short of its goal, but merely to point up the fact that wisdom literature never was intended to provide a theological system that operated in isolation from the historical revelation of God through the Law and Prophets.

Biblical humanism is lacking at the very point for which it aims—a personal relationship to God. The fear of the Lord was to involve the individual in a personal encounter with God, to turn him away from himself to the Creator. The failure, however, becomes visible when man cannot penetrate beyond the creation to the truly personal nature of the Creator God.

While the Creator was personal and involved with His creation, the wisdom person lacked the penetrating insight into the genuinely personal nature of the God who not only created but also redeemed. It is only in the Redeemer God that man meets the Deity as Person. Only in the Redeemer God does the image of God the Creator become personalized. The Creator God, while admittedly personal, is more remote, more transcendant than the Redeemer God who comes down, reveals Himself in history, and walks among His human creatures.

MORAL GUIDANCE

Wisdom supplies certain deficiencies in modern culture and society. The need to find an anchorage for moral conduct is met by wisdom's accent on the Creator God as the source of life and the reference point for all human actions and attitudes. The one Creator of all men and all things is the Absolute against which all relationships must be measured and all actions weighed.

The modern view that religious faith is at best only a catalyst in a process is detrimental to the well-being of mankind. The psalmists knew that faith itself was the process. God was both transcendent over and immanent in the lives of men and women. A faith whose God is transcendent promotes a high view of the deity, but a faith whose God is immanent produces a high view of man. Both components are found in the biblical faith of the poetic books. One is not exclusive of the other but they are companions of divine revelation.

The basic element of what is morally permissible and what is not is based upon a double relationship, that of the horizontal and vertical, or a person's relationship to his world and to his God. Wisdom literature, while drawing the horizontal lines very heavy, does not neglect the vertical. In a society plagued by relativism, the missing element of moral guidance can be supplied by wisdom.

While this may be said of other biblical genres as well, it is strikingly true of wisdom because this movement and literature made moral conduct one of its primary concerns. Social stability could never be achieved without moral integrity, and moral integrity, whose reality is validated and tested by interpersonal relationships, was anchored in relationship to God. Perhaps modern society will find less offensive a literature in which social concerns and human justice are so central, but which employs moral admonitions rather than divine imperatives. But once one has accepted the didactic mode of wisdom, one will find that its urgency is as pressing as the imperative of the Prophets and the prescription of the Law because it, too, originates in the moral character of God.

In a culture where religion is often considered a scourge rather than a badge of honor, true piety may be held in contempt. Yet wisdom literature and the Psalms call the church to recover genuine piety, not piety caricatured as "a hypocritical life-style which imprisons an individual in a repressive straight jacket."[28] It is not legalism, but the performance of duty from a sense of love. A mature attitude of spiritual growth and enjoying God is part of its makeup (Ps. 131:1-2).

The church in any age cannot experience genuine renewal without a revitalization of piety. As the Psalter illustrates so well, man's double bond to God, creation and redemption, is the only context in which the meaning of human existence takes intelligible form. Before the God who is both transcendent and immanent, Creator and Redeemer, the only appropriate human posture is prostration before His majesty. The Psalms are a frequent witness to the truth that personal happiness and inner security are found in the praise of God. The recognition that human destiny is fixed in direct proportion to the praise of God will free the heart to soar to Him, oblivious of personal gain. For only when God is exalted does man find his rightful place in the universe.

Wisdom has its own term for this dimension of faith, the "fear of the Lord." The necessity for the recovery of this disposition is written in the defiance and chaos of the modern social order. A world view that gathers all the

28. Bruce L. Shelley, ed., *Call to Christian Character: Toward A Recovery of Biblical Piety*, preface and p. 1.

threads of human experience and puts them in proper relationship to the religious life is of vital importance to the survival of a world of such technological complexity and diversity as ours.

In fact, we need to recapture the pervasive power of our Christian faith, which includes and addresses all human experience within the wide circle of life. As for Old Testament wisdom, so for the unsearchable wisdom of Christ, man is a totality that must come under the light and scrutiny of faith. He cannot be dismembered and his constituent parts distributed among the various disciplines, leaving only his elusive "spirit" within faith's circle. Instead, all facets of life and experience must turn their faces toward the encircling and enlightening God. The fear of God in its fullest proportions as taught by the wisdom sages can serve as a model for those who would undertake this challenge.

# 3

# THE BOOK OF JOB

Perhaps no problem has engaged man's mind and occupied his heart so universally as the perplexity of human suffering. All of the major religions have been compelled to come to grips with it.[1] The Hebrew and Christian faiths have conducted a valiant struggle in this regard, and the book of Job is the classic formulation of the Hebraic position on the matter.

The Christian faith has fallen grateful heir to this statement. Indeed, the spirit and theology of the book are so much a fundamental part of Christianity that numberless Christians have read this book, identified with its hero, fed upon its whirlwind revelation, and have had the strange sense that, despite the pre-Christian context, they stood within the encompassing bounds of the incarnation. Yet it is not a Christian book but Hebraic through and through, and the sense of kinship that is experienced is due in part to the universal issue that it treats and the unexcelled heights of anticipation to which it rises.

## THE CENTRAL ISSUE OF JOB

The most obvious issue in the book is the suffering of the righteous. Yet the range of the book is multiform. The basic approaches to explaining the central problem may be viewed in two categories, the theological and the existential. The focus upon a universal question, such as justice or evil or unmerited suffering, with the aim of providing an explanation, constitutes the theological approach. The existential, in comparison, is not concerned with theological issues per se but with theological experience, the way a person relates to God and universal issues.

Addressing the book of Job theologically, some view the central issue to be the problem of evil. Although this may be the larger context, the author made no effort to resolve this agonizing problem. Actually we are probably closer to precision by being less precise and viewing the central issue as a complex of ideas rather than a single one. The issue(s) is (are) attracted to two poles, the justice of

1. John Bowker, *Problems of Suffering in Religions of the World.*

God and the integrity of the righteous. Clustering around these poles are other issues inherent in any consideration of the two, the mystery of evil, the prosperity of the wicked, and the suffering of the righteous. As Kaufmann has correctly observed, the suffering of the righteous leads inevitably to the larger question of whether there is a moral order in the world at all.[2] Job entertained this question (9:22-24). The author peeled off the layers of Hebrew life and thought and exposed the bare core in a daring adventure—when the justice of God and the righteousness of man clash, what resolution exists? Pedersen astutely observes the resolution in the God speeches.

> [Job] must subject himself to the mighty will of God, trusting to the fact that man has *his* righteousness and God *his*; and when they do not harmonize, then it is not that God's justice goes against that of man and suspends it, but that it transcends it and goes deeper than man is able to penetrate.[3]

While we regard the theological interpretation of Job as the primary mode, the existential approach advances a complementary understanding of the book. The assumption of this hermeneutical mode is that the experience of Job is paradigmatic of what others, regardless of time in history, have suffered. They, therefore, find their experience in Job and identify with him. The cathartic element of great literature is recognizably important for its enduring impact on mankind. And Job does not fall short of that characteristic. That Job launched upon a journey of faith can hardly be denied, and we can identify with his regress and progress. Snaith, affirming the existential interpretation, has proposed that the sufferings of Job are discussed to highlight the problem of the transcendent God: "How can the High God ever be imminently concerned with the affairs of men?" In his view, the eventual answer of the book to this question is submission: "God still far away, unapproachable and incomprehensible, but with a working rule for man."[4] Habel also declares in favor of the existential approach by stating that the book "is the intense struggle of a great poet to probe the very meaning of life, especially life where suffering and injustice prevail for no apparent reason."[5]

Job indeed struggled with life, moved from humble submission (prologue) to daring challenge (dialogue), and eventuated in a more informed submission after the God speeches. As important as his journey was, it was complementary to the theological-issue complex, the vehicle for communicating it and evoking its many facets. It was the verbal expression of the substantive matter, the latter being the justice of God and the integrity of the righteous. But is one more im-

2. Yehezkel Kaufmann, *The Religion of Israel*, p. 334.
3. Johannes Pedersen, *Israel, Its Life and Culture*, 1-2:373.
4. Norman H. Snaith, *The Book of Job: Its Origin and Purpose*, p. vii.
5. Norman C. Habel, *The Book of Job*, p. 1. See also Alexander Di Lella's article, "An Existential Interpretation of Job." *Biblical Theology Bulletin* 15 (1985):49-55.

portant than the other? Put another way, can God do without man? The answer is only implied in the book—indeed He can! But man was His doing and not God man's devising. God took the initiative—"Have you considered My servant Job?" And God resolved the issue by answering Job out of the whirlwind. Job's significance and the meaning of his religious experience began and ended with God, whose inherent nature (not Job's) committed Him to His human creature— "there is no one like him on the earth." Thus the relationship between the theological and existential interpretations of Job is one of both substance and perspective. The theological is primary because God is omnipotent Creator—"Where were you when I laid the foundation of the earth!" (38:4*a*). Yet the fact that God was speaking those words to Job involves the existential truth that man is very important to Him.

## SOME INTRODUCTORY MATTERS ABOUT JOB

### PURPOSE

Once the central issue is put in perspective, the purpose of the book has already assumed its outline. The book of Job was written in order to probe the vast regions and recesses of the justice of God in the world. It is our prime biblical example of a theodicy, a work that seeks to investigate the problem of divine justice. The wisdom schools of ancient Israel were known for this intellectual and spiritual exercise. Job is that exercise incarnate. The philosophical and theological dimensions of divine justice are given a personal and experiential form, thus bringing the hypothetical into the practical arena of life. It is on that level that the discussion must eventually take place, and only at the point where the theoretical touches the practical can man find ease for his aching heart and satisfaction for his questing spirit. The book of Job provides a real example of extreme suffering, and it is precisely its reality (as well as the profound faith of its hero) that has been a source of comfort and reassurance to those who have suffered through the ages. In Job the suffering saint has one with whom to identify.

### DATE

The difficulty of dating the book of Job is suggested by the wide range of dates that have been assigned to it, extending from the patriarchal period to the postexilic age. Recognizably one of the problems is that the author had no interest in historical details. At least they did not serve his purpose. Other considerations that bear upon date are the relation of the language of the dialogue to the Ugaritic, Aramaic, and Arabic languages, the development of wisdom literature in general, the importance of the individual in ancient Near Eastern culture, and the concept of the afterlife. All of these have been utilized in attempts to locate this incomparable book at an approximate place in the historical continuum. At the outset, therefore, we must sense the insecurity of dogmatism on the matter and agree with A. B. Davidson that here we have entered a region "which is not that of argument but of impressions."[6]

Most likely the rabbis were influenced toward a patriarchal date by the author's use of *El* and *Eloah* for God, measurement of Job's wealth in terms of his cattle and flocks, Job's patriarchal role as priest, and his longevity. The Babylonian Talmud preserves rabbinic speculation on the subject.[7] Delitzsch examined Job in relation to other biblical books and concluded on the basis of language that the psalms of Heman and Ethan (Pss. 88, 89), both contemporaries of Solomon (1 Kings 4:31), were minted from the same age as Job. Thus he assigned the book to the Solomonic age.[8]

In chronological order, the next assigned date is the monarchical era between Solomon and the Babylonian Exile. Yehezkel Kaufmann[9] cautiously opts for a preexilic date, as does also Pope,[10] but for different reasons. Kaufmann believes the classical Hebrew style pleads for the age that produced the great prophetic and moralistic literature of the Old Testament, whereas Pope is largely convinced by the absence of any allusions to the great tragedy of Judah in the early sixth century, along with the probability that the advanced development of wisdom literature in the preexilic age provided the context for such a masterpiece.

The Exile has also had its proponents. Davidson believed that divine providence was no longer calmly accepted, and that the background of the poem was some great disorder, the Exile being the most viable era.[11] Guillaume built an impressive hypothesis largely from certain allusions to lawless conditions that might have obtained for a Jew during the Babylonian domination (cf. chap. 30). The restoration of Job's fortunes suggested to him the end of the Babylonian occupation. Thus he dated Job's misfortunes during the occupation of Tema by Nabonidus (c. 552 B.C.).[12] Such precise dating of Job is unusual, not to mention precarious.

An early postexilic date is favored by Gordis, who views Job as the "high-water mark of biblical Wisdom."[13] Dhorme, following a comparative Scripture approach, has suggested 500-450 B.C. Believing Job 12:17-19 to be an allusion to the Exile, he established Judean captivity as the *terminus a quo*, with Malachi marking the *terminus ad quem*, since that prophet suggested the method and complaints of Elihu (cf. Job 1:1 and 33:31 and, Mal. 3:16).[14]

6. A. B. Davidson, *The Book of Job*, p. lxvi.
7. The Babylonian Talmud, ed. I. Epstein. *Baba Bathra* 14b, 15b; *Sanhedrin* 106a; *Sotah* 11a.
8. Franz Delitzsch, *Biblical Commentary on the Book of Job*, 1:23.
9. Kaufmann, p. 338.
10. Marvin H. Pope, *Job*, p. xl.
11. Davidson, pp. lxiii, lxvi.
12. A. Guillaume, *Studies in the Book of Job*, pp. 3-14.
13. Robert Gordis, *The Book of God and Man*, pp. 20, 52.
14. E. Dhorme, *A Commentary on the Book of Job*, pp. clxvii-clxix.

Although we do not seek specificity, some observations are in order and may help us in settling on some broad era as a date range. Wisdom compositions in the ancient Near East are as old as the second millennium B.C. S. N. Kramer has translated a Sumerian wisdom poem that he dates roughly about 1700 B.C.[15] W. G. Lambert has collected many examples of Babylonian wisdom from the second and first millennia B.C.[16] Thus the literary milieu as well as parallels to Job extend far into the preexilic era. Further, since these compositions treat the suffering of individuals, the prominence of concern for the individual cannot be relegated to the late preexilic or postexilic eras. Nor can we continue to confine the afterlife concept to Israel's postexilic age,[17] particularly when the popularity of afterlife thought in Mesopotamia and Egypt is considered along with the biblical data. Finally, the citation of other biblical materials and the attempt to establish the chronological priority of one over the other is a risky task.

In view of all the considerations, we may agree with Kaufmann and Pope that there are no cogent reasons to deny a preexilic date. To be more precise than that would require more data than we have on hand.

### PROVENANCE AND AUTHORSHIP

Suggestions for the origin of the book or the identification of the author are almost as varied as those for date. The range of proposals for provenance includes Egypt, Arabia, Edom, and Israel.[18] It may be helpful to speak of provenance on two levels, geographical and religious. As to Egypt, nothing so profound as Job has come forth in Egyptian wisdom documents. Arabia may be rejected for its polytheistic religion and primitive culture.[19] Edom has probably enjoyed the greatest popularity because of the identification of Uz with Edom in Lamentations 4:21, the two occurring in parallel lines. Another tradition has located Uz near Damascus; however, Gordis suggests that Edom is most likely because the proper names in Job are drawn from the genealogy of Esau in Genesis 36 (esp. vv. 4, 11).[20] Although we are ready to acknowledge this likelihood, the religious provenance is another matter. Our knowledge of Edomite religion is insufficient to speak intelligently on the matter, but we can confidently say that Job's concern for the poor and oppressed was typically Hebraic (4:3-4; 29:12-17). And the challenging spirit was not foreign to the Israelite religious experience either. Moreover, to understand why an Israelite would have a long established

15. S. N. Kramer, "Man and His God: A Sumerian Variation on the 'Job' Motif," WIANE, pp. 170-82.
16. W. G. Lambert, *Babylonian Wisdom Literature*.
17. See Herbert C. Brichto, "Kin, Cult, Land and Afterlife—A Biblical Complex," HUCA 44 (1973):1-54, esp. p. 51.
18. See Gordis, pp. 209-12, for a discussion of the proposals.
19. Ibid., pp. 210-12.
20. Ibid., p. 66.

residence in Edom is not difficult, for it was not unusual for Israelites to take up residence in neighboring countries (cf. Ruth 1:1). We may suggest then that geographically the provenance is Edom, although in spirit and language the book is Hebraic.

There is simply no way to determine who wrote this marvelous piece of religious literature. We can be confident, however, that the author was a Hebrew or Israelite who espoused a pure monotheism and whose faith in the omnipotent and just God was unshakable. It was because of that spiritual security that he was capable of challenging Almighty God to lay bare the inner workings of His universal order and thereby expose a part of His nature that, to the author's mind, was too obscure. He challenged the spirit of man to rise above the purely mechanical explanation of the moral order and to enter the realm of divine perspective where cosmic mystery is resolved in the nature of God Himself. He was no commonplace thinker, the likes of whom the world has known very few. He may remain anonymous in name, but let us hope that his spirit and faith will forever be written indelibly upon the heart of man.

## THE LITERARY STRUCTURE

In this section we shall concern ourselves primarily with literary structure because of its significance for the meaning of the book. To illustrate, if Elihu does not belong to the essential structure of Job and was not part of the author's original plan, as some scholars contend, then our interpretation of the book as a whole will be greatly affected. Job is a book whose literary structure and meaning are so intertwined that they stand or fall together. While we shall subsequently discuss the content of the book in more detail, it becomes obvious that we cannot speak about literary structure without discussing interpretation to some extent.

The book of Job defies all efforts to establish its literary genre. While it has been viewed as an epic,[21] a tragedy,[22] and a parable,[23] upon close analysis it is none of these even though it exhibits properties belonging to each of them.[24] As Robert Gordis observes, the author of Job has created his own literary genre.[25] The book is didactic in the sense that the author seeks to teach religious truth, a task that he executes primarily by means of lyrical poetry expressive of deep emotions.[26]

21. See, e.g, Nahum M. Sarna, "Epic Substratum in the Prose of Job," JBL 76 (1957):13-25.
22. Horace M. Kallen, *The Book of Job as a Greek Tragedy*, esp. pp. 3-38.
23. Moses Maimonides, *The Guide of the Perplexed*, p. 486.
24. See the list of genres that have been proposed in William Sanford Lasor, et al., *Old Testament Survey*, pp. 572-75.
25. Gordis, p. 7.
26. Ibid.

As the book has come to us, the literary structure is as follows:

### LITERARY STRUCTURE OF JOB

| PRO-LOGUE 1-2 | | DIALOGUE 3-27 | | | | THREE MONOLOGUES 28-37 | | | GOD SPEECHES 38:1–42:6 | | EPI-LOGUE 42:7-17 |
|---|---|---|---|---|---|---|---|---|---|---|---|
| Scene 1, Ch. 1 | Scene 2, Ch. 2 | Job's Opening Monlogue, Ch. 3 | First Cycle 4-14 | Second Cycle 15-21 | Third Cycle 22-27 | Poem on Wisdom, 28 | Job's Closing Monlogue, 29-31 | Elihu Speeches 32-37 | 1st Speech 38:1-40:5 | 2d Speech 40:6-42:6 | Job's Restoration 42:7-17 |

Many scholars believe that the present structure shows signs of disarrangement and editorializing. Although we should not assume that passages were not occasionally misplaced in the process of scribal transmission, the drastic rearrangement that has sometimes been proposed may be too easy a way out of a difficult dilemma. We should also be aware of the risks involved, one of which is superimposing our literary logic upon an ancient piece of literature. Further, if an earlier form of the book existed and was popularly known, we may wonder how extensive rearrangement could be perpetrated without its being detected by the readership of the book and thus subsequently corrected. A basic principle of biblical hermeneutics, which is sometimes ignored, is that the interpreter must deal initially and finally with the form in which the literature has come to us. Nor should we disregard the work of the Holy Spirit in the total process. Thus we will attempt to interpret the book of Job in its present arrangement.

### PROLOGUE-EPILOGUE AND DIALOGUE

The prologue (chaps. 1-2) and epilogue (42:7-17) are written in prose, with the poetic dialogue sandwiched in between. Yet the portrait of the faithful Job in the prologue (1:21; 2:10) hardly prepares us for the near-defiant Job of the dialogue. The problem has two facets, the literary and dialectic, which are really one. Some scholars have tried to solve the literary by proposing that the prose narrative originally had nothing to do with the poetic dialogue. Yet, if the story of Job's life and faith prior to his tragedy is the mere occasion for the author of the dialogue to engage his literary skill, we lose the impact of the suffering, innocent man who moves from unquestioning faith in God through the depths of trouble (prologue), and subsequently challenges God's justice (dialogue).

Rick D. Moore shows how the Joban poet interfaces the prologue and the dialogue by the thematic structure of Job's lament in chapter 3. In 1:21 the poet introduces Job's first utterance affirming life and God, broken down into a four-fold thematic structure, and in chapter 3 he provides a negative commentary on that utterance—A. Reverent acceptance of the womb (1:21a)/Denigration of the womb (3:1-10); B. Reverent acceptance of the tomb (1:21b)/Regret of his delayed death (3:11-19); C. Reverent acceptance of God as the Giver of life (1:21c)/Indirect questioning of God (3:20-23); D. Theocentric praise (1:21d)/ Egocentric lament (3:24-26).[27] Thus the lament becomes a swing text that provides smooth passage from the prologue to the dialogue.

The Job of the prologue was a man whose religion was the interpretative factor for all aspects of life. When trouble struck, the natural thing for him was to interpret it in terms of his faith. Even when personal loss was compounded by physical affliction, he still held fast to his religious integrity (2:10). Yet subsequently the dark depths of emotional and physical suffering evoked reexamination of the theological tenets that had initially enabled him to respond so trustingly.

Dialectically there is ample evidence in the dialogue that the author is working with the portrait he has painted of Job in the prologue. Dramatic irony is operating in the prologue, because the audience knows about the heavenly council, is aware of the wager between God and Satan, and is informed of the reason for Job's suffering, whereas Job is not. It is a test, not to refine an imperfect man, but to bring out the sterling character that God knows Job already possesses. The author has presented him as "a man in whom all ethical and religious qualities are raised, as it were, to the highest power, and whose external circumstances leave nothing to be desired."[28] Even though Job is ignorant of the metaphysical events, momentarily at times he receives keen insight into that transaction, although he still is not aware of its reality. In 23:10 he verbalizes the reason for his suffering:

> But He knows the way I take;
> When He has tried me, I shall
> come forth as gold.

Immediately Job follows this by a reaffirmation of his loyalty to God (vv. 11-12), and then acknowledges that He performs what He has appointed for him (vv. 13-14). Unbeknown to our protagonist, he has just articulated God's rationale for putting him to this test.

27. Rick D. Moore, "The Integrity of Job," CBQ 45 (1983) 26:17-31.
28. Roderick A. F. MacKenzie, "The Transformation of Job," *Biblical Theology Bulletin* 9 (1979):52.

In 24:1 Job asks:

> Why are times not stored up by the Almighty,
> And why do those who know Him not see His days?

A rhetorical question for Job, the audience knows that God does have special days when He entertains queries about His righteous servants on earth (1:6; 2:1).

In Job's famous speech about wisdom, he concludes by quoting God's own declaration about wisdom, and in doing so sums up God's assessment of Job's character in the prologue (1:8; 2:3):

> And to man He said, "Behold,
> the fear of the Lord, that is wisdom;
> And to depart from evil is understanding."
>
> (28:28)

The poem on wisdom claims that no one but God knows the way to wisdom. That is, God's ways are really incomprehensible, and no one but He can understand them. This is Job's ultimate concession, corresponding to his confession and repentance in the God speeches. How true that neither Job nor his friends understood what God was doing. Yet the one truth of which he is sure is the description of wisdom of verse 28, and that truth operates in a very practical context. The philosophical dimensions are not so perceivable to him. God's summation of true wisdom here and in His character description of Job in the prologue coincide. Moreover, Job is in agreement. He is not so far from God, and God not so far from him, as he had claimed in his diatribe.

Perhaps the capstone to this uncanny insight into the metaphysical events of the prologue, momentary though it may be, is Job's confession that he had spoken without adequate knowledge of God's ways and motives:

> Therefore I have declared that
> which I did not understand,
> Things too wonderful for me,
> which I did not know.
>
> (42:3)

While it is true that this confession comes in response to the God speeches, it is also true, as indicated above, that Job already had remarkable insights into the metaphysical realities of the prologue, and the God speeches merely enabled him to stabilize that mental posture and act upon it.

The problem of the prologue versus the dialogue must ultimately be solved on both the literary and dialectical levels. The two portraits are quite different, but not so different as to justify the theory of literary discontinuity. Already in the unsettling lament of chapter 3, Job justifies God's vote of confidence in him, for Satan had laid down the challenge that Job would curse God to His face (2:5). His wife actualized that challenge in the earthly situation (2:9), but Job rejected it, and cursed only the day of his birth. On that note of confirmation the dialogue gets under way, and Job is right to maintain his innocence. Further, he is right to establish his innocence with a whole series of oaths in 31:5-40, an innocence that God Himself first affirmed, then Job maintained, and God ultimately vindicated (42:7).

The theological affirmations of the prologue (1:21; 2:10) may have a darker side, and when suffering is held in their light, it will not always reflect their meaning in the same way. Faith too can ask, must ask, What is the meaning of suffering? The symphonic theme, though stated in a major key, can have its minor expressions also. In the dialogue we hear both majors and minors. Job had committed himself to a theological position that had to be explored. The dialogue is the record of that, filled with allegations against a God who, in Job's estimation, was immanent in suffering but distant in justice (e.g., 9:1, 19; 19:7-12; 23:3-7). Yet out of the depths of Job's troubled soul an occasional glimmer of faith's light shone forth (e.g., 19:25-26; 23:10). He had entered the arena where faith and reality meet, and the fight that ensued was neither invalid nor dispensable. The friends acted to an extent as a counterbalance in the first cycle, but in the second and third they had lost patience with Job and no longer counterbalanced but counteracted. Their defense of God turned into a defense of their own theology at the expense of their friend Job.

The relationship between the dialogue and the epilogue is also of great import. If the friends' theology of retribution was so wide of the mark, then why was the restoration of Job a necessary sequel to the story? God's elusive answer to Job's questions did not commit Him to such a system of justice. So He was not obligated to this plan of action. So far as the theology of the God speeches is concerned, Job could have been left suspended in his suffering, and he still would have responded to the deity in the same submissive way. Satan, now fallen out of the picture completely, had been proved wrong—God does have at least one servant who serves Him with no ulterior motive, and even if only one such person is found, religion is genuine. Job's repentance, apart from any promise of restoration, is the self-vindication of God's opinion of him; but God's declaration that Job, in contrast to his friends, had spoken what was right of Him, is God's final vindication of His servant (42:7). Moreover, this latter statement assumes the extensive interchange between Job and his friends in the dialogue.

More than being God's vindication of Job, the epilogue moves justice to the earthly level. The God speeches informed Job that justice was sometimes a mystery, incapable of being translated into human language. However, if that is all, if justice is merely metaphysical, then Job's challenge was right. How can we be sure that weal and woe are not all the same to God (9:22)? The epilogue there-fore necessarily bears out the truth that, although justice is often a mystery, it is also real, capable of translation in terms of this world. Thus Job's restoration supplies a necessary part of the answer. It does not follow, however, that divine justice will always be transcribed in physical terms. But sometimes it must be so that we do not mistakenly conclude that it is a matter for heaven only and not for earth.

THE POEM ON WISDOM

Scholarly opinions on chapter 28 may be subsumed essentially under three headings:[29] (1) those who consider this poem an extraneous composition by an author different from that of the dialogue, (2) those who regard it as a composi-tion by the same author but out of place in the present structure of the book, and (3) those who believe it to be composed by the same author and serving a literary function where it stands.

The exponents of the first position point out the difference in language and mood and conclude that the poem is out of character with the dialogue on both counts.[30] Yet they must deal with the fact that Job (12:2, 12-13) and the friends (11:6; 15:7-8) were concerned specifically and generally with wisdom. Further, the mood of the poem is hardly decisive because Job's emotional disposition fluctuated.

The proponents of the second position point out that the literary character of the poem is worthy of the author of the dialogue, but in its present position it is anticlimactic.[31] Some have suggested that it is the climaxing speech of Zophar (esp. vv. 8-23), since in the third cycle there is no speech for him.[32] Another opinion is that this is an earlier attempt by the author of the dialogue to deal with the mystery of human suffering, and that a later editor included it in its present position.[33]

Yet the third position, that the poem is at home both in literary quality and position, has its proponents too. David Neiman notes the literary excellence of the composition and considers it a lyrical interlude between the verbally harsh debate and the final soliloquy of Job, concluding that it is an integral part of the book.[34] Delitzsch understood the poem to be a confirmation of the assertion in 27:13-23 that evildoers will have their punishment. By the discourse on wisdom and his final declaration that the fear of the Lord is wisdom (28:28), Job taught

29. None of these categories should be considered exclusive, since many scholars would find them-selves straddling two of them. But they will serve as handy pegs for the varying positions.
30. S. R. Driver and G. B. Gray, *A Critical and Exegetical Commentary on the Book of Job*, 1:232-36.
31. Gordis, p. 102.
32. E.g., Habel, pp. 7, 141.
33. Gordis, p. 102.
34. Neiman, pp. 99-100.

that although he could not see through the mystery of his suffering, he had to still hold fast to the fear of the Lord, and that those who fear Him had to be judged by a different principle than the cause-effect principle that the friends had used.[35]

## THE ELIHU SPEECHES

The Elihu speeches (32:1–37:24) have undergone as much critical analysis as the poem on wisdom. The reasons for viewing them as a disparate composition include the observation that Elihu appeared unexpectedly (not having been mentioned in the prologue or dialogue and ignored in the epilogue),[36] that he added little that was new to the argument of the dialogue,[37] and that the language of the speeches is different from the rest of the book.[38]

The reason for Elihu's unanticipated appearance, however, is explained in his opening speech (32:6-7)—he was young and deferred to older men in matters of such importance. Wisdom was believed to reside with the aged (12:12; 15:10), and Elihu respected that tradition.

That he was introduced by the author as an angry young man (which fact is mentioned four times in 32:3-5) is obviously significant. Pfeiffer held that these speeches were an interpolation by a later author who was incensed by the explanation that God's ways are incomprehensible (chap. 28), and despite appearances to the contrary, that they were in line with what human beings believed was right (chaps. 38-41).[39] Though this may account for Elihu's anger, it does not explain why one so incensed would not just substitute his own solution for the God speeches. The author may have tried to give the clue that Elihu's response was more angry than rational. He was angry at the friends because they had not successfully refuted Job (32:11-12, 15-16), and he was angry at Job because he had maintained his innocence at the expense of God's own justice (33:9-12).

The author ignored Elihu in the prologue and dialogue because of his youth, and made no mention of him in the epilogue because he did not live up to his claims that he would not use the friends' words (32:14),[40] that he would teach Job wisdom (33:33), and that he would convince wise men that Job was wrong (34:34-35). The author thus appropriately observed protocol and let the

---

35. Delitzsch, 2:116.
36. Pope, p. xxvii.
37. Driver and Gray, 1:41.
38. For a discussion of language resulting in favor of the genuineness of the Elihu speeches, see Gordis, pp. 106-7, and Delitzsch, 2:210.
39. Robert H. Pfeiffer, *Introduction to the Old Testament*, p. 673.
40. In fact several ideas propounded by Elihu had already been employed by the friends: similar allegations against Job are 34:7/Eliphaz—15:16; 34:8/Eliphaz—22:15; similar approaches to Job's problem are 34:11/Bildad—8:4; 35:5-8/Zophar—11:7-9 and Eliphaz—22:2-3, 12.

aged and experienced speak first. Yet he recognized that they contributed little toward a solution to Job's problem. So to avoid the criticism that the young, to whom wisdom literature was so frequently directed,[41] had not had their opportunity to speak, the author permitted Elihu to unburden himself. Thus he demonstrated the truth that wisdom lay neither with the aged and experienced nor with the young, but only with God. In this manner he prepared us for the God speeches.

The second reason for viewing Elihu as a literary intruder—that he added little new to the arguments of the dialogue—is in a sense true. Yet although he did not live up to his claims, he did expand a theme that had been only briefly suggested by Eliphaz (5:17-18)—that suffering is a form of divine discipline (33:16-28; 36:8-11, 15). Definitely that theme functioned as part of the author's total treatment of the problem of suffering. But in light of the prologue and Job's constant insistence upon his innocence, it fell far short of solving Job's problem, even though it may serve us well in other circumstances. As with so many of the arguments of the friends, there was truth in this approach, but Elihu applied it to the wrong situation.

Thus the Elihu speeches do not solve the problem, but they do bring to the fore a point that should be made clear before the argument is done. Nor should we be surprised to find the name of this angry, young, presumptuous man missing in the epilogue. We may speculate that the idea he propounded so well was one of the less acceptable explanations for suffering and would be likely to come from an inexperienced and youthful mind. In a sense, although protocol demanded that the elders be heard first, their experience and age became obstructions in the path of truth and reason. When experience became for them the measure of truth, as Ellison well says, it turned itself into falsehood.[42]

In respect to the third reason for excising these speeches from the book,[43] arguments on the basis of language are relative and not absolute.[44] A writer may use some terms more frequently in one composition than in another. And if we are dealing with real dialogue, then we can expect Elihu to have a vocabulary different from, though similar to, that of the friends. We should be open to the idea that a real dialogue occurred and that the author's vocabulary reflects the style and language of the different speakers. Further, Elihu's familiarity with the content is supportive of the literary legitimacy of this composition. It is both an interaction with and a reaction to the speeches composing the dialogue.

---

41. In the book of Proverbs, for example, the pedagogical term "my son" occurs twenty-two times. Further, the constant stress upon sexual morality implies that these were young men. See Gordis, *Koheleth—The Man and His World*, p. 32.
42. H. L. Ellison, *From Tragedy to Triumph*, p. 36.
43. Driver and Gray, 1:xli, consider them superfluous to the book.
44. Gordis, p. 107.

THE GOD SPEECHES

We now approach the God speeches (38:1–40:2; 40:6–41:34), which can be expected to form the most determinative part of the book when we confront the question of innocent suffering and theodicy. Or to state it more simply— Does the author of Job offer a solution? If he does, the crux of it must occur here in the God speeches. Job has demanded that God answer him. That kind of challenge cannot go unanswered in a work of this nature.[45] Thus the majority of scholars view these speeches as an essential part of the book, although a few question their authenticity in part.

A representative of this position is Georg Fohrer, who is troubled by the double structure that contains two speeches by God (38:1–40:2 and 40:6–41:34) and two replies by Job (40:3-5 and 42:1-6). He assumes there was only one God speech, which was interrupted later by the insertion of the superscriptions and introduction in 40:1, 6-7, followed by a single reply from Job. He proposes that the speech of God consisted originally of chapters 38-39; 40:2, 8-14, and Job's reply comprised 40:3-5; 42:2-3, 5-6. Further, proposes Fohrer, the songs about the hippopotamus (40:15-24) and the crocodile (41:1-34) are later expansions, although the description of the ostrich (39:13-18) is genuine to the original.[46]

Although the duplications are undeniable (38:1/40:6; 38:3/40:7, and 40:2 is similar), it is a mistake to reason upon the assumption that duplications in an ancient text hint at textual tampering and expansion. Nor should we require the same logical consistency of the author of Job that we require of ourselves. Further, the double structure is stylistic for the author. For example, the introduction to the Elihu speeches exhibits the double structure:

> Then these three men ceased answering Job, because he was righteous in his own eyes. But the anger of Elihu the son of Barachel the Buzite, of the family of Ram burned; against Job his anger burned, because he justified himself before God. *And his anger burned against his three friends because they had found no answer,* and yet had condemned Job. Now Elihu had waited to speak to Job because they were years older than he. *And when Elihu saw that there was no answer in the mouth of the three men his anger burned.* So Elihu the son of Barachel the Buzite spoke out and said, . . . (32:1-6a, author's emphasis).

As the italicized words show, the fact of Elihu's anger against his three friends because they had been unable to answer Job is repeated. But this is stylistic, and we need not conclude that either statement has been interpolated into the text.

45. See the discussion on the meaning of the God speeches, pp. 106-109.
46. Georg Fohrer, *Introduction to the Old Testament*, pp. 327-29.

There is really no passage in the God speeches that cannot be accommodated rather comfortably within their structure. The matter, however, may be pursued further in the critical literature.

## HERMENEUTICAL ISSUES OF JOB

One of the most critical questions the church has faced throughout its history is that of correct biblical interpretation. The reason, of course, is obvious. Upon the Scriptures the faith of the Christian church rests securely. Prerequisite to grasping the meaning of any passage or book is knowledge of the proper way to interpret that particular type of literature. The book of Job deserves a preliminary engagement of this question as much as the Revelation of John or the book of Genesis.

Although we cannot or need not discuss all the hermeneutical issues and procedures involved with wisdom literature (some of which are discussed in the introduction), we are compelled to deal with four fundamental issues that decisively affect the interpretation of Job: the literary unity of the book, mythology, the Satan of the prologue, and the relation of the book to the New Testament.

### LITERARY UNITY

The first hermeneutical principle that we will observe for interpreting this book is to view it as a whole.[47] However many strata one may believe oneself to find, a stratigraphic interpretation at the expense of the all-inclusive approach is difficult to justify. The literary unity of Job should be assumed so that the message of the book as a whole may be determined.

Although the question of the integrity of such a passage as chapter 28 to the overall message and literary structure may be valid, we must determine first if we can discover its meaning as a part of the total message before we excise it or move it to another literary neighborhood in the work. Strange indeed are some biblical passages where they stand, but the unexpected environment may provide the setting necessary to highlight the significance of their message.

Though Elihu, for example, was by his own admission an intruder into the dialogue (32:6-10), he must not be assumed a literary intruder until his speeches have been examined minutely to find out whether he contributed anything to the book. However, the reasons must be deeper than mere presuppositions. And to presuppose that an ancient writer would have shared our concepts of style and logical sequence exposes not the writer's but the interpreter's inadequacies. Thus the wholistic approach takes precedence for the sake of literary integrity.

47. See also previous section "Literary Structure," pp. 74-83.

MYTHOLOGY AND JOB

Some interpreters have recognized certain mythological elements in Job and have capitalized on them. Obviously there may be allusions to mythological creatures (e.g., 3:8; 9:13; 26:12-13), but how should we view them? If we examine the works of a classicist like John Milton, we discover that he alluded frequently to Greek mythology, but he did not espouse such a system. Poetic language may derive vocabulary and illustrations from mythology without embracing its religious system. The book of Job originated in a world where mythology was part of everyday life. The language of that world also bore the impress of the pagan religious systems. And the writer of Job made no more of an effort to expunge those elements from it than we do to eliminate such mythological allusions as "fortune" and "tantalize." In fact, world mythologies have contributed certain concepts to language that have become vehicles of meaning.

Job did not embrace a mythological system. Some scholars have begun with the textual allusions and extrapolated that a mythological substratum lay beneath the theology of the book.[48] Such a substratum may indeed lie at the base of the language, but the theology of the book, which is the determinative factor, points in the other direction. Even Eliphaz's reference to the "holy ones" (5:1) is likely a taunt against Job. There and in Psalm 89:5 the term does not bear the idea of deity.[49]

Further, the famous figures in the God speeches, Behemoth and Leviathan (40:15-24; 41:1-34), are thought by many scholars to be creatures of mythology. Pope tentatively associates Behemoth with the monstrous bullock of the Ugaritic myths, both of which, he suggests, may be identified with the Sumero-Akkadian "bull of heaven," which Gilgamesh and Enkidu killed in the Gilgamesh Epic.[50] While Pope admits that the only allusion to a bovine character is 40:15c, he speculates that if verse 23 were moved to an appropriate place in the Leviathan description (e.g., following 41:23), then the amphibious nature of Behemoth would be eliminated,[51] thus strengthening the postulation that Behemoth is a mythological creature that is restricted to the land. Because 1 Enoch 60:7-9 assigns Behemoth to the land and Leviathan to the sea, the amphibious nature of this beast (40:21-23) has inclined interpreters toward identification of Behemoth with the hippopotamus, an option that Pope finds troublesome to his mythological interpretation. Though his manipulation of the text is ingenious, we must reject it as a subjective effort to coerce the passage to yield a meaning the interpreter, rather than the author, intended.

48. W. A. Irwin, "Job's Redeemer," *JBL* 81 (1962):217-29, esp. pp. 221-22, where he extrapolates that the descent of Ishtar into the netherworld is the basis of Job 19.
49. See E. Smick, "Job," *The Zondervan Pictorial Encyclopedia of the Bible*, 3:615.
50. The text is found in James B. Pritchard, ed., ANET, pp. 83-85.
51. Pope, pp. 268-70.

Further, Pope would identify Leviathan (41:1) with the sea monster called Lotan in the Ugaritic myths.[52] This same name appears in Isaiah 27:1, Psalms 74:14, 104:26 (in the last passage it may be the whale),[53] as well as in Job 3:8, but in all these instances the language is poetic, and the figure may be viewed as mere allusion to mythology, devoid of belief in the real existence of such a creature.

In light of the highly poetic nature of both these passages, we must reject the mythology approach and align ourselves with those scholars who view Behemoth as the hippopotamus and Leviathan as the crocodile.[54] A further reason for viewing these creatures in this manner is a theological one—if they are mythological, this destroys the validity of the God speeches. If God was so badly informed about His own creation, then He had no right to speak at all. If, however, one objects that the author was limited by his own time and world view, then we are hardly dealing with a genuine divine revelation, but rather with a literary composition that rises no higher than the author's own world view.

Job knew that God was his only resource. He gave no hint that he could appeal to other divine beings if the one he knew as God failed to answer him. Yet he wished with all his heart that he could (9:33; 16:21). For the very reason then that God was the only one who could resolve the question of justice and truth, Job appealed to Him alone. If he had espoused a mythological system, he might have easily appealed to a member of the pantheon as his "umpire." But he did not. If he had espoused a dualism, he could have returned to the Satan of the prologue to resolve the dilemma. The fact that Satan does not appear in the dialogue (although Rashi sees a reference to him in 16:9) inclines us toward the position that a solution to the problem that confronted Job must ultimately come to light within a monotheistic, non-mythological framework.

Further, since the Mosaic law forbade assimilation of such elements (Ex. 20:3-6), it would truly be incongruous with Old Testament theology for a book with so prominent a mythological substratum to survive the prophetic era (if we assume an early date) and the divestment of the faith of idolatrous practices during the exilic period. Ezekiel remembered Job, along with Noah and Daniel, for his righteousness (Ezek. 14:14, 20). In light of that prophet's opposition to pagan worship and idolatry (Ezek. 8:9-18; 14:6-8, etc.), it is inconceivable that he would hold forth such figures as Job and Daniel for their exemplary righteousness if he had any notion that they had maintained idolatrous associations.

---

52. Ibid., pp. 276-78.
53. Delitzsch, 2:365.
54. E.g., Delitzsch, 2:357-74; Otto Eissfeldt, *The Old Testament: An Introduction*, p. 458; Gordis, pp. 119-20; 336, n. 4.

THE SATAN OF THE PROLOGUE

Another consideration that may help us clarify some of the hermeneutical issues is that of the Satan of chapters 1 and 2, which has long been an obstacle for interpreters of Job. In the first place, the role of Satan in Job is not that of chief opponent of God as it is in the New Testament. Moreover, he does not reappear in the book. Further, the use of the definite article has been viewed as an indication that the term is not a proper noun and should be translated as "the adversary."

In consideration of these problems, we admit that we do not have a full disclosure of the archenemy of God in Job 1-2. For that matter, we do not have it at all in the Old Testament, although here and in Zechariah 3:1-2 and 1 Chronicles 21:1 he is by no means a friend of God. His role in the prologue of Job is to impugn God's righteous servant. And although he is not presented as the archfiend, he operates antagonistically toward Him and with malicious intent toward Job:

> Then the Lord said to Satan, "Behold, all that he has is in your power, only do not put forth your hand on him."
>
> (1:12)

> And Satan answered the Lord and said, . . . "However, put forth Thy hand, now, and touch his bone and his flesh; he will curse Thee to Thy face."
>
> (2:4-5)

The author obviously was aware of certain hazards as he told his story. Thus he took care to avoid two misconceptions. The first was that Satan not be identified among "the sons of God." After a full statement about their appointed consultations with God, he added, "And Satan also came among them" (1:6; 2:1). Although "among them" could denote his legitimate rank as one of them, we are struck by the manner in which the author appended this to the main statement, which seems to distinguish not only his role but also his station from that of "the sons of God." He did not want his readership to confuse Satan—"the adversary"—as one of the legitimate sons of God.

The other latent idea that could emerge in the wrong form was that Satan constituted a viable challenge to the sovereignty of God. In both of Satan's appearances before the Lord, the author took pains to show that he could not act without divine permission (1:12; 2:6). A dualistic theology is cleverly avoided by this permissive note and further by the fact that Satan's challenge that Job would curse God to His face miscarried. He cursed the day of his birth (3:1), but he did not curse the Lord.

Some scholars have explained the introduction of Satan into the prologue on the basis of Jewish contact with the dualism of Persian Zoroastrianism and its doctrine of two universal forces—Ahriman, the god of darkness and evil, and Ahura-Mazoa, the god of light and righteousness.[55] Yet a comprehensive view of the Scriptures casts doubt upon that hypothesis. Delitzsch objects that since both Jesus and His apostles regarded His work as the overthrow of Satan, it is incongruous that they made so much of the satanic kingdom and the suffering endured to overthrow it if this Satan were a mere copy of the Persian Ahriman. If so, Jesus and the apostles worked against a mere phantom. His opinion was that the concept of Satan was extant earlier than the Solomonic period, being expressed in the serpent of paradise (Gen. 3) and by the Mosaic term "Azazel" (Lev. 16), to whom the scapegoat bearing Israel's sins was dispatched on the Day of Atonement.[56] John identified him as "the serpent of old who is called the devil and Satan" (Rev. 12:9), the "serpent of old" being an allusion to the serpent in Genesis 3.

The biblical theologian must view the phenomena of Scripture in both their immediate and larger contexts. Therefore, the New Testament view of Satan becomes a part of our consideration. We should refrain, however, from reading the New Testament concept into the Job prologue, but the Satan of the prologue needs to be understood in view of the larger scriptural context. We do not deny that the arguments in respect to Persian influences present some pertinent questions that should be faced. Yet they are not decisive. Moreover, proponents of the Persian dualism hypothesis are frequently oblivious to the doctrine of special revelation, opting for an organic evolution of concepts in history while leaving little room for divine impartation of the mysteries of the universe. Thus we would view the Satan of the prologue much like the Old Testament concept of the Messiah. He was not fully disclosed in the pre-Christian era any more than the incarnate God in Christ was fully disclosed before His advent in the first century. And we may recognize the wisdom of God inherent in this fact. It is a tribute to the work of the Holy Spirit that He did not disclose the full reality of Satan and the demonic world except in chronological proximity with the full disclosure of God in Jesus Christ, the conqueror of sin and death, and victor over Satan.

The argument that the definite article disqualifies the term as a proper noun is weak. An example of a proper noun occurring with the definite article is *Elohim* ("God"), which frequently is prefixed by "the" but should be translated simply "God," referring to Israel's God. Moreover, in Genesis 1-2 *ādām* generally occurs with the article, but a few times without it (1:26; 2:5, 20). Yet the text of Genesis 3 treats him as an individual man with its reference to "her husband" (v. 6) and "to Adam" (v. 17), as does the narrative of chapter 5 where Adam is clearly a proper noun without the article. Thus a proper noun may occasionally occur with the article.

55. Gordis, pp. 69-71.
56. Delitzsch, 1:28-29.

We may conclude that, although the Satan in Job 1-2 is not God's archenemy, he is His adversary. Yet he is not a match for God even though he may set forth imposing claims—he must work within the range of divine permission. And the author, not setting out primarily to prove Satan wrong but to prove Job right, finds no compelling necessity within the framework of his story and theology to return to the person of Satan. His role was an initiating one, not a concluding one. Integrity between God and man was something that not even God's and man's adversary could destroy.

JOB AND THE NEW TESTAMENT

Finally, one temptation we should avoid is to use New Testament concepts as tools to hammer and chisel the book of Job into New Testament shape. The meaning of Job and its full impact are far more beautiful and striking if we let them speak out of their own environment. To illustrate, let us not take the doctrine of the incarnate God in Christ and shape Job's "redeemer" (19:25) according to it, tempting though that may be. Rather let us sit in silence, as did his friends, until Job has spoken. For only when he has had his say can we begin to sense the wonder of this book. His hands reach out to grasp the more tangible forms of revelation that God would graciously offer in the future, yet he is poignantly aware that they evade his grasp. Even in the presence of the solution at the end of the book, we receive only that which enables us to live with our dilemma. The groping hands are partly withdrawn.

Obviously we cannot take off our Christian robes and don the regalia of the ancient mind and spirit, but we can of a certainty be aware of our theological dress and not require that Job be dressed accordingly. By this hermeneutic our understanding of Job becomes richer. Admittedly we hear his message in a much larger sound chamber, which produces numerous overtones that would not have been possible in the pre-Christian era. That Job wished fervently for an intermediary is undeniable. That he predicted our intercessor, Jesus Christ, is not so plausible. Yet he drew attention to the vacuum that existed, the need that every troubled heart recognizes. In this respect he anticipated the incarnate Savior. Yet there is an important difference between anticipation and prophetic prediction—the one a fervent wish, the expression of a void needing to be filled, the other a promise, the intangible presence of a future reality. The latter is not found in Job. The former definitely is. And in the midst of the human dilemma, Job's "redeemer" has always found a home. Yet on the basis of that "redeemer" alone, we could not have ventured a guess that He would be so much at home among us, so tangibly present, as He came to be in Jesus Christ.

DETAILED ANALYSIS OF JOB

PROLOGUE: THE DILEMMA DELINEATED (1-2)

*Job and his faith*. Job's righteousness was remembered by the sixth-century prophet Ezekiel (14:14, 20) in company with Noah and Daniel. His religious and moral integrity was predicated first by two words, "blameless" and "upright" (1:1). The first word is likely a description of his relation to God and is explained by the additional clause "one who feared God." The second describes his behavior in relation to his fellowman. Yet we should not press the separate nuances of these words too far but view them more as a hendiadys[57] describing Job's religious faith in general. The author further elucidates the piety of Job by reference to his priestly function on his family's behalf (1:5). The fact that he offered sacrifices for the sins of his children would suggest a patriarchal setting for the story, since before Mosaic times the family patriarch was also the priest (Gen. 8:20; 12:7-8; 15:9-10). Perhaps these were for inadvertent sins his children might have committed during their festive celebrations.

The essence of Job's faith, however, was expressed in God's confident assertions about him (Job 1:8; 2:3) and Job's own declarations of personal trust in God (1:20-21; 2:10), as well as the author's confirmation (1:22; 2:10*b*). These expressions of religious integrity stood in contrast to Satan's distrust of him and his allegation that Job's faith was conditioned by his wealth and well-being (1:9-11; 2:5). He thought that faith and prosperity were correlates, and if the latter were removed, the former would disintegrate. God, however, was willing to risk the reputation of His servant to prove Satan's thesis false. After all, when He put Job's reputation on the line, He also put His own there. So this book is not only concerned with the religious integrity of a human being, but also with the integrity of God, a fact that Job perceptively recognized, but the friends did not.

By virtue of the prologue we are placed on Job's side at the very outset, drawn into the struggle of a human being whose light is all but extinguished. This struggle into which Job entered was the ground of his progress. His friends did little more than "spin their wheels," repeating theological platitudes without appropriate regard for the situation and the person to whom they spoke. Yet, though they remained suspended in their own theological apathy, Job set out upon his spiritual journey through great pain of heart and body. We get the impression that the friends kept screaming their platitudes to him as he rode out of sight, howbeit at a slow and arduous pace.

The prologue has placed us in the theological center of gravity, that is, Job's religious integrity and divine justice, but we are still not immovably ·fixed in that place. The dialogue has a dislodging effect, tipping us off center, at times

---

57. A *hendiadys* is two terms conveying one idea.

turning us away from Job's arguments and tirades and turning us toward the friends and their defense of God. One of the marks of greatness that characterizes this book is that after the prologue we are never able to identify fully and fixedly with Job or with the friends until the epilogue. At times the force of the dialogue is centrifugal and at other times centripetal. By this skillful technique the author draws us into Job's struggle, forcing us to look at all angles. So we need not be overcome by guilt when we on occasion cheer Job on as he challenges God, nor by condemnation when we find ourselves nodding approvingly at the speeches of the friends.

*The tragedy.* The account of the tragedies that befell Job (1:13-19) is a continuous chain of action, one report of calamity interrupting another. Since Satan had contended that Job's faith was dependent upon his wealth (1:9-11) the tragedy first touched his possessions (1:13-17), which consisted of cattle, sheep, camels, and servants. The wealth of a man in the patriarchal age was measured in terms of his domestic animals and servants (cf. Gen. 12:16). The first phase of Job's tragedy climaxed in the catastrophic death of his children (1:18-19), which hurled him into an abyss of emotional suffering and left him prostrate before God in mourning[58] and humble submission (1:20).[59] The second phase of the tragedy came when Satan by divine permission afflicted Job's whole body with infectious sores (2:1-8). This phase was motivated by Satan's belief that if a man's price cannot be reckoned in terms of his possessions and offspring, it can indeed be computed in terms of his own life: "Skin for skin, yea, all that a man hath will he give for his life" (2:4, KJV).

By the complexity of Job's dilemma, the author of the book may point toward the complexity of the system of pain, suffering, and evil. That is, he did not choose merely to deal with the dimension of physical pain or with emotional suffering. Rather he combined them to present the worst possible predicament that could be imagined, and to this compound problem he addressed himself.

The first indication that Satan had lost his wager that Job would curse God (2:5) came when his wife tempted him to do just that, and he rejected this alternative. The rather long addition of the Septuagint after verse 9 further denigrates the character of his wife, but the Hebrew text offers no basis for this. There is no reason to assume that she had any motive except a genuine concern for Job and his welfare. Her problem was simply that she could not distinguish between the metaphysical proportions of human suffering and the physical and emotional dimensions, which seemed more immediate and real. She was very human. However, Job had the strength to resist her emotional overture, recognizing that there

58. Tearing one's clothes was customarily a sign of mourning (Gen. 37:34; 2 Sam. 1:11, etc.), as was also shaving one's head (Isa. 22:12; Jer. 7:29, etc.).
59. The verb for "worshiped" is one that occurs frequently in the Old Testament and connotes obeisance before a superior and occasionally before one's peers (Gen. 33:7; Ex. 18:7; 1 Kings 2:19). See Pope, pp. 15-16.

was a rationale that penetrated beneath the pain. Subsequently he fell into the same error, although he never took up her tantalizing challenge.

The friends came to "condole" (RSV; NASB, "sympathize") Job, a verb that literally means "to shake" (the head) as an expression of sorrow or pity.[60] In 42:11 it occurs as a synonym of the verb "to comfort." When they observed his disfigurement, they wept and mourned for seven days. They did not speak until Job himself opened the conversation. Yet their actions spoke louder than any words—they were deeply moved for their friend.

JOB'S DISORIENTATION (3)

The hero's theological orientation in the prologue, once tragedy had struck, was congruous with his reputation for religious integrity and piety. And before we conclude that this had been shattered, let us notice the rejected alternative. Satan had confidently claimed that when Job was deprived of his well-being he would curse God, a challenge that his wife also flung at him. So the author wanted us to see immediately that Job resisted that temptation: "Afterward Job opened his mouth and cursed the day of his birth" (3:1). This was quite different from what Satan had anticipated—he did not curse God at all, but his own birth-day.

The chapter contains three elements: a malediction of the day of his birth (vv. 3a, 4, 5, 11-19), of the night of his conception (vv. 3b, 6-10), and a general lament on life (vv. 20-26). The tone for the dialogue is set here. A faith that was stated in the prologue in a beautiful major key is now transposed into a mournful minor. The whole chapter is irrational. It is the lament of one who has become a total victim of his trouble. He pronounced a curse upon life in general because of his suffering in particular, as men measure their general experience by their particular ones. Surely Job's life had contained many joys; yet in pronouncing a curse upon the day of his birth, as did Jeremiah also (Jer. 20:14-18), he disclaimed the total entity of his bitter life.

Job had become completely disoriented to life. His rational, faithful affirmations of trust in the prologue had been turned inside out so that we see the other side of faith as, in the anguish of life's bitter experience, it writhes to raise its head above the distorted world. In fact, the humanness of Job is clearly discernible in this chapter and the dialogue. He had feared this kind of disaster (3:25). Although he was emotional throughout his speeches, he never again, as here, became purely irrational. But for those who endure emotional and physical pain, the irrational phase does not always immediately follow the trauma. Job first reaffirmed his faith and then denounced his bitter life. The plunge into the abyss of despair would only be reversed slowly and arduously.

60. Francis Brown, S. R. Driver, and Charles A. Briggs, *A Hebrew and English Lexicon of the Old Testament*, p. 626b.

*Leviathan (3:8).* This name also appears in 41:1 where it probably describes the crocodile. Pope and others, following Gunkel, amend "day" (Hebrew *yôm*) to "sea" (*yām*), a change that would accommodate the mythological interpretation very nicely. However, with Dhorme[61] and others, we view the logical interpretation as "day" in line with verse 1 where Job cursed "his day." The word in 8*b* rendered by the *New American Standard Bible* as "prepared" and the *Revised Standard Version* as "skilled" occurs also in 15:24 and Esther 3:14 where it means "ready," "prepared," and was so understood by the King James Version translators. The problem stated simply is: What is the connection between cursing the day and rousing up Leviathan? If we opt for Gunkel's emendation (which has no textual support), we satisfy the mythological sense, but Job does not seem to have given such credence to the mythology of his day.[62] The sense may suggest the courage of these professional mourners who were ready to engage in anything from cursing the day of their birth to rousing up the ferocious crocodile. If the mythological Leviathan is the object, Job was still hardly made a proponent of current mythology. In such a case, this is poetic metaphor drawn from mythological sources.

*"The knees receive me" (3:12).* We have a parallel to this custom in Genesis 30:3. E. A. Speiser[63] cites the Hurro-Hittite tale of Appu where the custom is mentioned. The father normally performed the rite, acknowledging the child as his own. In the Genesis passage, however, the mother performed it. Here the celebrant is not specified.

THE DIALOGUE: CYCLE ONE (4-14)

*The method of argumentation.* We should be aware that the dialogue does not proceed strictly by the method of point/counterpoint. Although one speaker would take strong exception to another's words, they often responded more to what they believed themselves to hear than to what the speaker actually said. It was an interpretative response, which read between the lines of the participants, at one point rebutting directly, at another indirectly. Yet Job's reply was not always restricted to what the immediate previous speaker had said. By the delayed reaction principle he spoke to issues raised by an earlier friend. Like chemical reactions, some words require a little more time to do their job. Solomon Freehof has explained the speeches as a configuration of circles that touch each other, some more, some less, rather than a chain of rectangles end to end.[64]

Although the friends heard Job's words, they only faintly read his heart. And sometimes his words were only the cinders expelled from the raging fire of

61. Dhorme, p. 30.
62. See earlier section of this chapter, "Mythology and Job," pp. 84-85.
63. E. A. Speiser, *Genesis*, p. 230.
64. Solomon Freehof, *The Book of Job, A Commentary*, p. 120.

his innermost being. The tone for the first cycle was set by Job's lament in chapter 3. Yet as the dialogue proceeded, it set its own tone, intensifying from detached sympathy to derogatory condemnation. After each friend spoke, Job replied, until all three had spoken. Then a new cycle began with Eliphaz and ran its course, followed by a third cycle in which only Eliphaz and Bildad spoke, Zophar remaining mysteriously quiet.

*Eliphaz and Job—Cycle One: First Exchange (4-5/6-7).* If Eliphaz was the oldest, as many surmise, protocol demanded that he speak first. He commenced courteously and ended gently. Yet after Job's pitiable lament, he could not restrain his words even if he had wanted to (4:2*b*). He brought together Job's manner of life (4:3-6) and his tragedy (4:7-11), attempting to discover from the former the element that caused the latter. His basic contribution to the dialogue was probably the universal principle that he propounded: the universe operates according to the law of cause-effect (4:7-11). Things do not happen without a reason. While this intimation was strong enough to put the idea of Job's guilt across, the only direct charge made against Job was that his behavior in this situation was not congruous with his past conduct (4:3-5).

To reinforce his philosophy, Eliphaz related a dream (4:12-21) in which he received information to the effect that mortal man cannot claim righteousness before God, and by intimation Job was no exception. The verses that follow (18-21) may be a continuation of the voice in Eliphaz's dream or his own meditation upon the content of it.

An interpretative problem occurs at 5:6-7 where Eliphaz endeavored to explain human misery by a general statement. If his theme that man's trouble is self-spawned (4:7-8) carried through the speech, then "man is born for trouble, as sparks fly upward" is incongruous since it suggests that man's trouble springs from the fact of his existence rather than from his own conduct, thus locating the cause in God. We may view 5:7 as the quotation of an apothegm that Eliphaz did not personally believe[65] ("Some people say, 'Man is born . . . ' "), or an alternative proposal is to deviate from the Masoretic vowels, thus making the passive verb "is born" an active—"Man gives birth to. . . . " The first alternative is preferable since no change in the vowel points is required. Thus his advice to Job in 5:8 was a counterstatement to the popular pessimism, asserting that God is just in all His actions.[66]

A second principle put forth by Eliphaz was that suffering may be viewed as the chastisement of God with the purpose of correction and healing (5:17-18). This is basically the idea that Elihu later set forth, claiming it to be a novelty in the discussion. Eliphaz's theology included a God who acts and sets things right

65. See Gordis, pp. 169-89, for an extensive discussion on the use of quotations in Job.
66. Freehof, p. 69.

(5:9-27). He was far more practical than theoretical, and experience confirmed that for Eliphaz. To such a God he advised Job to commit his cause (5:8).

Job's response (chaps. 6-7) to Eliphaz revealed the disappointed heart that expected far more from his friend. First, he again lamented his incalculable suffering (6:2-4), and then reaffirmed that he spoke for a good reason (6:5). Although 6:6-7 is variously translated, the verses likely refer to the insipid quality of Job's own life,[67] or his rejection of Eliphaz's argument as he rejected tasteless food.[68]

Outside of our Lord's own bitter loneliness during His passion, there must be no keener sense of having been forsaken by one's friends expressed in Scripture than here (6:14-21, 27). They had become like wadis that were fresh and flowing in the rainy season but dry and parched when one really needed water during the summer. When he really needed them, they offered no help, although he had asked nothing of them but friendship (6:22). Job further maintained the insinuations of Eliphaz (6:10b, 24) that he had done no wrong, thus beginning his forceful arguments in defense of his innocence.

Looking at human life through his own bitter experience, Job bewailed the hard service of man upon earth (7:1-2), like the slave whose only comfort was the shade, and a hireling whose solace was his wages. Job was so tormented by his troubles that he could not hide from them even when he slept (7:13-15). God pursued him and kept a constant surveillance over him (7:12). With nothing to lose, he launched his complaint to God (7:7-21).[69] Here he began his turbulent tirades against the Omnipotent. If he had sinned, why did God not forgive him, rather than pursue after him (7:20-21)? In any event, what was man that God should care to use him for sport (7:17-18)? Job's complaint was bitter. He wished God would only leave him alone for an instant ("until I swallow my spittle," v. 19). The speech had turned from a response to Eliphaz to a pungent accusation directed against God.

*Bildad and Job—Cycle One: Second Exchange (8/9-10).* Bildad well made up for the gentleness of Eliphaz. His speech was harsh, at moments even heartless, illustrated by his callous reference to Job's children (8:4). He had no time for oriental niceties, and his first sentence accused Job of windy speech (8:2). His whole speech was a resounding defense of the justice of God: "Does God pervert justice?" (8:3). Actually Job had not said that explicitly, rather that God was treating him quite harshly. But Bildad had read between the lines and reacted to what he thought Job said. In anticipation, however, he was right. For Bil-

---

65. See Gordis, pp. 169-89, for an extensive discussion on the use of quotations in Job.
66. Freehof, p. 69.
67. Ibid., p. 75.
68. Pope, p. 50.
69. Although the addressee is not specified, the singular verb of verse 7 ("remember") might suggest that he was addressing God rather than his friends.

dad's direct charge may have served to bring to the surface what was already submerged in Job's mind, and in his response to Bildad Job left no doubt about his friend's accurate perception.

Whereas Eliphaz had appealed to a dream to justify his message, Bildad appealed to past history (8:8-10). To illustrate his mechanical doctrine of divine justice, he cited the papyrus plant that grows in the marsh and withers as soon as it becomes green (8:11-13)—"So are the paths of all who forget God, and the hope of the godless will perish" (8:13).

Yet Bildad, like Eliphaz, had some positive words of promise for his friend should he implore God's mercy (8:5-7, 21-22). Maimonides saw in 8:6-7 the belief in compensation.

> If you are innocent and have not sinned, the reason for these great events is to make great your reward. You will receive the finest of compensations. All this is good for you, so that the good that you will obtain in the end be increased.[70]

At this point in the dialogue Bildad could well have meant that, as 8:20-22 might also suggest. However, we must remember that he prefixed the condition with a substantial "if." Job's innocence was not at all fixed in Bildad's mind.

Job's response began in agreement with Bildad's belief that God does not pervert justice: "Truly I know that it is so" (9:2, RSV). We wonder if this is not one of those deep affirmations of faith that scramble to the surface in the troubled, doubting heart—"Lord, I believe; help my unbelief." Could not this be the man of the prologue fighting to get out of the prison in which his suffering had confined him?

But prisons are known for their formidable confines, and Job only momentarily thought of the freedom of the world of faith that he had known. So his attention turned to the essential cause of the world—God. Bildad had spent no words describing God, but Eliphaz had (5:8-16). He was a God of action, setting things right by virtue of His omnipotence. In contrast, Job saw Him as a God of action to whom "might makes right" (9:3-13), outwitting man at every juncture (9:14-20), showing no rhyme or reason for His actions (9:17, 22). If we may speak in terms of morality at all, He was amoral (9:22-24).

This pondering about God and His governance of the world led Job into a lament over his own sad plight (9:25-35) in the same plaintive vein as earlier. Indeed he would like to be done with this complaining and be on with life, but that would mean accepting a guilty verdict when he was convinced of his innocence (9:27-28; also vv. 15, 20-21; and 10:7). Thus, again in the spirit of one who had nothing to lose, Job reiterated his intent to speak his mind before God. Yet all his words were not bitter, for he recognized God's loving care for him

70. Maimonides, *The Guide of the Perplexed*, p. 493.

(10:8-12); but that only highlighted God's perpetration of His hidden motives (10:13). So Job directly asked God why He brought him to birth and challenged Him to grant a reprieve before he died (10:18-22).

We, of course, have been cued in by the prologue to the "things Thou hast concealed in Thy heart." The passage reeks with irony. God's purpose was truly hidden from Job, but it did not have the malevolent design that Job attributed to it. This speech is sufficient evidence that Job never doubted divine omnipotence, but he did of a certainty call divine justice into question.

Note: The word *Rahab* (9:13) is not related to the name of the harlot of Jericho (Josh. 2:1); the two words derive from different Hebrew roots. Twice in the Old Testament (Isa. 30:7; Ps. 87:4) Rahab refers clearly to Egypt. However, the other four occurrences (Job 9:13; 26:12; Ps. 89:10; Isa. 51:9) seem to have a mythological background. Delitzsch[71] has correctly observed that here (and at 26:12) Egypt is not predicated since the book of Job makes no direct reference to events in Israel's history. Some rabbinic commentators take it in its literal sense of "pride" or "proud strength" (e.g., Metzudat Zion and Gersonides), although Rashi understands the word in 26:12 as the Egyptians.[72] The Septuagint renders the word in Job both times as "sea monster." Some commentators[73] extrapolate that these are a vestige of some ancient myth relating how Yahweh defeated a mythological sea monster, similar to Tiamat and her cohorts in the Babylonian creation story, Enuma Elish.[74] Although we do not deny that Rahab may be a mythological allusion, we should exercise caution in reading into Job a full mythology, and until further evidence is in, go no further than recognizing "some well-known extraordinary example of wicked enterprise which had been frustrated."[75] In any instance, the message is unharmed by the reference—God is sovereign over all forces of the universe, including those that pose a massive force of evil design against Him.

*Zophar and Job—Cycle One: Third Exchange (11/12-14).* The blatant Zophar spared no feelings with his blunt sarcasm and malignant accusation. First he alleged that Job was full of talk (Hebrew, "a man of lips"), one whose "babble," intended to silence his accusers, had been mere mockery (11:2-3). He assumed essentially the same theological position as his two companions—that the circumstantial evidence proved Job guilty. If only God would speak to him, he would discover that he had received less than he deserved (11:6). In view of Job's compounded tragedy, these words were as heartless as Bildad's reference

---

71. Delitzsch, 1:152.
72. These commentaries are found in *Mikraoth Gedoloth* (in Hebrew) at the appropriate citations in the Job section.
73. See Pope, p. 70; and T. H. Gaster, "Rahab," in *The Interpreter's Dictionary of the Bible*, ed. George A. Buttrick et al., 4:6.
74. For a discussion of mythology see pp. 84-85.
75. Delitzsch, 1:152.

to Job's children (8:4). Obviously the friends' theology was far more important than Job. It was well structured, and they would not permit even a friend's complex dilemma to alter it.

Zophar summed up Job's position as he had heard it (11:4), for Job had not claimed purity of doctrine, although he had certainly asserted his innocence. This third friend believed that Job had not even scratched the surface of wisdom, much less was in possession of it. Man must remain agnostic in relation to it (11:5-12). What is more, God knows Job's sins and will not forget to deal with him (11:11).

As hopeless as Job appeared to Zophar, however, he had an appropriate admonition couched in conditional language (11:13-19), holding forth hope to Job as had the other two members of the friendly trilogy. But woe unto him who did not heed the "gospel" (11:20).

All three friends having spoken, Job was ostracized, alienated from God and man, a lone challenger in an unfriendly universe. He was forced to face reality alone (so it seemed), to reduce life to its smallest common denominator. In Job's opinion, both candidates for that position, God and man, had disqualified themselves. At least God as the source of justice was out, but still in the running was God as the omnipotent (12:13-25). Countering the friends' thesis that wisdom resided with the aged,[76] Job admitted that the only candidate was God, an omnipotent God whose actions prove that He cannot be figured out. Essentially he offered the same argument as Zophar but with different meaning. The terminology was homonymous but not synonymous. In Zophar's view, a mere man like Job could not apprehend unfathomable wisdom, whereas for Job, divine wisdom was not so deep as to be unfathomable but so contradictory as to be incomprehensible. As in other instances, one person in the dialogue seized his opponent's sword and fought with it. Yet Job could hardly expect to succeed with the sword that had failed his friend.

It is too early in the debate to recognize that both theses, although containing a bit of validity, were not acceptable to the author. We have made no progress when we have only countered a false thesis with a false antithesis. Job was ahead of Zophar merely in that he located wisdom solely in God, not that he understood its content any better.

In a defensive tone, the leading character further declared that he was not inferior to his opponents in understanding (12:3; 13:1). He knew all they knew, but they did not understand his pain. They had defended God by ignoring his suffering. So they flattered Him unjustly (13:7-8), for which He would punish them (13:10). God does not need, indeed does not want, His justice and power defended at the expense of man's suffering. To be oblivious to human pain while cognizant of divine justice does not merit God's favor but His rebuke. For

---

76. 12:12 may be a summary of their thesis as Job had perceived it. Understood as Job's words, it would not harmonize with his position otherwise stated.

although God requires praise from His human creatures, He cannot appreciate flattery (13:7-10).

The translation of 13:15 in the King James Version is generally considered by present-day scholars to be incorrect.[77] Although we cannot rule out a glimmer of faith at this point in the hero's experience, the context seems to confirm the sense of the *Revised Standard Version*—"Behold, he will slay me; I have no hope; yet I will defend my ways to his face." That is, even at the risk of death, he will argue his case before God. This was a man who had nothing to lose and everything to gain.

Thus Job turned his attention upon God, whom he accused of harassing him senselessly, like frightening a driven leaf and pursuing dry chaff (13:24-28). His personal fate led him to consider the lot of man in general in one of the greatest laments in the Bible (14:1-22). Man's life on earth is ephemeral, and added to that is the uncertainty of an afterlife. To Job's knowledge, a tree was more likely to sprout again than man (14:7-12). Yet if he could have such a hope, his suffering could be endurable, and he could wait out his weary days (14:14). In the absence of such hope, however, Job saw God destroying man, somewhat as He ordains that nature decay and waste away (14:18-22).

Yet already a change had begun in Job's arguments. He had turned from his personal tragedy to the universal dilemma of man. When one is able to make such a transition, we may suspect that the reconstructive process has begun.

THE DIALOGUE: CYCLE TWO (15-21)

*Eliphaz and Job—Cycle Two: First Exchange (15/16-17).* Job had begged his friends to keep silent after their first round of speeches (13:5). Eliphaz, quite done with his initial conciliatory approach (chaps. 4-5) now shattered that hope and pronounced Job guilty by reason of his own words (15:6).[78] He, along with Bildad and Zophar, had made all the progress he could or would in understanding Job and his dilemma. What the friends would say thereafter was generally harsher and devoid of any sympathy that their words may have borne in the first cycle. If Job had been alone in the first round of debate, he was contemptuously abandoned in the second and third.

In defiance of one who dared challenge the meaning of human existence and divine justice, Eliphaz sarcastically quizzed Job:

> Were you the first man[79] to be born,
> Or were you brought forth before the hills?
> (15:7)

---

77. See the English commentaries, e.g., Pope, p. 95.
78. Compare 4:6/15:4; 4:7-11/15:5-6; 4:17-19/15:15-16; 5:2-7/15:17-19.
79. The generic term *'ādām* is used rather than the individual "a man" (*'îsh*).

Wisdom is resident in God, not man, Job contended (12:13). How, asked Eliphaz, could a mere man like Job state that claim so confidently, overlooking the sagacity of the aged (whom Eliphaz represented), unless he could at the same time claim primary status among God's creatures and a privileged audience in the divine council (15:7-10)? Job's ontological musing (14:1-22) evoked from Eliphaz his own sarcastic parody of "man born of woman" (15:14-16). God's distrust of man propounded in Eliphaz's first speech (4:17-19) was hurled at Job again.

To illustrate the profundity of his wisdom, Eliphaz presented a simple explanation for the prosperity of the wicked—although they seem to prosper, they are actually tormented by the expectation of misfortunes and punishment, thus nullifying what appears to be genuine prosperity (15:20-24). But if this is wisdom, we applaud Job's refutation.

Job's response was filled with scorn for his "miserable comforters" and their platitudinous mockery (16:2; 17:2). If he were in their circumstances he could compose calm speeches too (16:4).[80] He saw himself assaulted by his enemy (16:9); whether Satan (as Rashi held) or his human adversaries is not clear. And God had designs on his life that were not commendatory (16:11-14; cf. 10:13). Nevertheless, his friends having miserably failed him, and God having abandoned him to the ungodly, Job yet turned to God. In 9:33 he had wished for an umpire, or arbitrator, and again he expressed the yearning that God would intervene (16:20-21), but not until a glimmer of hope and faith had brightened the horizon: "Even now, behold, my witness is in heaven, and he that vouches for me is on high" (16:19, RSV). The conviction seems to have grown that if justice were to be done, the only hope was God, as unreliable as He may have appeared to Job at this time. Still the only thing that gave any semblance of reality to the situation was Job's conviction of his own innocence (16:17). To that he must cling tenaciously until all the other parts could be pieced together. If it is valid at all to talk of elements that bring coherence to this book, we may suggest two—God's omnipotence and Job's innocence. In the author's mind neither could be sacrificed for the other.

*Bildad and Job—Cycle Two: Second Exchange (18/19).* Job's sarcasm and directness touched a tender spot in the undeviating Bildad. The only one to mention the hero's deceased children (8:4) again snidely insinuated that Job's childless state was evidence of his wickedness (18:19). The purpose of Bildad's speech was to reaffirm the simple position he set forth in 8:11-19 that the wicked really do not prosper and that they receive their just deserts (18:5-21). They are pursued and victimized by their own sin. Obviously this theory is expressed elsewhere in the Scriptures and viewed as orthodox. However, Bildad's mistake

---

80. The gesture of shaking the head implies mockery and satire in those passages where it occurs (Ps. 22:7; Isa. 37:22; Ecclus. 12:18; Matt. 27:39).

was to assume that one generalization could apply to all cases. This discourse was really merciless, not even containing the brief element of reassurance to Job that Bildad incorporated into his first address (8:20-22). The need for self-defense had changed the tone. In the first exchange he had opened with a defense of God's justice (8:3), whereas here he promptly leaped to the defense of the friendly trio (18:3).

With the friends refusing to abandon their persistent verbal badgering, Job raised the hypothetical[81] question: "Even if I have truly erred" (19:4). If he had, it did not affect them. In superb language, with deep emotion, he laid open the pitiable plight of a man estranged from friends, forgotten by guests, repulsive to his wife, loathsome to his brothers, and abhorred by his friends (19:14-19). Ravaged by both emotional and physical pain, out of his troubled soul Job yet pleaded with his friends to have pity on him (19:21).

Then as lightning dispels the dark night for a brief moment, he reaffirmed the faith he had confessed in the prologue, wishing that his words could be inscribed in timeless stone as a witness against that day when his vindicator would acquit him in a juridical confrontation (19:23-27). He appealed to the God who pursues. Already Job had spoken of an "umpire" (9:33) and a "witness in heaven" (16:19) as his mediator, and now a "redeemer." Though some commentators view this redeemer as someone other than God, Gordis correctly observes that the Hebrew mind would consider this blasphemy.[82] In the Old Testament the "redeemer" in Israel could ransom fellow Hebrews sold into slavery (Lev. 25:47-55), redeem property for the family (Lev. 25:23-24), avenge his kinsman's blood (Num. 35:19), and preserve the line of a relative through marriage (Deut. 25:5-10). Even if we may not superimpose the New Testament doctrine of the God-man Redeemer Christ, certainly Job's statement pointed in that direction, although the concept of the incarnation is completely absent. Verse 26 has been interpreted as a declaration of belief in the bodily resurrection. However, Ellison probably comes closer to the truth of the verse by suggesting that Job asserts faith in continued conscious communion with God after death rather than in bodily resurrection.[83] Unquestionably this is one of the great passages of the Old Testament, soaring far above the spiritual heights normally reached in ancient Israel. It is, like lofty Nebo, a towering summit from which to get a glimpse of a blessed promised land.

*Zophar and Job—Cycle Two:Third Exchange (20/21).* As confident of the certain disaster of the wicked as he was in his opening speech (11:20), Zophar

---

81. Although the Hebrew lacks the hypothetical element "if," verse 6 quite definitely puts the sentence in the hypothetical strain, since there he charges God for his plight. Further, reading the conditional element out of the verse is not incongruous with standard Hebrew grammar.
82. Gordis, p. 88.
83. Ellison, p. 69. The doctrine of the bodily resurrection is twice spoken of in the Old Testament, in Isaiah 26:19 and in Daniel 12:2.

reacted to Job's insulting words with a defense of his initial thesis, that the success of the wicked is so ephemeral as to be a negligible factor (20:4-29). He did not reject the idea that some prosperity may accrue to his actions. Rather his essential approach was that this did not matter since one can expect the wicked man to disgorge his ill-gotten riches as surely as he swallows them down (20:15). The basic assumption of Zophar's thesis was that the universe protects the righteous and damns the wicked (20:27), an idea found elsewhere in wisdom literature.[84] Even though the concept is attractive, the evidence is dubious, and Job's friends seem to have been incognizant of that fact.

With the verbal mockery of the first two cycles of the friends' speeches wearily behind, and after Job's pitiable plea for mercy in his last speech, he proceeded fully convinced that mockery and falsehood would characterize their discourse henceforth (21:32, 34). Yet as long as they responded, he was compelled to reply. In this speech Job rephrased the question of theodicy.

Why do the wicked live, reach old age, and grow mighty in power (21:7)? Neither succumbing to the badgering of his friends nor capitulating to the scanty evidence they produced, Job took strong exception to their thesis and asked how many times in fact the lamp of the wicked is put out (21:17). Indeed the terminal point of the prosperous wicked and the poor righteous appears quite the same —death. In the absence of any vindication, Job believed the wicked have the better lot (21:23-26).

### THE DIALOGUE: CYCLE THREE (22-27)

*Eliphaz and Job—Cycle Three: First Exchange (22/23-24).* In the clearest and most caustic indictment yet, the once gentle Eliphaz recapitulated arguments from his initial speech, adding a liberal touch of sarcasm.[85] Who did Job think he was that he should expect God to value his righteousness so highly (22:3)? In his original speech Eliphaz had acknowledged Job's benevolent conduct (4:3-4), but now the intervening arguments and emotions had come to so dominate his objectivity that he was fully convinced that Job had required illegal pledges[86] and taken undue advantage of the poor generally (22:6-9).

Eliphaz's theological system had overpowered his objectivity. He now disbelieved what experience had once validated. Job's present plight was the evidence for his evil (22:10). Correctly Eliphaz charged Job with saying that God stood transcendently aloof (22:13-14), for Job had held that God was immanent in suffering but distant in justice. The imperative to Job was equivalent to "Repent!" If he would only concede that God was teaching him about his evil, all would be well between him and God again (22:21-28).

84. See Wisdom of Solomon 16:17.
85. Compare 22:2-3/4:3-5; 22:4/4:6; 22:6-9/4:3-4.
86. See Exodus 22:26; Deuteronomy 24:10-13.

Unlike Job's previous speeches, this reply seems to be, with possibly two exceptions (24:18-20, 25), a monologue. He was essentially alone now with God and his own confidence of personal innocence. His progress in the dialogue becomes evident here, for earlier (9:3, 14-20, 32-33) he expressed the belief that even if he could present his cause to God, God's might would prevail, whereas here he believed God would both hear and acquit him (23:6-7). But since God still evaded him, he was left with only his personal conviction of his innocence (23:8-12).

Whereas chapter 23 deals with Job's personal dilemma in particular, chapter 24 turns upon the human predicament in general. Again we may have an indication of Job's progress, for now he had broadened the dimensions of his personal tragedy so as to identify with others. He no longer demanded simply that others identify with him. Finally, in a defensive tone Job flung down the gauntlet, challenging someone to prove him a liar (24:25).

*Bildad and Job—Cycle Three: Second Exchange (25/26).* Only this speech of Bildad's and the second speech of Zophar (20:2) begin with a declarative sentence rather than a question containing some direct or indirect reference to Job. Due to its brevity, some scholars believe that this speech has been mutilated,[87] whereas others believe the brevity may be regarded as an indication that the friends had exhausted their arguments. Some would add 26:5-14 to it,[88] a section that is congenial to Bildad's own view. It is true that chapters 26-31, considered as a reply to Bildad's last speech, are very long compared to Job's other replies. Gordis tentatively assigns the portions thus:

## AN ANALYSIS OF JOB 25-31

| | |
|---|---|
| Speech of Bildad | — 25; 26:5-14 |
| Job's Reply to Bildad | — 26:1-4; 27:1-12 |
| Speech of Zophar | — 27:13-23 |
| Hymn to Wisdom | — 28 |
| Job's Soliloquy | — 29-31[89] |

If, however, we view 26:1-4 as sarcastic irony and not an admission that his friends have helped him, they fit Job's character role quite well. Further, 26:5-14 is congruent with Job's themes elsewhere (e.g., 9:5-13; 12:15).

Bildad obliquely suggested that since God is so terrible and powerful, Job should not dare criticize Him or claim innocence, as he had blatantly done (cf.

87. Driver and Gray, 1:214-15.
88. Gordis, p. 268.
89. Ibid., pp. 268-69.

9:20; 16:17; 23:10-12; 23:13–24:25). Job had already admitted the truth of Bildad's contention that man cannot claim righteousness before God (9:2), an idea that Eliphaz also propounded (15:14-16). Here we see a feature of the method employed by the author in the dialogue. Job and his friends utilized the same arguments, but each to his own particular advantage. Both Bildad and Job saw the universal forces as an expression of divine power, Bildad to show that there is a moral order, and Job to show that there is not[90] (cf. 25:4 and 9:2; 25:5 and 9:7).

*Zophar's "lost" speech.* The natural thing for the sake of literary symmetry is to look for the third speech of Zophar somewhere in the lengthy discourses of Job that follow. We have already mentioned that Gordis, for example, tentatively discovers it in 27:13-23, following Driver and others.[91] We, of course, cannot say definitely that some textual mobilization has not occurred, thus incurring the loss of portions of Bildad's speech and the whole of Zophar's. Admittedly 27:13-23 does not sound like Job, since it is a description of the fate of the wicked and the vindication of the righteous. Delitzsch, however, views 27:12 as an introduction and verses 13-23 as Job's rehearsal of the friends' position, giving back to them the doctrine they had imparted.[92]

In this connection, an interesting linguistic phenomenon occurs at 27:1 and 29:1, which may provide a clue, admitting, however, that this hypothesis too is tentative. In all other instances Job's speeches are introduced literally by "And Job answered and said," whereas these two sections are prefixed by "And Job again took up his discourse, and said" (RSV), suggesting that this might not have been expected were it not for some irregularity in the order of things. We may assume then that Job paused for Zophar to speak again and, the latter failing to come forth, resumed his own discourse. When at length he had finished and paused for a second time with the same resulting silence, he proceeded to deliver his final monologue. Elihu's anger is attributed partially to the fact that the friends "ceased answering Job" (32:1). Thus at 27:13 Job employs the very words with which Zophar closed his second speech (20:29), rehearsing the theological position of the three, whereas in chapter 28 he imparts the teaching that he promised in 27:11 to give them. If we may assume this as a working hypothesis, we get the following:

> Job paused for Zophar to speak.
> Zophar now silent, "then Job continued his discourse and said," 27:1.
> 27:11     Job promised to teach his friends about God's ways (a task that he fulfilled in chap. 28).

90. Neiman, pp. 91-92.
91. Driver and Gray, 1:226, also attributes verses 7-10 to Zophar. Dhorme, p. 387, and other commentators add 24:18-24.
92. Delitzsch, 2:71-72.

27:12       Job introduced his version of the friends' position by asking why, having seen the evidence, they continued to be foolish. (Whereupon he rehearsed their foolish stance on the evil and the righteous, vv. 13-23).

29:1–31:40 Job delivered a final monologue (summing up).

*Job's resolve unabated (27).* As in the past (cf. 9:20; 16:17; 23:10-12), Job still maintained that he was innocent, and the correlate to that is that God had deprived him of justice (27:2, 5-6). Therefore, he could not and would not relent. Even at this weary point in the debate, he was far from an admission that the friends were right (v. 5). Thus he reviews their erroneous theology (vv. 13-23) and pledges to set them right (v. 11).

POEM ON WISDOM (28)

The central figure in the drama and the three discussants had argued back and forth about the nature and provenance of wisdom. While the former maintained that it is found only with God and that the three friends had none of it, the latter insisted that they were imparting wisdom to Job all the time they were speaking. In a truly magnificent poem Job approached the subject again to stress that wisdom may not be traced to the wealth produced by the earth (vv. 1-6), that it is neither known by the birds who soar above the earth nor the beasts that traverse it, and that even the most ingenious creature of all, man, cannot discover where wisdom makes its home (vv. 7-11).

The question is posed succinctly in verse 12, "But where can wisdom be found?" In verses 13-19 the leading character recapitulates the ideas of verses 1-11, finally repeating the question and concluding that wisdom is to be found neither in the land of the living nor in the realm of death (vv. 20-22). Verses 23-28 constitute a beautiful literary climax and capsulate the author's religious position: Only God knows the way to wisdom. Yet although not detected by human ingenuity, it nevertheless manifests itself in human life:

> Behold, the fear of the Lord, that is wisdom;
> And to depart from evil is understanding.[93]
> (v. 28)

Thus Job's pilgrimage, though not yet at its destination, had brought him to the recognition of the good life and its association with wisdom—it is wisdom! The author used essentially the same terms to describe Job in the prologue (1:1, "fearing God, and turning away from evil"). This was a milestone on the way

---

93. Observe that this statement is the content of divine revelation, as is also the answer to Job in the God speeches.

to the faith that Job confessed consequent upon his encounter with the Lord in the whirlwind. Although God was not finished with Job, He had compelled him to climb to a spiritual plateau from which the panorama of human life was coherent.

### JOB'S CLOSING MONOLOGUE (29-31)

The chapter divisions provide a practical outline of this speech. In chapter 29 Job nostalgically reviews his past, certifying that the ground of his security and happiness had been God (vv. 2-5). His faith had not been invalidated by the intervening tragedy. Further, he rehearsed the honor in which his compatriots held him (vv. 7-11), resulting directly from his practical demeanor in life constituted by proper consideration of and care for the poor, the fatherless, and the widows (vv. 12-17). His practical righteousness was such a natural outgrowth of his inner being that Job could say, "I wore righteousness and it wore me" (v. 14, author's translation).

Such a recollection of his former state led naturally to the lament over his friends' ill treatment of him and his present pitiable state in chapter 30. And that in Job's mind was directly related to God's attitude toward him. The only direct address to God in this soliloquy (vv. 20-23) contained essentially the same charges Job had leveled against Him on other occasions in the dialogue.

To accentuate Job's conviction of his personal innocence, in chapter 31 he ended his final defense by taking oaths regarding deeds that could have brought about his disaster. Indeed this act revealed both his confidence of personal integrity and the gravity of the situation. We may mention also that the absence of the fulfillment of these curses (insofar as the epilogue informs us) confirms the judgment of the prologue that Job was a righteous individual. Moreover, the same fact constitutes an implicit denunciation of the charges of the friends to complement the Lord's explicit reprimand of their words (42:7-9). Alongside the terms "umpire" (9:33), "witness in heaven" (16:19), and "Redeemer" (19:25), we now have a fourth epithet for the advocate Job earnestly hoped for: "one to hear me" (31:35).

Ironically, someone in the audience yet unheard from was listening, and he had plenty to say in reply. Yet the young, budding Elihu, possessed of a confidence not tempered by time and experience as in the case of the other respondents (and thereby his speech may be less self-indicting), came no closer to solving Job's problem than had the three men with whom he had lost patience. But we may be sure the hope that had on occasion momentarily sparkled in Job's words had been kindled from the divine flame that often is eclipsed by crisis and human doubt. We must, therefore, bear with Elihu so that we may even more genuinely appreciate the true light from the whirlwind.

THE ELIHU SPEECHES (32-37)

The author of Job, having countered the thesis that age and experience are the source of wisdom (cf. 32:9), next suggested another proposition through the youthful Elihu[94]—that understanding (wisdom) is resident in man as a gift of God (32:8) and does not need to wait for the work and tempering of time before it can be called wisdom. This is true, of course, and Job said it quite as well or better (28:28). However, Elihu's inflated self-confidence (cf. 33:33) failed to justify his thesis that wisdom is a gift of God. And while age cannot lay exclusive claim to it, age and experience cannot be written off so glibly as Elihu did.

He brought an angry disposition to the debate; he was angry at Job because he "justified himself before God," and angry at the friends because they had found no answer even though they had declared Job to be in the wrong (32:2-3). The fact that the text states four times that Elihu became angry (vv. 2, 3, 5) cues us in on a certain quality of his speeches. They were more angry than rational, yet certainly incorporated worthy ideas. Believing himself to have clearly understood Job, he summarized the basic arguments set forth by him: Job had charged God with his trouble (33:8-11), had claimed that He would not answer him (33:13), that He had denied him justice (34:5-6), and that Job had advocated that the lot of the righteous was no better than that of the wicked (35:2-3). Elihu had listened well. Twice he challenged Job to answer his arguments (33:32; 34:33), but we can only speculate as to why he did not.

The gist of Elihu's contribution was that God sends suffering for man's discipline and correction (33:14-30; 37:13). Despite his boasting, Eliphaz had briefly formulated this idea in his first speech (5:17). Although we are left with an attractive formula that might explain suffering in some cases, the reader knows that Elihu had applied it to the wrong case because the prologue has provided the audience a higher level of understanding. When the garrulous Elihu is finished, we may have explored another forest more fully, but we are really no closer home than we were when the major discussants had exhausted their verbal arsenals.

THE GOD SPEECHES (38:1–42:6)

Job received the answer to his question partly from the fact of the Lord's appearances and partly from the content of His speeches. We probably should not debate which was the more important. They are complementary, thus observing the style of our author who has already presented parts of the answer in the dialogue. Indeed the friends were partly right—suffering is related to sin—

94. See discussion under "The Elihu Speeches," pp. 80-81.

but they were partly wrong, as this is not a universal rule applicable to all cases. Job was partly right—the innocent often suffer. And Elihu was partly right —suffering may instruct and correct.

Yet none of these explanations constitutes a whole. In fact, they leave much yet to be explained. The fact, therefore, of the Lord's appearance to the suffering Job is inexpressibly significant. However, theophanies alone convey an emotional content that cries out for verbal expression. Thus the verbal content gives substance to the theophanic form.

We may identify several basic approaches to the God speeches. Some who take the existential view contend that the Lord's appearance was quite enough to satisfy Job and answer his challenge that God confront him. Although there is an element of truth in this approach, it makes the words of the God speeches superfluous. Another attempt to explain them is to say that God just overwhelmed Job with a deluge of data about the beauty and mystery of the world, and that became an anodyne to Job's suffering.[95] But this explanation puts God's action in a devious light if He were just trying to make Job forget his question. Still others take the pastoral approach and explain that God wanted to show man what was the proper conduct in suffering.[96] If that were the case, however, then God could be expected to indict Job for improper conduct in the dialogue. If there is any indictment in the God speeches, however, it is only implicit. If this had been God's purpose, we should have expected Him to be far more explicit. One other explanation is that the Lord informed Job that justice is not one of the pillars of the universe, and in this way his problem was resolved.[97] It was a matter of correcting his presuppositions.

Significantly, the direct answer to the question "Why do the innocent suffer?" is nowhere spelled out in the God speeches. The Lord did not accommodate Himself to so simplistic a formulation of so profound a mystery. Job had begun with the challenge that God explain his own personal dilemma, momentarily drawing the circles big enough to include others who were oppressed. But whereas Job's concern was essentially egocentric, even though he probed for the answer to a universal question, the Lord's answer was phrased almost altogether in universal terms. He proceeded to draw a series of tightening circles around Job. He began with the creation of the world (38:4-11):

> Where were you when I laid the foundation of the earth!
> Tell Me, if you have understanding.
>
> (38:4)

95. E.g., Gordis, passim.
96. E.g., Fohrer, p. 334.
97. Matitiahu Tsevat, "The Meaning of the Book of Job," HUCA 37 (1966):73-106.

Then He moved to the operation of the world (38:12-38):

> Have you ever in your life commanded the morning,
> And caused the dawn to know its place?
>
> (38:12)

Sarcastically the Lord alluded to Job's egotism:

> You know, for you were born then,
> And the number of your days is great!
>
> (38:21)

He drew the circle in still more—could Job understand and maintain the animal kingdom? (38:39–39:30):

> Can you hunt the prey for the lion,
> Or satisfy the appetite of the young lions,
> When they crouch in their dens,
> And lie in wait in their lair?
> Who prepares for the raven its nourishment,
> When its young cry to God,
> And wander about without food?
>
> (38:39-41)

Man had been instructed to subdue the animal kingdom when God assigned him to the lordship of the world (Gen. 1:28). Or, to take something even more familiar, the world of human beings, the Lord challenged Job to set it right (40:10-14):

> Adorn yourself with eminence and dignity;
> And clothe yourself with honor and majesty.
> Pour out the overflowings of your anger . . . .
> Look on everyone who is proud, and humble him;
> And tread down the wicked where they stand.
>
> (40:10-12)

Still further, if man was too much for Job, the Lord had other challenges for him among His irrational creatures. He might tackle the hippopotamus (40:15-24) or the crocodile (41:1-34).

The God speeches remind us that the universe is essentially theocentric. Further, although much about divine justice had not been clear to Job, God had not left the world quite so destitute of moral implications as Job had alleged. The natural world with its beauty and orderly design presents man with an indicator of an ordered moral universe even though it be beyond man's cognitive perception. By revealing transcendence in meticulous details, the Lord simultaneously revealed His immanence. So near is He to man that He appeared to Job personally. So near is He to His world that He causes the rain to fall on the subhuman creatures even though man knows nothing about His activity there (38:26-27). By impugning God for His evasiveness, Job had committed the same offense against God that the friends had committed. They justified God at Job's expense, whereas Job justified himself at God's expense (40:8).

In summary, although the theophany delivered a declaration, it also presented Job with a challenge. If he knew so much about the order of the universe, suppose he reproduce the details of creation, unravel the secrets of the cosmos, demonstrate that he could control nature! If he could meet God's challenges, then God Himself would acknowledge that he was self-sufficient (40:14).

The first speech of the Lord was met by a brief, submissive response from Job in which he conceded that he was unable to answer Him (40:3-5). God's questions had not been merely rhetorical—He challenged Job to answer (40:2). The Lord's second speech was met by Job's recantation (42:1-6), conceding that he did not and could not know the full mystery of the moral universe. Suffering is sometimes a mystery. We must affirm both the mystery and God Himself. The paradox remained, but now, at least, Job knew that it belonged there—that it is built into the moral and physical orders and into the very nature of God as He has permitted us humans to perceive Him. In a world where the universal principle is cause-effect, the book of Job reminds us that the principle is a reflection of the mysterious, self-revealing God. It is subsumed under Him, however, and He cannot be subsumed under it. The God speeches remind us that a Person, not a principle, is Lord.

EPILOGUE (42:7-17)

Although the God speeches are the climax of the book, the story has yet another chapter, which is related here. It is important that the metaphysical be translated into phenomenal terms at some point in human experience. We need not suppose, however, that the theophany was insufficient for Job—his repentance and recantation point to its sufficiency. Nor should we assume that the particulars of God's moral universe will at some time be translated into physical terms in every case. That divine justice certainly exists is indicated by the God speeches. But it does not follow that the double restoration of the hero's fortunes was or will be a regularly recurring expression of it. Rather the epilogue reveals more of God's love, forgiveness, and benevolence than of His justice. There is more to His nature than justice. He could call Job His servant because Job had recognized that the moral fabric of the universe is an entity to be reckoned with in human experience, though at times it may evade our sight. Job now knew that justice is not the sum of human life or the whole of God's essential being. Further, just because God's justice is real, human integrity is an entity that God cannot and will not ignore. Job had defended his own, and in so doing had defended God's.

### QUMRAN FRAGMENTS OF JOB

Qumran so far has not been generous in its yield of fragments on the Hebrew text of Job. One fragment from Cave 2 (2Q15) contains Job 33:28-30 and is said to be of the Masoretic type. Part of Job 36 has come from Cave 4 (4Q Job[a,b]) along with a third fragment written in paleo-Hebrew (4QpaleoJob[c]).[98] Yet Cave 11 has yielded an Aramaic translation (Targum) of a significant portion of Job (11QtgJob).[99] Although the scroll possibly dates from the first Christian century, the translation likely was made a century or so earlier. The first sixteen chapters are missing, but beginning at 17:14, parts of all chapters except chapter 23 are contained among the fragments, breaking off with 42:11. The final passage (42:12-17) is missing, but it is not certain whether it was once included in this Aramaic translation or not.[100]

The significance of this Targum is that it agrees in general with the Hebrew text as it has come to us, and furthermore, it corroborates the order of the Hebrew text.[101] The poem on wisdom, the Elihu speeches, and the God speeches occupy the same position they do in the Hebrew Masoretic text. Moreover, this text virtually assures us that written Aramaic translations predate the Christian era and were not first written down only in the second century A.D., as some scholarly opinion has proposed. Linguistically this Targum provides us with a larger picture of the Aramaic language in the first century A.D.[102]

98. Joseph A. Fitzmeyer, "Some Observations on the Targum of Job from Qumran Cave 11," CBQ 36 (1974):524.
99. The text was first published by J. van der Ploeg and A. S. van der Woude, *Le Targum de Job de la Grotte XI de Qumran* (Leiden, 1971). For facsimiles, see this volume. Sokoloff, mentioned below, gives a transcription with an English translation and commentary.
100. Michael Sokoloff, *The Targum to Job from Qumran Cave XI*, p. 5.
101. John Gray, "The Masoretic Text of the Book of Job, the Targum and the Septuagint Version in the Light of the Qumran Targum," ZAW 86 (1974):332.
102. See Joseph A. Fitzmyer, "The Contribution of Qumran Aramaic to the Study of the New Testament," NTS 20 (1974):382-407.

# 4

# THE PSALMS

Old Testament history and theology are impressed upon this book in fragmented and unsystematic form. The dynamism of history and personal encounter with God exudes from these songs. They have not only arisen out of history and personal encounter, but have also stood the test of the same. To read and pray the Psalms is to join the voices of numberless people who too have read and prayed them, have felt their joy, anguish, and indignation.

Rarely has human history enjoyed the luxury of a literature so cathartic. And seldom has a people opened their souls so freely to all mankind as has Israel in the Psalms. There is no better way to enter the spirit of Israelite history and the faith of this people of antiquity than through this book. For the cognitive quality of these songs is reinforced by the emotional content. One acquires not only a historical knowledge of this elect people but also an orientation to the psychology of their mind and spirit.

Yet the Psalms are more than an eye into Israel. They stand as a monumental witness to the timeless and universal nature of man. His heart is turned so easily to sin. Hatred, greed, and disobedience are part of his infamous baggage. Without God, his Creator, he is orphaned in the world. But despite who man is, God sees him as His special creation (Ps. 8) and seeks to redeem him. The essential nature of man is counterbalanced, indeed countermanded, by the essential nature of God. The Psalms capture the qualitative essence of man and God, and lay them out in juxtaposition, thus revealing the insufficiency of the one and the all-sufficiency of the other.

It is hardly an exaggeration to say that in the arena of faith the book of Psalms has been a cloud by day and a pillar of fire by night for Israel and the church. The reasons are not elusive. This collection of ancient hymns represents a wide spectrum of life experiences, a broad range of social ranks from kings to commoners, a microcosm of human emotions and situations, and a catalogue of spiritual experience. The simple and sublime of both human experience and ancient Hebrew poetry exist side by side in this book. Wherever an individual finds himself on the journey of faith, the Psalms provide a place of rest and a time of repose and reflection, as well as a stimulus to send him on his way. As the occasions of life diversify and emotions intensify, the value of the Psalms increases proportionately.

## INTRODUCTORY MATTERS ABOUT PSALMS

### TITLE

Our English title, "The Psalms," has been routed through the Greek and Latin versions of the Old Testament. The Septuagint used the word *psalmos* to render the Hebrew *mizmôr,* the technical term for a song sung to the accompaniment of musical instruments. The Vatican Greek manuscript (fourth century A.D.) has the title "Psalms" (*psalmoi*), which has good precedent in the Lukan writings. Jesus referred to "the book of Psalms" in Luke 20:42, and Peter spoke of it by the same title (Acts 1:20). The Alexandrinus Greek manuscript of the Old Testament entitled the book *Psaltērion,* meaning a stringed instrument. From this title the Christian church has taken the name "Psalter" as a designation for the book. The Hebrew Bible, however, appropriately entitled the book "Praises" (*tehillim*), a word that occurs a number of times in the various psalms but only once to designate an individual psalm (Ps. 145).

### NUMBER

The Hebrew Bible contains 150 psalms, and Protestant Bibles have followed the Hebrew numbering. The Greek Bible, however, contains an additional psalm at the end of the book. Further, two of the Hebrew psalms have been subdivided in the Septuagint (followed also by the Latin Vulgate), and twice a pair of psalms in Hebrew have been fused into one, as indicated below:

## TWO SYSTEMS OF NUMBERING PSALMS

| *Hebrew and Protestant Bibles* | *Greek and Roman Catholic Bibles* |
|:---:|:---:|
| 1-8 | 1-8 |
| 9 | 9 |
| 10 | |
| 11-113 | 10-112 |
| 114 | 113 |
| 115 | |
| | 114 |
| 116 | 115 |
| 117-146 | 116-145 |
| | 146 |
| 147 | 147 |
| 148-150 | 148-150 |
| | 151(Gk.) |

Therefore, we must be aware of this different system of numbering when reading the works of scholars who refer to the Septuagint or Vulgate.

DEVELOPMENT AND COMPILATION

We must speak of two lines of development in regard to the book of Psalms: the development of Hebrew poetry and psalmody, and the growth of the Psalter up to its present form.

*Old Testament psalmody.* Although no comparable collection of songs from biblical times has come to light, a variety of hymns of Egyptian, Sumero-Akkadian, and Hittite origin does exist.[1] Among the Ras Shamra texts, however, no hymns as such have been discovered to date.[2] Yet they have become an important source for linguistic studies and a comparative literature for the study of poetry. Both aspects of Ugaritic studies have brought a new dimension to the study of the Psalms. Mitchell Dahood in particular utilized the Ras Shamra (or Ugaritic) literature in his three-volume commentary to elucidate Hebrew words, phrases, and concepts. Moreover, significant studies have been done in Ugaritic poetry in an effort to understand more fully the dynamics and nature of Hebrew poetry.[3]

While an interdependence of ancient Near Eastern literatures was definitely a reality, the Hebrew faith, especially with its monotheism and ethical aptitude, could be expected to produce a superior hymnody. We may draw such a conclusion also in regard to Hebrew prophecy, based upon the prophetic literature from Mesopotamia[4] as compared to its Old Testament counterpart. A superior religious faith will inevitably create a superior religious literature. Therefore, Hebrew psalmody stands in a class by itself and deserves to be studied as distinctive.

We may confidently trace the history of Hebrew psalmody back at least to the time of Moses. The Israelites celebrated their victory at the Red Sea with hymns, the songs of Moses and Miriam (Ex. 15:1-18, 21). In like manner was celebrated the victory of Deborah and Barak over Jabin the king of Canaan (Judg. 5). With time the Hebrews even collected their poetry. It is thought that the Book of Jashar, which contained the hymn commemorating Joshua's victory over the Amorites (Josh. 10:13) and David's lament over the death of Saul (2 Sam. 1:17-27), was a book of poetry, or at least contained poetic materials. It is certainly plausible that by the time the books of Joshua and Samuel were written, some Hebrew collections of poetry existed.

1. James B. Pritchard, ed., ANET, pp. 365-92; Pritchard, ed., ANET Supp., pp. 573-91.
2. Mitchell Dahood, *Psalms*, 1:xxxii.
3. See the previous discussion of Old Testament poetry on pp. 31-38; also Peter C. Craigie, *Psalms 1-50*, pp. 48-56.
4. Pritchard, ANET Supp., pp. 623-32.

It would seem to me, therefore, that the tradition of psalmody that the Chronicler associated with David was no romantic invention. It had at least three aspects: (1) David's musical abilities;[5] (2) David's role as founder or organizer of Temple musicology;[6] and (3) David as founder of Hebrew psalmody.[7] Further support comes from King David's poetry, which is preserved outside the book of Psalms as well as within. Two extended hymns help to corroborate the evidence: his beautiful lament over the death of Saul (2 Sam. 1:19-27), and the song of thanksgiving when he had been delivered from all his enemies (2 Sam. 22:2-51, a near duplicate of Ps. 18). These are augmented by the brief lament over Abner (2 Sam. 3:33-34) and his longer, superb last words (2 Sam. 23:2-7). Kirkpatrick remarks: "[Psalm 18] has all the freshness of creative génius. It can hardly have been the solitary production of its author. If such a Psalm could have been written by David, so might many others."[8]

Although the Psalter is our primary evidence that hymnody continued to develop in Israel and became indelibly stamped upon the heart of this people, the Old Testament contains many other hymns of invaluable worth. The songs of Moses and Miriam (Ex. 15:1-18, 21) are Pentateuchal examples, and the former prophets contain such hymns as the song of Deborah and Barak (Judg. 5:2-31), which is by the testimony of most scholars a very ancient poem. The prophetic books have their songs too, for example, Isaiah 5:1-7; 23:16; 26:1-6; 27:2-5; Ezekiel 19; Hosea 6:1-3; and Habakkuk 3, to name only a few. The internal testimony of the Old Testament then is that the hymn as a popular literary genre spanned most of Old Testament history.

*Process of growth.* With its many authors and widely ranging dates, the Psalter obviously came into being over a period of centuries. Its composite nature is further suggested by the presence of duplicate psalms:

DUPLICATE PSALMS

| | | |
|---|---|---|
| 53 | – | 14 |
| 70 | – | 40:13-17 |
| 108 | – | 57:7-11 and 60:5-12 |

Moreover, subordinate groupings within the book testify to the aggregate nature of the Psalter. For the most part, Book I is composed of psalms "of David" (except 1, 2, 10, 33), whereas Books II and III contain the collections "of

5. 1 Samuel 16:18, 23; 2 Samuel 6:5; Nehemiah 12:36; Amos 6:5.
6. 1 Chronicles 15:16; 16:7; 25:1; Ezra 3:10; Nehemiah 12:24, 46 (the last reference includes Solomon).
7. Nehemiah 12:24, 36, 46.
8. A. F. Kirkpatrick, *The Book of Psalms*, p. xlii.

the sons of Korah" (42-49) and "of Asaph" (73-83), and Books IV and V "of David" (138-45). Songs of Ascents (120-34), the "hodu" Psalms (all beginning with the Hebrew imperative for "give thanks" [*hodu*], 105-7), and two groups of the "Hallelujah" Psalms (all beginning and/or ending with the Hebrew imperative "praise the Lord," or "Hallelujah," 111-18; 146-50). In addition to these collections, we have others connected by obscure titles, two Maschil groups (42-45, 52-55), and one Michtam collection (56-60).[9]

A further clue to the growth of the Psalter is the use of the divine names. Psalms 1-41 (Book I) employ the name *Yahweh* predominantly, with *Elohim* occurring only a few times. In Psalms 42-72 (Book II) the controlling name is the generic Elohim, whereas Psalms 90-106 (Book IV) use only Yahweh. Psalms 73-89 (Book III) alternate the predominance of each name between two sections, Psalms 73-83 (Elohim), and Psalms 84-89 (Yahweh).[10] This has led some scholars to postulate the existence of an "Elohistic Psalter" (Pss. 42-83), which was composed of still smaller collections.[11] The reason the authors of these psalms preferred Elohim over Yahweh is no longer evident. Peter C. Craigie advanced the suggestion that the "Elohistic" collection was compiled for the Temple at a time when the name Yahweh was used with great hesitation.[12] We know that by the time the Hebrew Old Testament was translated into Greek (Septuagint) the name *Adonai* (Lord, Master) had become a substitute for Yahweh, for the translators consistently rendered the name with the Greek equivalent (*Kurios*, "Lord").

The preference for one divine name over the other can be seen in the duplicate psalms. Psalm 14 employs the divine name Yahweh whereas its duplicate in Psalm 53 (in the so-called "Elohistic Psalter") uses the name Elohim. The same clarity, however, is not evident in Psalm 40:13-17 and its duplicate, Psalm 70. Psalm 40 employs Yahweh in all instances, as we might expect, except verse 17 where Elohim occurs. In like manner, Psalm 70 uses Elohim, as is the pattern of the "Elohistic" collection, but in verses 2 and 6 both Elohim and Yahweh occur (in that order).

Although some of the smaller collections probably came into being independently, the origin of others is likely tied to the development of a larger collection. For example, the Maschil group, Psalms 42-45, is incorporated into a series of Korah psalms, Psalms 42-49.

When the book was finally edited, it was given a fivefold division. Although the antiquity of this division cannot be established, the Midrash on the

9. See Derek Kidner, *Psalms 1-72*, p. 38, for a discussion of suggested meanings of *maschil* and *michtam*.
10. S. R. Driver, *An Introduction to the Literature of the Old Testament*, p. 371.
11. The collections can be identified: Psalms of Korah (42-49), the Psalms of Asaph (50, 73-83), and Psalms of David (51-65, 68-72). See S. R. Driver, p. 371.
12. Peter C. Craigie, *Psalms 1-50*, p. 30.

Psalms, codified in the tenth century A.D., attests to it and makes the fivefold division analogous to the five books of the Torah.[13] The five divisions are as follows:

### TRADITIONAL DIVISIONS OF THE PSALMS

| | |
|---|---|
| Book I | Psalms 1-41 |
| Book II | Psalms 42-72 |
| Book III | Psalms 73-89 |
| Book IV | Psalms 90-106 |
| Book V | Psalms 107-50 |

Each of the first four books is concluded by a doxology: 41:13; 72:18-19; 89:52; 106:48. The first three are plainly distinct from the psalms they follow, whereas the fourth is not. Yet it belonged to the psalm in antiquity, since it was a part of the psalm in 1 Chronicles 16:35-36. The fifth book is concluded with a series of doxologies (Pss. 146-50). Psalm 150 sometimes is called the "Great Hallelujah." To the concluding doxology of Book II is added, "The prayers of David the son of Jesse are ended" (72:20).

*Dating the process.* Specificity in dating the final editions of the several collections as well as the completed book itself is a precarious undertaking. Yet some general remarks are necessary.

The continuum of this collection process probably extended from the Davidic period well into the postexilic era. Alexander's approach of taking Psalm 90 (attributed to Moses) as the central column separating the two parts of the book (the first belonging to the times of David and the last, with a few exceptions, to post-Davidic times)[14] is too simplistic, although Psalm 90 did historically become a dividing point between Books III and IV. A much more complex effort by Moses Buttenwieser,[15] which seeks to arrange the psalms into three historical eras (preexilic, exilic, and postexilic psalms), reaches overconfidently in the opposite direction. Yet the three eras are natural categories for dating the hymns of the Psalter even though we may not be able to accept Buttenwieser's groupings and chronological conclusions in many instances.

Four possible eras of Old Testament history when such collecting and editing efforts may have occurred are suggested in the historical books: the periods of David, Jehoshaphat, Hezekiah, and Ezra. The Chronicler has preserved the tradition that David assigned a division of the Levites to the musical services of the Temple (1 Chron. 23:2-6). To engage in conjecture, it is logical to suppose that a collection of Davidic psalms would have come into existence toward the

13. William G. Braude, trans., *The Midrash on Psalms*, 1:5.
14. J. A. Alexander, *The Psalms*, 1:xiii.
15. Moses Buttenwieser, *The Psalms, Chronologically Treated with a New Translation*.

end of David's reign or soon after his death. Another similar flurry of Levitical activity and literary fervor is recorded during the reign of Jehoshaphat (first half of the ninth century), although no mention is made of any psalmic efforts. That revival was focused upon the Book of the Law (2 Chron. 17:7-9). Well over a century later Hezekiah revitalized Temple worship, including the musical responsibilities of the Levites (2 Chron. 29:25-30). That monarch's literary interest is also recalled in Proverbs 25:1. Therefore, we may assume that by the end of Hezekiah's reign (c. 715-685 B.C.) hymnody had reached a new plateau. The next and possibly final state in the growth of the Psalter can be seen in the time of Ezra and Nehemiah. When the wall of Jerusalem was dedicated, the singing Levites were summoned for the occasion. The narrative gives evidence that the musical activities of the Levites had become institutionalized by that time, for "the singers had built themselves villages around Jerusalem" (Neh. 12:27-30, 45-46). In fact, the honored status of the Temple singers at the time of Ezra had begun during the governorship of Zerubbabel, when the Temple was rebuilt (Neh. 12:47).

Some scholars have extended the growth of the Psalter into the Maccabean Period (second century B.C.), whereas others have objected strongly to the idea of "Maccabean" psalms. Buttenwieser contends that the Hebrew language had degenerated too much by that time to allow the literary excellence that the Psalms exhibit.[16] Dahood, upon the basis of the Ras Shamra texts, has demonstrated that much of the phraseology of the psalms was current in Palestine-Syria long before the time of David. Further, he has maintained that the Septuagint translators in the third century B.C. revealed a lack of knowledge of biblical poetry and a lack of acquaintance with biblical images and metaphors, suggesting to him a wide gap in time between the writing of the psalms and their Greek translation.[17] Consequently, he has opted for a preexilic date for most of the psalms. This position certainly seems to be within the bounds of the evidence, even though all scholars recognize that some of them are exilic and early postexilic (e.g., Ps. 137).

*Authorship.* Often the titles of the Psalms include the Hebrew preposition *lamedh* (generally meaning "of," "to," or "for") prefixed to the names of important persons. It may in some cases imply authorship ("of" as a subjective genitive), and in others mean "for the use of," or "to" (dedicated to), and still in other cases it may carry the meaning of "belonging to" (a collection).[18] While we cannot determine with certainty how many of the seventy-three Psalms that have David with the prefixed *lamedh* in the title were actually composed by him, there is good reason to believe that many were. David's musical ability and ac-

16. Ibid., pp. 10-18.
17. Dahood, 1:xxx.
18. Craigie, pp. 34-35.

tivity is too generally attested in the Old Testament to deny him a role in the composition of the Psalms. He is called the "sweet psalmist of Israel" (2 Sam. 23:1), inventor of musical instruments (Amos 6:5), the organizer of the Temple musicology (1 Chron. 15:16-24; 16:7, 31; Ezra 3:10; Neh. 12:24), and the composer of psalms (2 Sam. 1:19-27; 22:1-51; 23:2-7; 1 Chron. 16:8-36). Such an image of David cannot be ignored.

In addition to David's name, the names of Asaph (one of David's chief musicians—1 Chron. 6:39; 15:17), the sons of Korah, Solomon, Moses, Heman, and Ethan (1 Kings 4:30-32) are associated with the Psalms, as the table on the following page will indicate.

CLASSIFICATION

There is no system of classification to which all the psalms are easily accommodated. That is not a criticism of the book but rather a confession of our inability to comprehend the scope of this collection. However, two methods are generally used, grouping by *content* and grouping by *function*. The first is the older method, and even with the rise of form-critical scholarship and its application to the Psalms, it has remained a helpful system. At the end of the last century, S. R. Driver listed seven rubrics based upon content, which, although not comprehensive, are helpful:

1. Meditations on various aspects of divine providence
2. Reflections on God's moral government of the world
3. Expressions of faith, resignation, joy in God's presence
4. Psalms with distinct reference to the circumstances of the psalmist
5. National psalms
6. Historical psalms
7. Royal psalms[19]

Other recognized classifications are messianic, wisdom, imprecatory, and so forth. Moses Buttenwieser, to cite another example, attempted to treat the psalms in their historical sequence, dating some of them as early in the preexilic period as the time of the Judges and none of them as late as the Maccabean age.[20] For the scholars who have followed the historical method, the precondition for proper psalm interpretation was understanding the historical circumstances that produced the song.

19. Driver, pp. 368-69, provides examples of these types as follows: (1) Psalms 8; 19:1-6; 33; 36; (2) Psalms 1; 34; 75; 77; 90; (3) Psalms 11; 16; 23; 84; 121; 133; 139; (4) Psalms 3-7; 9-10; 12; 30; 40:1-12; (5) Psalms 14; 44; 46; 60; 74; 79; 87; 124-26; (6) Psalms 78; 81; 105; 106; 114; (7) Psalms 2; 18; 20; 101; and 110.
20. Buttenwieser, passim.

## THE AUTHORSHIP, DEDICATION, AND COLLECTION OF THE PSALMS

| | Book I Pss. 1-41 | Book II Pss. 42-72 | Book III Pss. 73-89 | Book IV Pss. 90-106 | Book V Pss. 107-50 | Totals |
|---|---|---|---|---|---|---|
| David | 3-9 11-32 34-41 (37) | 51-65 68-70 (18) | 86 | 101 103 (2) | 108-10 122, 124* 131, 133 138-45 (15) | 73 |
| Asaph | | 50 | 73-83 (11) | | | 12 |
| Sons of Korah | | 42 44-49 (7) | 84-85 87-88 (4) | | | 11 |
| Solomon | | 72 | | | 127 | 2 |
| Moses | | | | 90 | | 1 |
| Heman the Ezrahite | | | 88 | | | 1 |
| Ethan the Ezrahite | | | 89 (one of two titles) | | | 1 |

*The few headings preserved in the Qumran Psalms Scroll from Cave 11 confirm those of the Masoretic text, but Psalm 123 in the Q scroll is attributed to David.

The second system of classification has been produced, not by investigating the historical background, but by identifying the "type," or genre (*Gattung*), of the song and tracing that back to its origin in the life of Israel. The rudimentary pursuit focused on the "setting in life" (*Sitz im Leben*), that is, the situation that brought the particular psalm into existence. For example, Psalm 24 according to many form critics was chanted at the gates of the Temple as the Ark was returned after a battle. Herman Gunkel[21] pioneered this method and insisted that the important question was not the historical background but the function of the song in the life of Israel. He believed that the earliest songs of Israel were connected to the religious shrines, although many of them were later spiritualized and used as personal prayers. He proposed seven types or classes:

1. Hymns, sung on holy days at the Temple
2. Community laments, chanted by the people when disaster had struck
3. Songs of the individual, sung by pious persons
4. Thank-offering songs, sung by one who had been delivered from great distress, and accompanied by a thank offering
5. Laments of the individual, intoned by one who had suffered physical or emotional affliction
6. Entrance liturgies, chanted by those who desired to enter the place of worship
7. Royal psalms, sung in honor of the king

Gunkel's protégé, Sigmund Mowinckel, built upon the form (or type) criticism developed and applied by his teacher, concluding that, "It is the non-cultic character of a psalm which has to be proved, the contrary being the more likely supposition."[22] He therefore set out to define the specific celebrations or festivals when each psalm was sung.

As an example of the historical approach or the content method as compared with the form critical, we may again cite Psalm 24. Many scholars admit that this song may have celebrated David's transfer of the Ark of the Covenant from Kiriath-jearim to Jerusalem (2 Sam. 6:12-23), although the occasion is not specified. That, or a similar occasion, provides the backdrop for interpreting the psalm. Those who seek the "setting in life," however, view the psalm as a composition that came into being to celebrate the New Year festival in Israel[23] when, as some scholars surmise, Yahweh was reenthroned, as was the Babylonian god Marduk, in a comparable New Year festival, the Ark being His visible representative. According to the latter view, the psalm was primarily liturgical, although form criticism is not incognizant of historical details.

21. For a synopsis of Hermann Gunkel's thought, see *The Psalms: A Form-Critical Introduction.*
22. Mowinckel, *The Psalms in Israel's Worship,* 1:22.
23. Ibid., 1:170 and passim.

Many scholars have come to recognize, however, that not all the psalms have a liturgical origin, and that many were probably never used at all in the liturgy of the Temple. Psalm 23 may be such a song, and even Mowinckel recognizes the difficulty of assigning this psalm to a cultic origin, admitting: "What gives it a priceless value to all ages may be the very fact that it stands there as a pure expression of confidence in God, unhindered by all special historical circumstances, an adequate expression of the confidence of faith of all sorts of people, and at all times."[24] This illustrates the extent to which Mowinckel carried the work of Gunkel.

Claus Westermann has critically evaluated the work of Gunkel and pointed out that he failed to define what a hymn was, in spite of its importance in his system of classification. Further, he did not give sufficient evidence that the cult was the *Sitz im Leben* of the hymn. Westermann insisted that there was no difference in category between the hymn and the song of thanksgiving, and he called them both psalms of praise.[25] He reduced Gunkel's types to essentially two, psalms of praise and psalms of lament, shifting the focus away from cult to worship. By worship he meant the broad history and development of the interaction between God and man,[26] and that, submits Westermann, is the real *Sitz im Leben* of the Psalms. The praise of God was a common occurrence, not limited to the Temple and its formalities: "Therefore the praise of God in Israel never became a cultic happening, separated from the rest of existence, in a separate realm, that had become independent of the history of the people and of the individual. Rather it occupied a central place in the total life of the individual and the people before God, as for instance the concept of faith does for us."[27] Thus Westermann has recognized that the origin of the Psalms has to be found in the common religious life of Israel.

## TITLES

Even though thirty-four psalms in the Hebrew Bible have no title (superscription),[28] we are still left with titles for more than two-thirds of them. The Septuagint, however, has supplied all but Psalms 1 and 2 with headings. We can distinguish five different categories among the titles in the Hebrew (and English) Bible:

1. Authorship
2. Historical origin

---

24. Ibid., 2:41.
25. Claus Westermann, *Praise and Lament in the Psalms*, pp. 18, 31.
26. Ibid., p. 21.
27. Ibid., p. 155.
28. These psalms have no title: 1, 2, 10, 33, 43, 71, 91, 93-97, 104-7, 111-19, 135-37, 146-50.

  3. Literary features
  4. Liturgical use
  5. Musical notations

Thirtle in his extensive study of the titles has shown that some elements belong not to the psalm that they superscribe but to the preceding one.[29] In particular, basing his conclusion upon the psalm in Habakkuk 3, which he believes to set forth a structural pattern, he has proposed that the musical notations preceding a psalm really belong to the previous one.

*Authorship.* In addition to the above remarks about authorship, we might add that recent scholarship has filled in the ancient cultural and literary context in which the attribution of certain psalms to ancient worthies is quite plausible. Dahood's application of Ugaritic studies to the language of the psalms, for example, led him to the conclusion that the literary tradition necessary for the composition of many psalms thought to be late had long been in place in Canaan. He lists examples of those he believed were Davidic (2, 16, 18, 29, 50, 58, 82, 108, 110).[30]

*Historical origin.* The thirteen titles belonging in this category all refer to David's life and experience.[31] Despite objections raised in the scholarly literature on the Psalms,[32] the historicity of these titles still stands rather firmly. Upon examination we can detect the organic connections between title and psalm, admitting, of course, that they were not always composed on the spot but during subsequent reflection upon the event.

*Literary features.* By this designation we mean those words that describe the literary character of the psalm. They include the terms psalm, song, *maschil, michtam, shiggaion,* prayer, praise. It is not our purpose to attempt a definition of these words in this study. However, we want to recognize the frequency of their usage in the Psalter and offer further study suggestions.[33]

*Liturgical use.* The few notes referring to the special usage of the psalms in the Temple liturgy may be indicative of the early completion of the book. By the time of the Septuagint translation, several of the psalms had become liturgically attached to certain days. The Septuagint notes that Psalm 24 (LXX, Ps. 23) was

---

29. James William Thirtle, *The Titles of the Psalms, Their Nature and Meaning Explained.*
30. Dahood, 1:xxix-xxx.
31. David's conflict with Saul, Psalms 7, 34, 52, 56, 57, 59, 142; culmination of his reign, Psalm 18; Suro-Ammonite War, Psalm 60; adultery with Bathsheba, Psalm 51; flight from Absalom, Psalms 3, 63. Some include Psalm 30, "A Song at the dedication of the house."
32. Brevard S. Childs, "Reflections on the Modern Study of the Psalms," *Magnalia Dei: The Mighty Acts of God,* pp. 377-88, proposes that the titles represent a later stage of interpretation and "represent an important reflection on how the psalms as a collection of sacred literature were understood and how this secondary setting became normative for the canonical tradition" (pp. 383-84). In agreement with Westermann, he believes the *Sitz im Leben* of the Psalms is to be found in the common life of the people (p. 384).
33. See Kirkpatrick, pp. xix-xx; Kidner, 1:37-38.

used on the first day of the week, Psalm 48 (LXX, Ps. 47) on the second, Psalm 94 (LXX, Ps. 93) on the fourth, and Psalm 93 (LXX, Ps. 92) on the sixth. A considerable lapse of time between the completion of the Psalter and the fixed liturgical daily use of some of the psalms would be necessary.

The Masoretic text has one such reference in Psalm 92, entitled "A Psalm, A Song for the Sabbath Day." Other abbreviated liturgical notes occur, but they are nonspecific: "to bring to remembrance" (Pss. 38, 70), "a psalm of thanksgiving" (Ps. 100), "a song at the dedication of the house" (Ps. 30), "to teach" (Ps. 60), and "a song of ascents" (Pss. 120-34). The standard commentaries[34] will provide some elucidation, but we must be careful that we not demand too much specificity from these vague annotations.

*Musical notations.* Some titles incorporate cryptic words and phrases that are intended to suggest something about the musical setting or the way the psalm should be sung. The phrase "to the chief musician" is prefixed to fifty-five psalms (in Habakkuk's prayer it is a subscript, Hab. 3:19),[35] and seems to suggest that these were used in the Temple services. Kirkpatrick advocates a special collection known as *The Precentor's Collection*, much like the Psalms of David.[36]

Although not occurring anywhere in the titles, the enigmatic *selah* is interspersed in the Psalter seventy-one times, and three times in Habakkuk 3, but nowhere else in the Old Testament. It may denote an instrumental interlude, some appropriate response by the congregation, or, as the ancient Jewish tradition understood it, "forever."

Other less frequent notations occur and are discussed in the commentaries referred to above.

## HERMENEUTICAL CONSIDERATIONS ON PSALMS

### PRELIMINARY OBSERVATIONS

Two preliminary observations may furnish us with a simple orientation to the task of interpreting the Psalms.

*Historical background.* The Psalms embody historical elements of the Israelite people, the result being that the true meaning of a psalm cannot be fully grasped apart from those historical elements. In the myriad of instances where the historical data are allusive and the interpreter is left to conjecture, the situation as it appears in the psalm must still be assessed. For example, although Psalm 2 arises out of international turmoil, the specific historical occasion is not

---

34. E.g., Kirkpatrick, pp. xxvii-xxix; Kidner, 1:32-46.
35. Based upon its position in Habakkuk's prayer, Thirtle, p. 13, proposes that wherever this phrase occurs it really belongs to the preceding psalm.
36. Kirkpatrick, p. xxi.

clear. Yet the historical crisis, whatever it was, lends definite orientation to the psalm. God asserts His sovereignty over those circumstances:

> He who sits in the heavens laughs,
> The Lord scoffs at them.
> Then He will speak to them in His anger
> And terrify them in His fury.
>
> (Ps. 2:4-5)

Out of that historical situation comes the prophetic decree that the Lord will establish His messianic king who will ultimately bring the nation under control:

> I will surely tell of the decree of the Lord:
> He said to Me, "Thou art My Son,
> Today I have begotten Thee.
> Ask of Me, and I will surely give the nations as Thine inheritance,
> And the very ends of the earth as Thy possession."
>
> (Ps. 2:7-8)

The political disorder and foreign attempts to frustrate God's designs in His people Israel have occasioned a messianic prophecy. It is often true in the Psalms and prophetic literature that historical frustration elicits promises of the messianic era and the Messiah Himself (cf. Isa. 7:1-16).

Other historical interests are involved in studying the Psalms. In addition to historical events and eras, we discover information about the national institutions of Israel, both social and religious. These must not be ignored if we are to interpret correctly. The central place of the Temple in many of the psalms illustrates the dominance of this religious institution in the life of Israel. However, the fact that the Temple is frequently the center of interest in the Psalms should not lead us to conclude that the book is purely a liturgical collection. The private and the corporate, the personal and the liturgical, balance one another. Yet we must admit that if any one institution of Israel lends coherence to the book, it is the Temple.

Thus the Psalms bring us in touch with ancient Hebrew life and worship. At the risk of overstating the case, we might compare them to the popular literature of our time, which supplies many details about our lives and world that would not be found in the standard history books. Although the Psalms do not provide historical outline, they bring flesh and spirit to the skeleton of Israelite history and are therefore indispensable to understanding the history of Israel.

*Religious significance.* The Psalms partially supply the material for reconstructing Israel's history of faith. They are the spiritual logbook for Israel. The elements include the major historical events through which the Lord revealed Himself to Israel, the personal struggles of the individual soul to appropriate the privileges and execute the responsibilities of that revelation, and the eschatological eventualities of the faith. Thus the first questions one must ask when beginning to interpret a psalm are, "What is the historical situation?" and "What, if any, historical events are celebrated, and what was their religious significance?"

PROCEDURAL PRINCIPLES

In addition to these observations, we need to ask specific interpretive questions. Although an exhaustive list is not possible, the following will prove helpful.

*Personal/corporate perspective.* Decisive to interpreting the Psalms is a determination of who is speaking, an individual or the community of faith. The speaker in Psalm 27 is an individual, whereas the congregation speaks in Psalm 44. Both prayers reveal that the speakers have fallen into difficult circumstances at the hands of their enemies. We should not, of course, assume that the "collective I," referring to the whole community, will never be used, but that seems to be the exception rather than the rule.[37] The Psalms are predominantly personal.

*Historical circumstances.* Unfortunately the historical dilemmas that called forth the Psalms are too frequently past finding out. A few of them[38] have superscriptions that provide some data. In most of these instances the connections between historical event and psalm are readily discernible, even though some scholars have viewed them as superficial.

Most of the hard data, however, is internal and must be gleaned from the psalm itself. This makes the interpreter's task difficult and frustrating. Although the general circumstances can usually be detected (war, defeat, victory, personal humiliation, and so forth), conjecture often becomes the only tool at that point. Yet the lack of specificity does not close the door to the interpretation of the psalm.

*Emotional orientation.* Emotionally, the Psalter oscillates between praise and lament. The tone of each psalm should be determined, even though some will contain elements of both. The poem's emotional orientation supplies a hermeneutical component for the total task of interpretation.

*Liturgical usage.* Even though we cannot accept the form-critical position of Mowinckel that the Psalter is largely, if not completely, liturgical,[39] that is, meant for Temple worship and written for that purpose, it is self-evident that many of the psalms have found their place in the Temple liturgy, and that some were probably written expressly for it. Psalms 118, 129, and 136, among many others, are examples of liturgical adaptation. After the Psalter was completed, certain psalms became customarily used on certain festival days.

---

37. Gunkel, p. 15, contends that the community "I" is infrequent.
38. Psalms 3, 7, 18, 30, 34, 51, 52, 54, 56, 57, 59, 60, 63, 142.
39. Mowinckel, 1:22 and passim.

Ascertaining the liturgical function of a psalm will contribute to a fuller understanding of it. For example, Psalm 30 is a Davidic psalm that was used "at the dedication of the Temple" (Hebrew, "the house"), even though we do not know which Temple or "house." Yet the joys and sorrows as well as the defeats and victories of Israel converge at that point to highlight the Lord's power and favor toward His people. It was a day of confirmation for the psalmist as well as for Israel.

*New Testament usage.* A major source of help for the interpretation of the Psalms is the way they are used in the New Testament. We need to take seriously the interpretive dimensions found there. For example, if the New Testament views a psalm messianically, then we may accept without question the validity of that approach. Even in those instances when the author of the psalm could hardly have been aware that his words capsulated such future extensions, the Holy Spirit opened up the deeper dimensions of the words (*sensus plenior*) through the New Testament spokesmen. Obviously the use of the Psalms in the New Testament indicates that the interpreters elevated the spiritual above the physical, and the eschatological above the historical.

## The Theological Content of Psalms

### A Repository of Israel's Faith

Since the first century the church has made a practice of formulating corporate expressions of her faith and the proper conduct of her life. Nineteen centuries of church history yield scores of both major and minor confessions and creedal statements. These are sometimes representative of many tributaries that have flowed into the mainstream, and sometimes of a major tributary that has become the mainstream.

Some scholars have maintained that Israel's faith was basically creedal, that she too confessed her faith corporately, and subsequently that creedal statement was incarnated in historical event, thereby creating history around creed. The evidence for this hypothesis, however, is meager. If Israel's faith could be called creedal in the Christian sense of the word, it was only because the content of her creed was already tendered in the Sinai covenant. To this she was required to pledge her loyalty, and she made her confession of God in terms of it. Yet in the Old Testament we do not have the formal and corporate expression of theology such as the church has found it both necessary and beneficial to make.

The Psalms do not qualify as such a corporate expression, for they are preponderately individual. They might be compared to a corporate fund to which many contribute and from which both individual and corporate withdrawals can be made. Although the individual nature of the Psalter is a witness of the importance of the individual in the Old Testament, it is nevertheless possible to deduce certain ideas from the book that are as valid when applied to the corporate faith of Israel as to the private faith.

*Diversity*. We may then recognize the great diversity of the Psalms—first a diversity of authorship, as we have seen above. The literary courage of an editor(s) who would permit such diversity to stand within one collection is admirable. Kings, priests, prophets, and commoners alike are given the same opportunity to speak to God and Israel. In general no apparent attempt has been made to legitimize anonymous psalms by assigning them to a famous person (except in the LXX). The Psalms represent the voice of "everyman." They give us a cross section of spokesmen from Israelite society. This would immediately suggest the diversity of moods, life situations, and viewpoints. We are not speaking, however, of an ancient social pluralism, but rather of a representative approach to life and faith, with the controlling element being the covenant between God and Israel. With such a pervasive control, we can anticipate some unanimity of expression.

*Unity*. This brings us to the second observation, that of the unity of the Psalter. It is a unity enriched by the diversity that we have discussed, and held in bounds by the covenantal element of Israel's faith. Two component parts may be mentioned here. The Psalms reveal a unity of faith in Israel's covenant Lord, and a unity of faith in covenant responsibility. There is no room in the Psalter for nonfaith.

"The fool has said in his heart, 'There is no God' " (Pss. 14:1; 53:1). Yet there is ample accommodation for a faith that can question and inquire about God's enigmatic ways (Ps. 22:1-2). Further, the introduction to the book clearly sets forth the covenantal responsibility:

> How blessed is the man who does not walk in the counsel of the wicked,
> Nor stand in the path of sinners,
> Nor sit in the seat of scoffers!
> But his delight is in the law of the Lord,
> And in His law he meditates day and night.
>
> (Ps. 1:1-2)

Thus the Psalter affords an excellent illustration of how diversity and unity can be mutually enriching and reinforcing when clear boundaries are drawn and observed. The book is far more a repository of the spirit than of the letter of Israel's faith.

THE PRAISE OF GOD

Claus Westermann has remarked that in ancient Israel when one was confronted with something beautiful, the typical reaction was not contemplation nor passing of judgment, but praise, "joy expressing itself in speech."[40] The Hebrew language offers a rich praise vocabulary.[41] Yet the vocabulary of praise is only the framework, or structure, to which descriptive praise is attached. Although the Psalms are full of the special words for praise (e.g., "Praise the Lord"), they are also replete with descriptions of who the Lord is and what He has done. The vocabulary of praise and the descriptive content are complementary.

For example, David did not stop with the language of praise in Psalm 103, but complemented it with a description of what the Lord continued to do:

> Bless the Lord, O my soul;
> And all that is within me, *bless* His holy name.
> Bless the Lord, O my soul,
> And forget none of His benefits;
> Who pardons all your iniquities;
> Who heals all your diseases;
> Who redeems your life from the pit;
> Who crowns you with lovingkindness and compassion.
>                                     (Ps. 103:1-4)

In fact, the language of praise dominates the opening (vv. 1-2) and the closing (vv. 20-22), whereas the main body of the hymn describes the Lord in terms of what He has done and who He is. At some point, the person who praises must endow the vocabulary of praise with content. We can praise God without using the special language of praise, but we cannot long maintain the genuineness of that language without relating His being and works. In fact, the form is validated by the content. It is the relationship between liturgy and gospel. The gospel validates liturgy, not vice versa.

Yet the Psalms, as any casual reader observes, are not all praise. The emotional disposition of the Psalter alternates between praise and lament. But the nature of the Psalter is such that the power of gravitation is in the direction of praise. Indeed the worshiper finds coherence and meaning for his life in praise, not in lament. Yet to find oneself closer to the pole of lament is not a reason for disdain. As the penitential psalms[42] inform us (esp. Ps. 51), self-recognition that occurs in the presence of the omnipotent God propels us toward the One who

---

40. Claus Westermann, *Creation*, p. 64.
41. Verbs for praise are *bērēk* (from which we get the term for "blessed"; it may derive from the noun *berek*, "knee," and suggest the gesture of bending the knee or bowing); *hillēl* (from which we derive "hallelujah," which consists of the imperative and an abbreviated term for Yahweh, or Lord, *yāh*, the full expression meaning "praise [you, pl.] the Lord"); *hôdāh* (which is probably derived from the gesture of stretching out the hands [the basic verb may derive from the noun "hand"], meaning "to confess"); *shibah* which means "to laud," or "to praise"); and *zimmer* (meaning "to praise" with instruments or "to sing praise").
42. The penitential psalms as distinguished by the early church are Psalms 6, 32, 38, 51, 102, 130, 143.

can turn our reasons for lament into occasions of joy. Thus the lament frequently breaks forth into praise or intersperses praise with lament.

With that in mind, we may recognize Gunkel's distinction between community lament (e.g., Ps. 44) and individual lament (e.g., Ps. 22; the penitential psalms also fall within the broader category of individual lament). The former includes Psalms 12, 36, 44, 60 (an individual lament of David that has been utilized by the congregation), 74, 79, 80, 83, 90, and 137. The individual lament is more frequent, including Psalms 3-7, 13, 17, 22, 25-28, 35, 38-40, 42-43, 51, 54-57, 59, 61, 63-64, 69-71, 86, 88, 102, 109, 120, 130, and 140-43.[43] The lament is occasioned by national or personal adversity, such as war, famine, personal illness, and persecution.

As we have observed, however, some psalms do not fall neatly into the classification of praise or lament. Rather they enfold both. Examples are Psalms 6, 13, 22, 28, 30, 31, 41, 54, 55, 56, 61, 63, 64, 69, 71, 86, 94, 102, and 130.[44] We may validly speak of praise and lament, therefore, as two poles in the Psalter, the full value of one unrecognizable without proper consideration of the other.

The nature of praise has been astutely described by Westermann:

> Praise elevates another person
> it is other-regarding, directing attention to the One being praised
> it is conjunctive, calling upon others to join.[45]

C. S. Lewis has commented that praise completes the enjoyment.[46] It is a reminder of our own self-insufficiency, that we do not live in isolation, that the two complementary terms of human existence are the individual and his neighbor, and that together they find their fulfillment in God.

If the knowledge of God is not always the occasion, it is always the end of praise. In Psalm 104 the created world evokes praise from the worshiper; however, it is not praise of the creation but of the Creator. The phenomenal world constitutes the cause. Yet in Psalm 8:1 the poet begins with the knowledge of God:

> O Lord, our Lord,
> How majestic is Thy name in all the earth!

And, interestingly, he moves from the Creator to the creation:

43. This is Christoph Barth's list, *Introduction to the Psalms*, p. 15.
44. Ibid., p. 17.
45. Westermann, *The Praise of God in the Psalms*, pp. 27-28.
46. C. S. Lewis, *Reflections on the Psalms*, p. 95.

> When I consider Thy heavens, the work of Thy fingers,
> The moon and the stars, which Thou hast ordained;
> What is man, that Thou dost take thought of him?
> And the son of man, that Thou dost care for him?
>
> (Ps. 8:3-4)

Not only is creation the occasion for praise, but God's mighty saving acts in history frequently evoke articulate joy in the Psalms (e.g., 78). In many of the hymns of the Psalter, moreover, the law calls forth the praise of the psalmists (e.g., Ps. 119).

The praise of the Psalms, observably, is not a mysticism that merely contemplates God and ignores man and the world. Rather it seeks to see the Creator and the creation in their proper relationship. The Westminster confessors observed the need for that perspective when they asked, "What is the chief end of man?" and answered, "Man's chief end is to glorify God, and to enjoy him forever."[47] The glorifying and enjoying are intertwined. The psalmists generally recognized this truth; human fulfillment is found only in relationship to God:

> Why are you in despair, O my soul?
> And why have you become disturbed within me?
> Hope in God, for I shall yet praise Him,
> The help of my countenance, and my God.[48]
>
> (Ps. 42:11)

Yet if praise may be described as a process to God, to authentic fulfillment and self-identity, it is also the end of the process. David found the prospect of dwelling continually in the Lord's house most attractive (Ps. 23:6), and he advocated universal and eternal praise:

> My mouth will speak the praise of the Lord;
> And all flesh will bless His holy name forever and ever.
>
> (Ps. 145:21)

### THE PORTRAIT OF GOD

We have already observed that the Psalms incorporate the diverse cultural and religious aspects of Israel's life. The portrait of God is just as diverse, at one time transcendent and at another immanent. The boldness of description sometimes could give the impression of a low view of God or an inadequate human comprehension (e.g., Ps. 78:65-66). Yet the anthropomorphic tendencies in the

---

47. *The Westminster Shorter Catechism*, Question 1, Answer 1.
48. Observe the repetition of this refrain (42:5-6a, 11; 43:5).

Psalms counterbalance the transcendence and keep us reminded that God is close to man.

The features of the God-portrait present us with a Deity who ultimately cannot be comprehended by man, except to the extent that He unveils Himself. This is one of modern man's problems in relating to God—that He eludes man's scientific analysis. The Psalms present such a God. Yet just when He appears in all His ethereal glory, making man look like dust, that glory and transcendence are translated into terms of immanence. The effect upon man is to improve his self-image—that such a creature as he should be created and attended by so great a God and be delegated the dominion of the world (Ps. 8:3-8). The Psalms, therefore, have a therapeutic value. Those who read them seriously and appropriate their content prayerfully cannot long have a low view of themselves or a low view of God. One's view of God is determinative of one's self-image.

We may profit then by keeping in mind the two attributes of transcendence and immanence and build our portrait around them. As transcendent God, He is Creator of the world. That in itself puts Him out of man's reach. The Psalms do not espouse pantheism, which identifies the Creator with the creation. God is always distinct from the world, even when He moves in the intimate functions of everyday life. As Creator He manipulates His creation, mechanizes its parts as His own will:

> He makes the clouds His chariot;
> He walks upon the wings of the wind;
> He makes the winds His messengers,
> Flaming fire His ministers.
>
> (Ps. 104:3*b*-4)

Further, the ongoing process of the created world (which we call history) cannot function without Him. He controls men and gods (97:6-9). Even when the enigma of history baffles its observers, God resolves it in His own Person (Ps. 78). That Person, of course, in some way remains a wonderful enigma Himself.

Distinct from other national gods, Israel's God created the universe, rules it, and reveals Himself in it. He is indiscriminate in His general revelation:

> The heavens declare His righteousness,
> And all the peoples have seen His glory.
>
> (97:6)

> The heavens are telling of the glory of God; . . .
> There is no speech, nor are there words;
> Their voice is not heard.

Their line has gone out through all the earth,
And their utterances to the end of the world.
(19:1*a*, 3-4)

Yet He is discriminate in His special revelation:

For He established a testimony in Jacob,
And appointed a law in Israel,
Which He commanded our fathers,
That they should teach them to their children.
(78:5)

Such differentiation, however, had a beneficent purpose, that the nations, too, might come to know Israel's God:

God reigns over the nations,
God sits on His holy throne.
The princes of the people have assembled them-
selves as the people of the God of Abraham; . . .
He is highly exalted.

(47:8-9)

He, therefore, is universal Lord, and seeks to be universal Savior. Israel is always His tangible sign of that intention.

Though the majestic and transcendent Lord is written in large letters in the Psalter, the immanent and condescending God is no less prominent. The latter portrait is sketched out in two obvious ways: the Lord's activity in and for the community of Israel, and His personal intervention and aid in the lives of individuals. Several psalms juxtapose His transcendent and immanent attributes by depicting the Creator and Sustainer of the universe condescending to work in Israel (e.g., Pss. 99:1-5 and 6:7; 136:1-9 and 10-25). It becomes evident that the Lord is the moving force in the history of Israel.

In a second and no less important way, the Psalms translate His immanence into comprehensible terms by relating God's interpersonal designs and activities as He helps individuals who appeal to Him. David found Him to be even a substitute for father and mother (27:10). As already noted, the Psalms are predominantly personal, and the imagery of the Psalter portrays God as personally involved in the world. He is depicted in terms of daily life, a shepherd caring for his sheep (23:1; 80:1), water for the thirsty (42:1-2; 63:1-2), a bird that protects her young under her wings (91:1, 4), the judge who dispenses justice (50:4,6), the warrior's shield of battle (18:2), a fortress when enemies invade (27:1), and the king of Israel and the earth (98:6). He appears in a myriad of circumstances, dispelling their complexity and dismantling their apprehension. The God of the Psalms is always there, even when He seems far away.

THE DESCRIPTION OF MAN

If the Psalms graphically describe God, they are just as descriptive of man. On occasion the question is formulated succinctly and candidly:

> What is man, that Thou dost take thought of him?
> And the son of man, that Thou dost care for him?
>
> (8:4)

> O Lord, what is man, that Thou dost take knowledge of him?
> Or the son of man, that Thou dost think of him?
>
> (144:3)

The first question is posed in the light of God's marvelous creation, the second in view of the brevity of man's life. The ephemeral, transitory nature of human existence is placed in sharp contrast to divine constancy, which is likened to the "rock" (144:1). To deny the valid existence of God is tantamount to denying man's own essence. You cannot deny God and affirm man, because God endows him with reality and purpose. Man does not validate God. The creation of man at the same time conveys God's esteem for him. The rabbinic statement is biblically grounded—"for my sake was the world created":

> The heavens are the heavens of the Lord;
> But the earth He has given to the sons of men.
>
> (115:16)

Thus man is not an accident in the world but the central feature of God's universal design.

Moreover, the Psalms view man as corrupted by sin. The portrait of man in the Psalms is a realistic one. Though there is no extensive effort to explain the origin of his evil, that man is sinful is a foregone conclusion, a basic presupposition of the Psalms. The realism of the Old Testament spirit would not allow a glossing over of his sin. Rather the Psalms meet him where he is and extend hope to him that he may find redemption in God, even though his sin has victimized him.

The only remedy for the human condition is reorientation toward God. Divine forgiveness is readily available to those who turn to their Creator and Redeemer. The psalmists reach out pleading hands toward God, who is their deepest desire, and in whom alone they find completion:

> Whom have I in heaven but Thee?
> And besides Thee, I desire nothing on earth.
>
> (73:25)

CREATION AND REDEMPTION

We have already observed the polarity of God and man that is typical of the book of Psalms. That polarity, however, is resolved by God's own saving deeds, or, to put it another way, by intersection of the two doctrines of creation and redemption. What a marvel that the Creator of the world should have intertwined His creative and redemptive designs like warp and woof, as the New Testament spokesmen transparently affirm.[49] Creation is more than the presupposition of redemption. It is God's commitment to redemption. Even though we may not have this position so lucidly set forth in the Psalms, the two doctrines are interdependent.

Although Israel's ancient neighbors had their creation stories too, it has been observed that in no instance was creation a central doctrine in the religion in which it was found.[50] This observation sets the Hebrew faith in a category by itself. The doctrine of creation is basic in the Psalms, and even where it is not explicitly stated, it is presupposed.

Although the literal order of the two concepts may not be creation-redemption, that is the theological order. Even when the redeeming acts of God constitute the main theme, as in Psalm 74 (vv. 12-15), and the creation theme follows (vv. 16-17), the basis for the psalmist's faith in God's past saving acts (vv. 12-15) and His plea for the future acts of redemption (vv. 18-23) is precisely His creative power and work. The inability of the gods of the nations to do anything in the world (if they existed at all) is explained by the fact that they did not create it:

> For great is the Lord, and greatly to be praised;
> He is to be feared above all gods.
> For all the gods of the peoples are idols,
> But the Lord made the heavens.
>
> (96:4-5)

As Genesis 1-2 reveals, the doctrine of creation is basic to the Old Testament generally. But even if we looked only at the Psalms, we would discover the same centrality because the doctrine of creation is the validating doctrine, the legitimizing idea. It forever secures God's place in theology and fixes Him at the center of all things.

49. John 1:1-18; Romans 11:36; 1 Corinthians 8:6; 2 Corinthians 4:6; Hebrews 1:1-3; 1 Peter 1:19-20; Revelation 13:8. Observe this motif also in Isaiah 40:12-31; 42:5-9; 43:1-7; 44:1-8, 21-27; 45:12-17.
50. C. S. Lewis, p. 78.

## BASIC TYPES OF PSALMS

As we have already noted, the classifications of the psalms may follow a functional or content method. Since either method falls short of being adequate, we find it necessary to employ both in an effort of systematization. The following categories will both indicate that and serve the student as an ingress to a study of the psalms by types. The list is by no means exhaustive.

### HYMNS

The hymn is a diversified classification and belongs to the "functional" method.[51] Gunkel pioneered the study of this type of psalm. His basic criteria were that it was a song of praise and that it was sung on holy days in the Temple,[52] either by the Temple choir or by the congregation. We will briefly discuss two categories within this type, hymns of praise and hymns of Zion. Weiser lists the following psalms among the hymns: 8, 19, 29, 33, 65, 67, 100, 103, 104, 105, 111, 113, 114, 135, 136, 145, 146, 147, 148, 149, 150; also Psalms 46, 48, 76, 84, 87, 122 (hymns of Zion) and Psalms 47, 93, 96, 97, 98, 99 (so-called enthronement psalms)[53] belong among the hymns.[54]

Frequently the hymns of praise open with a call to praise the Lord, followed by the praise itself, which takes varied forms of expression (vocabulary of praise like "hallelujah," and descriptions of what the Lord has done). Sometimes the psalm concludes with a final call to praise (e.g., Pss. 145-50). In general the basis for praise was the saving deeds of the Lord in Israel, but creation also was frequently the psalmist's reason for praise.[55]

The hymns of Zion constitute another subgroup. Lists vary from commentator to commentator, but we may include Psalms 46, 48, 76, 84, 87, and 122, although some commentators would be more restrictive. The religious context of these hymns is, in general, the three pilgrimage festivals when all Hebrew males were required to appear in Jerusalem for worship: the feasts of Unleavened Bread, Weeks, and Tabernacles (Deut. 16:16). The city of Jerusalem and the Temple with all the paraphernalia and joy that attended those festivals are celebrated in these psalms. One group of psalms (Pss. 120-34, called "Songs of Ascents"), only one of which is generally designated as a Zion hymn (Ps. 122), may have been sung by the pilgrims as they made their way in companies to Jerusalem for those occasions.

---

51. See "Classification" of the psalms, pp. 118-21.
52. Gunkel, p. 10.
53. See "'Enthronement' Psalms," p. 142.
54. Artur Weiser, *The Psalms, A Commentary*, p. 53.
55. See previous section, "The Praise of God," pp. 127-30, and Westermann's helpful book, *The Praise of God in the Psalms*.

PENITENTIAL PSALMS

Although the ancient Christian church designated seven psalms as "penitential" (Pss. 6, 32, 38, 51, 102, 130, 143), only three of them contain the element of penitence. Psalms 51 and 130 are the clearest examples, both being genuine prayers of penitence, as also is Psalm 38, yet the psalmist there views his sin as the cause of the illness from which he suffers and over which he laments. Although Psalm 143 is not penitential in the strict sense of the word, it does take cognizance of the larger context of the sinfulness of the human race (143:2). Two of these psalms (32, 102) are laments about some illness that the worshiper has endured, whereas Psalms 6 and 143 lament the ill treatment of the psalmist at the hands of his enemies. Yet the tone of all seven psalms is one of submission to God and appeal for His favor.

WISDOM PSALMS

In addition to the "higher" wisdom of the Old Testament, of which Job is the example par excellence, much "lower" wisdom is contained in the Old Testament (e.g., Proverbs), with a fair amount in the Psalter. Those psalms that, like Proverbs, seek to describe and prescribe the way to achieve the good life are of the "lower" wisdom type. Others may struggle with the problems of why the wicked prosper; Psalms 37, 49, and 73 treat this question. Of interest are the answers given, which remind us of the explanations offered by the friends of Job. We may recall that their solutions were not invalid per se, but they were given as the full explanation of the problem. That was the invalidating quality.

It is doubtful that these psalms are intended to give an easy and comprehensive explanation for the prosperity of the wicked. In Psalm 37 the solution is that their prosperity is transitory, whereas righteousness is enduring. The solution of Psalm 73 is similar, for there the wicked are said to pass away suddenly like a dream. The explanation of Psalm 49 seems to stretch forth toward the doctrine of the life to come. The psalm declares that death will come to the wicked and righteous alike, but even then the righteous will come off better.

> But God will redeem my soul from the power of Sheol;
> For He will receive me.
>
> (Ps. 49:15)

This is reminiscent of the degree to which Job's faith soared when he affirmed that his eyes would behold the Redeemer after his body has decayed (Job 19:25-27).

Psalms 1, 112, 127, and 128 complete the wisdom psalms, and these are largely composed of maxims, proverbs, and the wise counsel for which wisdom teachers were known.

## MESSIANIC PSALMS

As we have observed, the idea of redemption is a dominant one in the Psalter. Although redemption for ancient Israel was a present reality, it was also both immediately and distantly future. In the Old Testament the idea of future redemption par excellence took the form of the personal Messiah. That is, redemption would ultimately be accomplished by a superhuman Person. This concept is prominent in Israel's literary repository of faith, the Psalms. Due to the influence of the form-critical school, however, the separate distinction of "messianic" psalms has been rather generally neglected[56] and the emphasis placed upon the "royal" psalms.

Although we do not want to slight history and its significance, we must contend that on some occasions the historical context was merely the skeleton for a composition that was primarily future. We may suggest, for example, that Psalm 2 was occasioned by historical events, but Psalm 110 had the future Messiah as its center of gravity. Yet the implication of the psalm for David's time was that, however uncertain the times, the Lord would establish His kingdom through the future Messiah. That reassurance might not have stabilized the Davidic times, but it certainly would have stabilized the heart. Therefore, we must view the messianic psalms as a legitimate classification by the content method.

Yet, because history and not eschatology is most often the center of gravity, we may agree that the "royal" psalms form a valid subgroup. And where they do not speak directly of the Messiah, we can affirm Ringgren's statement that "The royal psalms prepare the way for the Christian belief in the Messiah, and thus form an important and essential part of the history of revelation."[57]

Our study may be facilitated by dividing the messianic psalms into two subdivisions, those that refer to the king and his rule (2, 18, 20, 21, 45, 61, 72, 89, 110, 132, 144), and those that treat man and his life generally (8, 16, 22, 35, 40, 41, 55, 69, 102, 109). It is not too much to say that the New Testament view of the Person of Christ identified Him with the aspirations and frustrations of both royalty and commoner.

*Messiah and His rule.* Using the New Testament as our guideline, we observe that from the first group only Psalms 2, 18, 45, and 110 are quoted, although many allusions may be cited, whereas quotations from all these of the second group (except Ps. 55) are applied to Christ by the New Testament spokesmen. When such is the case, we have the messianic character already determined for us by our Lord and the first-century disciples. Other criteria must be formulated for those not applied messianically in the New Testament.

---

56. Christoph Barth, p. 26, for example, advises giving up the distinction between messianic and non-messianic psalms, although he does not advocate an absence of the messianic idea in the Psalms.
57. Helmer Ringgren, *Faith of the Psalmists,* p. 114.

The most obvious figure for the Messiah in this first group of psalms is "king." Psalm 2:6 speaks of the king's divinely appointed position in Zion, reassuring Him that He is God's Son (v. 7). This sonship of the king is cited in Hebrews (1:5) to reinforce the argument of Christ's superiority over angels. Although Psalm 18 is likely a historical statement by David, and although it could have been properly spoken by David in a limited frame of reference, the absolute reference is to the Messiah (esp. vv. 20-30).[58] Paul quoted verse 49 to show that the promises to the patriarchs were also meant for the Gentiles (Rom. 15:9). A third psalm about the king, also quoted by the author of Hebrews (1:8-9), is Psalm 45, which may celebrate the king's wedding. The divine honors enumerated in verses 6-7 are taken at full value by the author of the epistle, applying them, as he did Psalm 2, to his argument for the Son's superiority over angels. Psalm 110, said Jesus, records David's homage to the Messiah (Mark 12:36-37). This psalm was also quoted by Peter on the day of Pentecost (Acts 2:33-35) and by the author of Hebrews to establish the priestly function of Christ as eternal priest after the order of Melchizedek (Heb. 5:6, 10; 7:1-28).

What then are the criteria for designating the other psalms "messianic" when the New Testament does not identify them as such? We suggest three:

First, when the language outruns the abilities of the subject, presenting achievements that are not humanly attainable, we may detect messianic overtones. To illustrate, the accomplishments requested in prayer for the king in Psalm 72 are so universally sweeping as to disallow the absolute fulfillment by an Israelite king.

Second, when messianic terms occur, such as "anointed" and "son of man," we may suspect a messianic inclination. Although "son of man" occurring in Psalm 144:3 means "mankind," the description that follows leads some commentators to look more closely for messianic associations.

Third, when the New Testament circumstances fit those described in the psalm, permitting prophetic inferences from it, messianic associations may be suspected. For example, Psalm 55:12-13, 20 applies very well to Jesus' betrayal and passion. In fact, a similar verse (41:9) was applied by Jesus Himself to Judas (John 13:18). Although these criteria may be helpful, they are not foolproof. Further, the application of more than one of them to a psalm in question enhances the messianic credibility. We may find any one or a combination of these criteria helpful when we study Psalms 20, 21, 61, 72,[59] 89, 132, and 144 in the first subgroup mentioned above.

*Man and his life.* The second division of the messianic psalms, those treating man and his life in general (8, 16, 22, 35, 40, 41, 55, 69, 102, 109), is composed of psalms quoted in the New Testament (except Ps. 55). Although some

58. Kidner, 1:93.
59. The Targum adds "Messiah" to "the king" in 72:1.

of them may have been spoken by the king, they do not deal with his royal position but rather with the general lot of man or with the particular dilemma of the worshiper. Psalms 35, 69, and 109 (Ps. 55 is similar) are designated "imprecatory psalms" and will be treated later.

Generally the terms of these psalms are viewed as perfectly fulfilled only in Christ. The human aspirations and frustrations have their ultimate extensions and resolutions in Him. David's cry of abandonment in Psalm 22:1 was used in its Aramaic form by our Lord on the cross (Matt. 27:46), and the author of Hebrews applied 22:22 to Christ (Heb. 2:12). Psalm 16 centers upon the importance of finding one's true identity in God. Peter quoted verses 8-11 in his Pentecost sermon to say that David's personal affirmation was fulfilled absolutely in Christ's resurrection (Acts 2:24-32). Our Lord Himself used Psalm 41:9 in reference to Judas' betrayal of Him (John 13:18), although the real situation was that the psalmist had experienced some illness because of his sin (v. 4). There was a definite sense in which the human dilemma described in these psalms could not exhaust their meaning, and was, in fact, only a relative fulfillment. The absolute satisfaction of the terms of the psalm was effected only in and by Jesus Christ.

IMPRECATORY PSALMS

The prize for the most perplexing of the psalms has long been held by the imprecatory psalms, or the "cursings." At least three fall clearly into this classification—Psalms 35, 69, 109. In addition, many scattered verses qualify.

At the outset we should recognize that all questions relating to Scripture cannot be solved like a mathematical problem. We can profit from the attitude the apostle Peter expressed toward the epistles of Paul, "There are some things in them hard to understand" (2 Pet. 3:16, RSV). In light of the difficulty, therefore, we want to avoid either of the two extreme approaches to the imprecatory psalms—ignoring them because they throw our theology out of focus, or declaring the spirit of them good because they are contained in the Bible. Although both of these approaches have their own strengths, neither is completely satisfactory.

A third alternative is to face them squarely, struggle with the spirit of them, and ask how they are God's Word.

Mowinckel believed these psalms represented a religious climate of black magic, the psalms being an "effective curse" against an enemy.[60] However, the Old Testament is relatively free of this kind of sympathetic magic; if any bits appear, the practice is not endorsed. Moreover, the allegation is leveled against the psalmist that he was filled with a vindictive spirit and overwhelmed by rage.

---

60. Mowinckel, 2:49.

But if we look very closely at these three psalms, we discover something quite important—what is identified as personal vindictiveness is placed in a larger context. The psalmist consigned the matter to God. There was absolutely no effort on his part to take personal revenge. He seemed to have been aware of the Mosaic principle, "Vengeance is Mine" (Deut. 32:35). And we may observe that in all three psalms he was innocent; his adversaries had perpetrated their evil designs "without cause."

The larger context is the kingdom of God, that is, God's people and His cause. In Psalms 69 and 109 the psalmist clearly states that it was for God's sake (69:7; 109:3, 21) that he prayed. We sometimes forget that God's reputation is intricately tied up with ours. Thus the larger context of these psalms is God's own nature and kingdom.

Yet this still does not remove the fact that the psalmist violated the spirit that Jesus clearly taught:

> You have heard that it was said, "You shall love your neighbor, and hate your enemy." But I say to you, love your enemies, and pray for those who persecute you.
>
> (Matt. 5:43-44)

We may try to solve the problem by saying that the psalmist represents the old dispensation whose ethic was inferior to the new. And there may be some relative truth to that. But when we look at the upper limits of the Old Testament ethic (Ex. 23:4-5; Lev. 19:18) to love one's neighbor as oneself, we must conclude that in the final analysis the Old and New Testaments stand or fall together. Therefore, the old-and-new-dispensation explanation is not satisfactory by itself.

Another approach is to view these texts as purely messianic, strictly future. But this denies the historical situation, and if divine revelation is to make sense, we cannot ride roughshod over history. It is the receptacle of revelation. Yet it is interesting how the New Testament uses these psalms. Jesus explained the world's hatred for Him by citing Psalm 35:19/69:4:

> But they have done this in order that the word may be fulfilled that is written in their Law, "They hated me without a cause."
>
> (John 15:25)

When reflecting upon the cleansing of the Temple, the disciples remembered Psalm 69:9:

> His disciples remembered that it was written, "Zeal for Thy house will consume me."
>
> (John 2:17)

Further, the apostle Peter applied Psalm 69:25 and 109:8 to Judas:

> "Let his homestead be made desolate, and let no man dwell in it," and,
> "His office let another man take."
>
> (Acts 1:20)

Paul applied Psalm 69:9 to Christ and obviously heard Christ speaking in it:

> For even Christ did not please Himself: but as it is written, "The reproaches
> of those who reproached Thee fell upon me."
>
> (Rom. 15:3)

Again, Paul interpreted the judicial blindness of the Jewish nation as a fulfillment of the psalmist's imprecations (69:22-23):

> And David says,
> "Let their table become a snare and a trap,
> And a stumbling block and a retribution to them.
> Let their eyes be darkened to see not,
> And bend their backs forever."
>
> (Rom. 11:9-10)

We observe then that the New Testament writers discerned a prophetic spirit in these psalms, which, of course, was in no way a denial of their historical situation.

Yet there is another dimension that we should consider—do they teach us anything? C. S. Lewis has remarked that we may learn from them that the absence of indignation may be an alarming symptom.[61] We should be disturbed about sin and aroused for righteousness. A further lesson is that the most bitter feelings can be resolved in the presence of God. The psalmist did not take the matter into his own hands but laid it out before God. We should not jump to the conclusion, however, that God shares his feelings about the transgressor, although He certainly cannot endure sin. Moreover, these psalms help to renew our confidence in the fact that God is just:

> For He stands at the right hand of the needy,
> To save him from those who judge his soul.
>
> (Ps. 109:31)

61. Lewis, p. 30.

## "ENTHRONEMENT" PSALMS

The designation "enthronement" psalms is mainly associated with Sigmund Mowinckel and generally refers to Psalms 47, 93, 95-99, all of which speak of the Lord as King or use the language "The Lord [or God] reigns." Mowinckel formulated a theory that Israel celebrated a New Year festival at which the king was reenthroned to commemorate the annual reenthronement of the Lord.[62] His logic assumed that the Israelite festival (which he believed was Tabernacles)[63] was patterned after the Babylonian festival that annually celebrated the resurrection of Marduk (Bel) after his death and descent into the netherworld. Although Mowinckel has had an impressive following, the literary evidence for such a festival in Canaan cannot be found either in biblical or extrabiblical material. The declaration "The Lord reigns" does not mean "The Lord has become king." Nor did the Israelites invest their kings with deity. If such had been the case, the prophets would certainly have inveighed against it.

## HISTORICAL USE OF THE PSALMS

Probably no other book of the Bible has been so influential and widely used in both synagogue and church as has the book of Psalms. Our appreciation for the psalms and even our understanding of their power for life may be enhanced by a few appropriate observations on their use in the Jewish synogogue and in the Christian church.

### IN THE TEMPLE

Already at the time of the translation of the Hebrew Old Testament into Greek (about 250 B.C.), the translators acknowledged the use of certain psalms for each day of the week except the third and fifth days. This is in agreement with the prescribed daily psalms given in the Mishnah[64] (codified in late second century A.D.), tractate Tamid 7.4. This tractate concerns daily services in the Temple when the whole offering was made (Ex. 29:38-42; Num. 28:1-8). Certain psalms were prescribed to be sung by the Levites day by day as indicated on the following chart.They were sung after the offering of the sacrifice. Those psalms chosen because of certain appropriate words or phrases for a particular occasion are called "proper" psalms.

Other proper psalms were used for the special festivals. The *Hallel* (Pss. 113-18, so named because the first psalm and others in the group begin and/or end with "Hallelujah") was used at New Moon, Passover, Pentecost, Taberna-

62. Mowinckel, 1:106-92. For a brief presentation of Mowinckel's hypothesis, see A. R. Johnson, "The Psalms," in *The Old Testament and Modern Study,* ed. H. H. Rowley, pp. 162-209. For a criticism of his position, see K. A. Kitchen, *Ancient Orient and Old Testament,* pp. 102-6.
63. Mowinckel, 1:119.
64. Herbert Danby, trans. and ed., *The Mishnah.*

## TRADITIONAL ASSIGNMENT OF PSALMS FOR TEMPLE WORSHIP

| | | |
|---|---|---|
| First day | — | Psalm 24 (recounting God's creation of the world) |
| Second day | — | Psalm 48 |
| Third day | — | Psalm 82 |
| Fourth day | — | Psalm 94 |
| Fifth day | — | Psalm 81 |
| Sixth day | — | Psalm 93 (which seemed appropriate for the completion of creation) |
| Seventh day | — | Psalm 92 A Psalm: A Song for the Sabbath Day (which is so titled in the Hebrew Bible) |

cles, and Dedication. In addition, Psalm 7 was used at Purim, Psalm 12 for the eighth day of Tabernacles, Psalm 30 for the feast of Dedication, Psalm 47 for New Year, Psalms 98 and 104 for New Moon, and the penitential psalms for the Day of Atonement.[65]

### IN THE SYNAGOGUE

Abraham Millgram has remarked that the Psalms became "the spiritual girders of the synagogue worship."[66] It is generally believed that the worship of the synagogue was largely patterned after the Temple services. Thus the psalms for daily and festival use became part of the synagogue liturgy. Some scholars have attempted to show that the Psalter was read in the synagogue in a triennial cycle, like the Pentateuch, each of the five books of the Psalter begun simultaneously with the five books of the Torah. Although this lectionary custom in the synagogue was certainly true of the Prophets, if it was applied to the Psalter, it is strange (as Lamb has observed) that it has not continued in the modern prayer books alongside the Torah and Haphtarah readings (the latter being a selected but prescribed portion from the Prophets).[67] Whatever has been the history of the Psalter in the synagogue, it still continues to be used extensively in modern Jewish worship.

### IN THE CHURCH

The subject of the Psalms in the church is as broad and complex as that of their use in the synagogue.[68] And we should recognize the debt of the church to

65. John Alexander Lamb, *The Psalms in Christian Worship*, p. 13.
66. Abraham Millgram, *Jewish Worship*, p. 63.
67. See Lamb's discussion, pp. 14-16.
68. Lamb's discussion is very helpful and one to which I am indebted for my discussion.

the synagogue.[69] Although evidence for the practice of the first-century church is limited, we know by the frequent quotations from the Psalter in the New Testament that the early Christians valued it very highly. Only three times does the noun *psalmos* occur in a context of worship: 1 Corinthians 14:26; Ephesians 5:19; Colossians 3:16. And only in the first instance does Paul undoubtedly refer to public worship, whereas the second two could refer to either public or private worship. The fourth passage is James 5:13 where the verb "to sing a psalm" occurs, but the question is also appropriate here whether private or public worship is meant.

The evidence for the use of the Psalms in the second century is sparse, but toward the third Christian century more frequent mention occurs. Origen (A.D. 185-254) mentions both hymns and psalms, and it is likely that Psalm 34 was sung as a Communion hymn (v. 8, "O taste and see that the Lord is good"). Tertullian (A.D. 155-223) spoke of psalms in public worship and said they were taken over from the synagogue.

In the post-Nicene church (after A.D. 325) the popularity of the Psalter held strongly. Chrysostom cited Psalm 141 as having long been used as an evening psalm. With time, Psalm 63 became used as the morning psalm.

Since we cannot discuss the topic fully, the reader will need to refer to the special studies on this subject.

We might add that the Reformation brought about some changes, yet John Calvin had great respect for the psalms for liturgical use. The movement encouraged by him and others resulted in the publication of the *Genevan Psalter* in 1562. This contained the psalms transcribed into metrical form for singing. The influence of this movement can be traced to Scotland through John Knox under whose influence the *Genevan Psalter* was partly included in the *Book of Common Order* published in 1564. Thus began a long history of the use and publication of the metrical psalms in the Scottish church.

Although many Protestant churches have resisted the tradition of prescribing certain psalms for specific occasions, in actual practice the Psalter continues to be the most popular book in Protestant worship today. And the interest is not declining. The reasons are obviously those that have led the church through the centuries to cling to this ancient book of praises. With the Psalms, the worshiper can come before God without pretense, confessing his sin, expressing his deepest emotions. He finds in them the language to say those things that lie inarticulate in his heart, and the courage to affirm the unutterable. Hardly a human situation occurs to which the Psalms do not offer some direct word of comfort or exhortation. The church has drunk from the brook of psalmody through the centuries and has discovered that it originates at the eternal spring of living water.

69. See W. O. E. Oesterley, *The Jewish Background of the Christian Liturgy.*

## THE QUMRAN SCROLL OF PSALMS

For the past three decades, one of the major interests in biblical studies for scholar and student alike has been the contribution of the Qumran materials to our understanding of the Bible. Though their major significance remains textual and cultural, we may satisfy our curiosity in the area of Psalms studies by a few comments on the Psalms Scroll from Qumram Cave II (11QPs).[70] The vellum scroll, composed of four separable leaves, came to the attention of scholars in 1956. Including four fragments identified as belonging to it, the scroll contains parts or all of Psalms 93, 101-3, 105, 109, 118-19, 121-46, 148-51. The Tetragrammaton (Hebrew divine name) is always written in the ancient Palaeo-Hebrew script. Except for orthographic differences, the scroll largely confirms the Masoretic text. There are, of course, variant readings that are of considerable interest and continue to be taken into account in recent commentaries. Also of great interest is the presence of Psalm 151 in Hebrew, which in part parallels the same number psalm in the Septuagint. The Qumran version acknowledges David's musical abilities and relates how the prophet Samuel came and anointed David rather than one of his brothers as king.[71] There is wide disagreement on the dating of this psalm, and we can only speculate about its omission in the Hebrew Bible and its inclusion in the Qumran Scroll. However, J. A. Sanders rather convincingly argues that the Qumran psalm lies behind the Septuagint (Greek) psalm; the evidence is that the Qumran version fills in details that the Septuagint version omits.[72]

---

70. See J. A. Sanders, *The Psalms Scroll of Qumran Cave II, Discoveries in the Judaean Desert of Jordan*, vol. 4.
71. Ibid., pp. 54-60.
72. Ibid., pp. 59-60.

# 5

# THE BOOK OF PROVERBS

Many persons who have become overwhelmed by a theoretical approach to Christianity have been able to get a "handle" on the faith by reading the book of Proverbs. For this book represents the commonsense approach to life and faith. It touches the shared concerns of all who are given the gift of life and struggle with how to live it. For those who are recipients of the gift of faith, this book distills the theological substance of Old Testament religion into its practical essence.

## Introductory Matters About Proverbs

### PROVERBIAL FORMS

In its basic form, the proverb is an ancient saying that takes wisdom and endows it with youthful vigor. In a few, piquant phrases the proverb capsulizes a practical idea or truth in such a way as to lift the commonplace to a new level of mental consciousness. It reweaves the threadbare idea and shows the ordinary to be quite extraordinary.

Yet the proverb is not the kind of form that one can assimilate in large quantities at once. W. A. L. Elmslie has astutely called it "compressed experience,"[1] and in this kind of literature overindulgence has its peculiar consequences. One needs time for gaining insight into some proverbs. Only contemplation will unfold the full meaning of:

> He who pursues righteousness and loyalty
> Finds life, righteousness and honor.
> (Prov. 21:21)

---

1. W. A. L. Elmslie, *Studies in Life from Jewish Proverbs*, p. 16. I acknowledge my indebtedness to Elmslie's excellent chapter entitled "The Characteristics of Proverbs," pp. 13-27.

Although its face value is obvious enough, the meaning bears prolonged thought. Yet others are highly volatile and yield their content with a sudden burst, which is part of their appeal and power:

> Better is a dry morsel and quietness with it
> Than a house full of feasting with strife.
>
> (Prov. 17:1)

The face value is all that is intended. Still other proverbs convey their truth with a bit of humorous wit:

> Why is there a price in the hand of a fool to buy wisdom,
> When he has no sense?
>
> (Prov. 17:16)

Fundamental to the proverbial form is that it bears a time-tested truth. Fads have no place in proverbial literature, except as their shallow nature may need to be exposed. Time and experience have bestowed their blessing upon proverbial lore. They are the soil in which truth is germinated and sustained. But to that which does not possess the innate substance for life, they are stony ground.

Much more can be said on the nature of the proverb, or aphorism, that is the building block of the book of Proverbs. Some of that will become obvious as the discussion proceeds, but much will depend upon time and experience to appropriate the magnitude of this book and the necessity of viewing life and faith from its practical perspective.

THE BOOK TITLE

"The proverbs of Solomon the son of David, king of Israel" (1:1) was very likely the original title of the book. The Septuagint has the slightly different title "Proverbs of Solomon son of David, who ruled in Israel," whereas the Vulgate has simply "Liber Proverbiorum" (The Book of Proverbs). The abbreviated title "The Proverbs of Solomon" at 10:1 is a subtitle within the larger collection (chaps. 1-24), and another title at 25:1, "These also are proverbs of Solomon," begins the second Solomonic collection (chaps. 25-29). Many scholars assume that the title of the first collection (1:1) has been borrowed from one of the other titles as the opening title.[2] Actually the title of the first Solomonic collection may be 1:1-6, in which the author identifies himself and sets forth his purpose for the book. We shall consider this matter further on in our discussion.

---

2. See later section of this chapter, "Literary Structure and Growth," pp. 153-55.

NATURE, FUNCTION, AND PURPOSE

*Wisdom in Proverbs*. The basic nature of wisdom as viewed by the author of Proverbs is summed up in his statement "The fear of the Lord is the beginning of knowledge" (1:7; cf. 9:10). That is, the fundamental nature of wisdom was theological. Thus in Proverbs the underlying basis of life is one's relationship to God. Out of that relationship grow moral understanding and the ability to judge what is right (2:6-22), a proper attitude toward material possessions (3:9-10), industrious labor (6:6-11), the necessary equilibrium and sense of security for living in the world (3:21-26), and the right relationship toward one's neighbor (3:27-29), to mention only a few of the more practical benefits of that relationship.

Wisdom in this book capitalizes upon the horizontal dimension of life (one's relations with other human beings and the natural world) and offers instruction in affirmative and declarative tones[3] compared to the exhortative word of the Prophets. The person-to-person details of life are not dealt with in a theological vacuum, however, but are viewed within the context of the Mosaic covenant and law.[4] It deals with the question "How ought we then to live?"

The personification of wisdom in chapters 8-9 constitutes another dimension of wisdom in Proverbs. Although the descriptions in 1:20-22 and chapters 2-3 may be largely metaphorical, as in Job 28, in chapters 8-9 of Proverbs wisdom is personified as a woman who speaks, offers wealth and prosperity to her devotees (8:18, 21), witnesses of her existence before the creation of the world (8:22-23; see p. 171 for meaning of 8:22), assists the Lord in creation (8:30), and possesses a house and servants (9:1-6). Yet wisdom does not have the ontological distinction that it has in the Wisdom of Solomon or that the Logos (Word) has in John's gospel. The purpose of personification in this instance is to help us understand God by abstracting one of His attributes and endowing it with personality and consciousness. The author wants to teach that wisdom is a divine attribute that is eternally related to Him, understood only in relation to Him, and is an extension of His dynamic Being to mankind. The method of personification is the means by which the practical perspective of wisdom is connected to God. It is the closest thing wisdom has to the prophetic formula "Thus says the Lord." By means of personified wisdom, the knowledge of God's nature is delivered to and integrated with the everyday life of men and women.

Based perhaps upon this method of personifying abstract ideas or divine attributes, later noncanonical authors emulated the method and developed it more fully. In Ecclesiasticus, wisdom is a direct emanation from God (24:3-5), was created before the world (1:4; 24:9), and has an eternal nature (1:1; 24:9). The most advanced level of this kind of thought is represented in the noncanonical

---

3. R. B. Y. Scott, *Proverbs, Ecclesiastes*, p. 24.
4. See later discussion in this chapter, "Function of Proverbs," regarding the legal useage of proverbs, p. 151.

Wisdom of Solomon, which R. H. Charles dates after 50 B.C.[5] There wisdom is hypostatized (cf. Wisd. of Sol. 1:6-7; 6:12-24; and chaps. 7-8), that is, endowed with a distinct essence and consciousness, much as the Logos is portrayed in the prologue to John's gospel. Although scholars generally have viewed chapters 1-9 of Proverbs as a late composition, possibly even postexilic,[6] basing their opinion in part upon the personification in chapters 8-9, the idea of unilinear development of concepts and institutions in the ancient Near East is dubious. In both Mesopotamia and Egypt, the personification of truth, justice, intelligence, understanding, and other abstract ideas is known from the third and second millennia B.C.[7]

The word used to designate the contents of the book is *mashal*, usually translated "proverb." Although the root is disputed among scholars, the general opinion is that it derives from the verb *mashal*, "to represent, be like."[8] Thus the meaning of the noun would be "likeness," and a *mashal*, or proverb, would be a statement that seeks to reveal the true nature of one thing by comparing it to something else.[9] In the Old Testament generally the term is used variously. It may signify a simple folk saying (1 Sam. 10:12; 24:13), an allegory (Ezek. 17:2), an enigmatic saying (Ezek. 20:49), a taunt (Isa. 14:4; Hab. 2:6), a lament (Mic. 2:4), a prophetic discourse (Num. 23:7; 24:15), a didactic discourse (Ps. 49:4), or a plea (Job 29:1). In the book of Proverbs it signifies either aphorisms (as in 10:1–22:16) or discourses (as in chaps. 1-9; and 23:29-35; 27:23-27).[10]

*Function of Proverbs.* The function of the type of proverbs preserved in this book was basically that of shaping men and women into socially and religiously useful members of society. Whereas prophecy worked from the nation downward to the individual, wisdom worked from the individual upward to the nation. John Mark Thompson appropriately argues that the basic function of Hebrew proverbs is philosophical (I would stress the religious function so as not to give the erroneous impression that proverbs basically fill a secular role), with three subfunctions: entertainment, legal usage, and instruction.[11]

Although the book of Proverbs is not primarily entertainment in any sense of the word, there is honest humor involved in Proverbs from time to time. Elmslie words it well: "Humor, divine gift, is no merely ornamental or superfluous quality we can easily afford to do without, but is the active antagonist of many deadly sins."[12] The absence of discretion in a woman annuls her beauty, according to the witty expression in 11:22:

---

5. R. H. Charles, *The Apocrypha and Pseudepigrapha of the Old Testament in English*, 1:519.
6. E.g., Otto Eissfeldt, *The Old Testament: An Introduction*, p. 473.
7. K. A. Kitchen, *Ancient Orient and Old Testament*, pp. 126-27.
8. Francis Brown, S. R. Driver, and Charles A. Briggs, *A Hebrew and English Lexicon of the Old Testament*, p. 605a.
9. Scott, p. 13.
10. Crawford H. Toy, *A Critical and Exegetical Commentary on the Book of Proverbs*, p. 4.
11. John Mark Thompson, *The Form and Function of Proverbs in Ancient Israel*, pp. 68-82.
12. W. A. L. Elmslie, p. 237.

> As a ring of gold in a swine's snout,
> So is a beautiful woman who lacks discretion.

The seriousness of folly evokes a chuckle in 17:12:

> Let a man meet a bear robbed of her cubs,
> Rather than a fool in his folly.

The animal world also provides a humorous illustration for the danger of meddling in other people's arguments:

> Like one who takes a dog by the ears
> Is he who passes by and meddles with strife not belonging to him.
> (26:17)

The contentious woman somewhat amusingly reminded Solomon (and likely he had had many lessons!) of a constant dripping of water:

> A foolish son is destruction to his father,
> And the contentions of a wife are a constant dripping.
> (19:13)

Comically, he would even prefer to live in a corner on the rooftop or in a desert than to live with a contentious woman (he does not mention his own faults):

> It is better to live in a corner of a roof,
> Than in a house shared with a contentious woman.
> (21:9)

> It is better to live in a desert land,
> Than with a contentious and vexing woman.
> (21:19)

A bit of humor is involved when the slothful man is described as too lazy to feed himself:

> The sluggard buries his hand in the dish,
> And will not even bring it back to his mouth.
> (19:24)

In another funny analogy, trusting a faithless person is like having a bad toothache or a sprained ankle:

Like a bad tooth and an unsteady.foot
Is confidence in a faithless man in time of trouble.
(25:19)

These examples are enough to illustrate the entertainment element, but obviously it is entertainment that teaches.

The second subfunction is the mutual function of law and proverbs. Thompson is inclined to think that some laws were the product of proverbs, especially the apodictic laws of ancient Israel.[13] His examples, however, could just as easily be used to illustrate the other direction of movement, from law to proverbs. And in view of proverbs as a teaching instrument, it would seem only logical that legal principles and injunctions were couched in proverbial form to make them more verbally memorable. The taking of bribes and the use of false weights are subjects of legal proverbs:

Diverse weights and diverse measures,
are both alike an abomination to the Lord.
(20:10, RSV; cf. Deut. 25:13-16)

Deuteronomy 19:14 forbids one to remove his neighbor's landmark. A parallel is found in Proverbs 22:28:

Do not move the ancient boundary
Which your fathers have set.

Rephrasing laws in proverbial form was like the reweaving of an old fabric.

The third subfunction is that of ethical instruction. As in the Egyptian and Mesopotamian instructions, the sages addressed their students as "my son." The topics of the book of Proverbs, while appropriate to the broad spectrum of age, are clearly directed to the young whose surging emotions and untried idealism needed to be tempered by experience. Their lives could still be shaped in the ways of wisdom. The products of both theory and experience are offered in short, pithy sayings that might be used as a rule of thumb for personal conduct. R. B. Y. Scott has identified seven proverbial patterns according to which these principles for living are expressed:

1. Identity (equivalence):
   A man who flatters his neighbor
   Is spreading a net for his steps (29:5).

---

13. Thompson, p. 112.

2. Nonidentity (contrast):
A sated man loathes honey,
But to a famished man any bitter thing is sweet (27:7).

3. Similarity:
Like cold water to a weary soul,
So is good news from a distant land (25:25).

4. Contrariety (indicative of absurdity):
Why is there a price in the hand of a fool to buy wisdom,
When he has no sense? (17:16).

5. Classification (persons, actions, or situations):
The naive believes everything,
But the prudent man considers his steps (14:15).

6. Valuation (priority of one thing):
A good name is to be more desired than great riches,
Favor is better than silver and gold (22:1).

7. Consequences:
The sluggard does not plow after the autumn,
So he begs during the harvest and has nothing (20:4).[14]

In addition to the proverb, the book contains the longer, more reflective passages (e.g., 1:8-19; 5:1-23; 23:29-35; 27:23-27). Based upon the reflective type of wisdom, we know that it involved more than just memorization of terse, practical sayings. The reflective and the pragmatic belonged together. Even in the highly reflective book of Job we have brief proverbs imbedded in the discourses (e.g., Job 4:8; 12:11; 21:19).

*Purpose of Proverbs.* The didactic nature of this book is a function of its purpose. In fact, the introduction to the book (1:2-6) sets forth the purpose: to initiate the reader into wisdom and instruction. The book then purports to be a primer of right conduct and essential attitudes toward life, aimed at producing lives in conformity to the divine will. The immediate object was to train and educate for the preservation of the family unit, and social stability of the society as a whole. Therefore, prominent in wisdom was the recognition that fulfillment of God's will is actualized in the personal and social conduct and institutions of ·His people.

Proverbs is an instructional manual, much like the ancient instructions of Egypt and Mesopotamia. The collecting activity associated with Hezekiah's reign (25:1), which produced chapters 25-29, may have been connected with the

14. Scott, pp. 5-8.

reform of Hezekiah in the early part of his reign (2 Kings 18:1-6; 2 Chron. 29-31). The didactic purpose then assumed greater proportions as a religiously and socially decadent society began its arduous road back to spiritual health and social stability.

LITERARY STRUCTURE AND GROWTH

The consensus of current scholarship is that the literary structure of the book is indicated by the titles heading up each section. Although these are rather obvious in the Hebrew text, they are sometimes obscured in the English translations. Three times the title "the proverbs of Solomon" appears, the first time (1:1) applied to the entire book, while the other two occurrences (10:1; 25:1) are applied to sections within the book. At the end of the section begun at 10:1, two shorter collections were inserted, simply titled "words of the wise" (22:17–24:22) and "Also these are for the wise" (24:23-34, author's trans.).

Yet this consensus has not gone unchallenged. K. A. Kitchen has done a form-critical study of the instructions of ancient Egypt and Mesopotamia and proposed that there are two types of these documents. Type A is composed of a title and main text. Proverbs 25-29, the words of Agur (30:1-33), and the words of Lemuel (31:1-31) are Type A. Type B has a more elaborate structure, composed of title, prologue, and main text, with subtitles optional. Proverbs 1-24, proposed Kitchen, are Type A, and 10:1, 22:17, and 24:34 are subtitles that do not signal a new document but only subdocuments within the larger work.[15] That Proverbs 1-24 contains a rather long title (1:1-6) in comparison to the short titles of 25:1, 30:1, and 31:1, is not inconsistent with the instructions, for they also contain titles of varying lengths. On the contrary, they fit the evidence quite well.[16]

Some scholars discount the historical value of the title that heads chapters 25-29 ("These also are the proverbs of Solomon which the men of Hezekiah, king of Judah, transcribed," 25:1).[17] Yet we really have no substantial reason for rejecting its historical reliability.[18] The "men of Hezekiah" is a technical phrase for Hezekiah's scribes maintained under the auspices of the royal court (cf. "David's men" in 1 Sam. 23:3, 5, and "Abner's men" in 2 Sam. 2:31;

---

15. K. A. Kitchen, "Proverbs and Wisdom of the Ancient Near East: The Factual History of a Literary Form," *Tyndale Bulletin* 28 (1977):73, 96.
16. E.g., Toy, pp. 457-58, contends that the Hebrew word for "transcribed" belongs to late literary vocabulary (in Gen. 12:8, KJV, it means "to remove"), and the time of Hezekiah was selected by the editor as an appropriate time for such literary activity, particularly in view of the activities of the prophets Isaiah and Micah and the tradition of Hezekiah's vigorous religious reform.
17. Scott, p. 17, finds no reason to disqualify the title. E. J. Young, *An Introduction to the Old Testament*, p. 317, cites the use of '*thq* in the Ras Shamra texts with the sense of "to pass" (of time) and suggests that the word may already have had different nuances in earlier philological history.
18. Ibid., pp. 78-79.

1 Kings 10:8). With the fall of the Northern Kingdom to the Assyrians in 733-722 B.C., a flurry of literary activity very likely occurred and involved not only wisdom writings but also prophetic literature. In the wake of the cataclysmic events in the North, the need for preserving the prophetic words, both fulfilled and unfulfilled, was impressed upon the Southern counterpart, and a renewed practical emphasis received strong encouragement from the eighth-century prophets, who clearly perceived that the religiosity of both kingdoms was contradicted by unethical personal actions (cf. Isa. 1; Amos 8:4-6).

While the prologue of Proverbs 1-24 (1:7–9:18) is quite long, more like Ahiqar of the fifth century B.C., Proverbs likely represents a transitional stage between the shorter prologue of the third/second millennia and the longer prologue of the late first millennium.[19]

The last three sections fit Kitchen's Type A identification. They are not Solomonic, but constitute an appendix of sorts. They could have been a product of Hezekiah's school, although the evidence for dating both the composition of these documents and their addition to the book is inconclusive. The first ("The words of Agur," chap. 30, and "The words of King Lemuel," 31:1-31—note that they are really his mother's words) appear to be non-Israelite in nature.[20]

The growth of the book can be viewed in the following stages:

## GROWTH OF PROVERBS

| Stage 1 | 1:1–24:34 | *First edition* of Solomonic proverbs, which were written and collected during the last part of the tenth century B.C. |
|---------|-----------|------------------------------------------------------------------------------------------------------------------------|
| Stage 2 | 25:1–29:27  +  1:1–24:34 | *Second edition* of Solomonic proverbs, prepared by "Hezekiah's men" in late eighth or early seventh century B.C. |
| Stage 3 | 30:1-33  +  31:1-31 | *Final edition* of book of Proverbs, edited at an indeterminable date after Hezekiah. |

19. Ibid., pp. 85-86.
20. See later section in this chapter, "Hermeneutical Considerations on Proverbs," pp. 161-65.

LITERARY STRUCTURE AND COMPOSITION OF PROVERBS

| FIRST SOLOMONIC COLLECTION | | | | | SECOND SOLOMONIC COLLECTION | APPENDICES TO PROVERBS | |
|---|---|---|---|---|---|---|---|
| Title | Prologue | Miscellaneous Proverbs of Solomon | Words of the Wise | Also These Are for the Wise | Miscellaneous Proverbs of Solomon Collected by Hezekiah's scribes | Words of Agur | Words of Lem- uel |
| 1:1-6 | 1:7–9:18 | 10:1–22:16 | 22:17– 24:22 | 24:23- 34 | 25:1–29:27 | 30:1- 33 | 31:1- 31 |

THE SEPTUAGINT ORDER OF THE TEXT

Following Proverbs 24:22, the Greek textual order diverges markedly from the Hebrew. The vast two sections (30:1-33; 31:1-9) have been inserted into the context of "words of the wise":

### CONTRASTING ORDER OF PROVERBS

| *Hebrew order* | *Septuagint insertions* |
|---|---|
| 22:17–24:22 | |
| ◄--------------------------------------------- | 30:1-14 |
| 24:23-34 | |
| ◄--------------------------------------------- | 30:15–31:9 |
| 25:1–29:27 | |
| ◄--------------------------------------------- | 31:10-31 |

Toy has seen in this different order the signs of an unsettled Hebrew text.[21] But in view of other difficulties associated with the Greek version of Proverbs, not the least of which is the translator's mistranslation of words and phrases,[22] caution must be exercised lest one put too much confidence in the Greek text. There is no reason whatsoever to distrust the Hebrew order. In fact the Greek order interrupts the long Solomonic sections. The probability is on the side of

21. Toy, p. xxxiii.
22. See following comments in this chapter on Proverbs 30, pp. 175-76.

the Hebrew arrangement, although the Greek translator evidently had editorial reasons for his rearrangement.[23]

## DATE AND AUTHORSHIP

One must keep distinct the questions regarding date of composition and date of compilation of the book; the first relates to authorship and the second to editorship. Here we shall discuss the first of these; the second has already been discussed under "Literary Structure and Growth." Of course, it is not possible to keep the two matters entirely separated, but the distinction must be maintained.

The Jewish tradition preserved in the Babylonian Talmud (*Baba Bathra* 15a) recalled the role of Hezekiah's men and ascribed the writing of Proverbs to them, but this tradition more than likely referred to the editorship of the book rather than to its authorship. Among the early church Fathers the opinion was expressed that the entire book was written by Solomon, but that was based upon the absence or obscurity of the titles of chapters 30 and 31 in the Greek and Latin manuscripts.[24]

The modern view generally represents 1:1–9:18 to be the latest collection. Eissfeldt concludes that it cannot be older than the fourth century B.C., a position based upon the long sentences in this collection and the personification of wisdom, both of which he attributes to Greek influence.[25] Yet Kitchen has observed that personification of abstract ideas was widely known in the ancient Near East as early as the third and second millennia B.C.[26] The implications of this, as Kitchen has remarked, are that "the first few chapters of Proverbs (cf. 1:1-7) is something more than just the idle fancy of some late scribe."[27] Young, responding to Eissfeldt's opinion, has assented to the position expressed by Kitchen on the basis of another contention, that the length of the passages in 1:1–9:18 is due to the subject matter and not to Greek influence.[28]

Delitzsch, in his thorough and helpful commentary, set forth the position that the allegorizing author of chapters 1-9 probably belonged to the beginning of Jehoshaphat's reign,[29] and that he based his composition on the Solomonic proverbs.[30] Delitzsch based his opinion upon the intensive teaching activities of Jehoshaphat's officials and Levites (2 Chron. 17:7-9), that king's reform (2

23. Toy, p. xxxiii, in a footnote, remarks that Frankenberg observed that the Greek arrangement divides the material into two Solomonic collections with only two titles (10:1 and 25:1).
24. Young, p. 312.
25. Eissfeldt, p. 473.
26. Kitchen, *Ancient Orient and the Old Testament*, pp. 26, 126-27 and n. 56.
27. Ibid., p. 26.
28. Young, p. 313.
29. Delitzsch, 1:29.
30. Ibid., p. 34.

Chron. 17:3-6; 19:4), and the fondness for allegorical forms during this general period (2 Kings 14:8-11; 2 Chron. 25:17-21).[31]

The reasons for attributing chapters 1-9 to an author other than Solomon are understandable and somewhat attractive to the occidental mind, but the presupposition that Solomon could not have written the longer, more reflective proverbs, even utilizing the method of personification, is unjustified.

Further, that the general editor(s) of the book believed Solomon to be the author of this section (1:7–9:18) is beyond doubt. We do not question the fact that this document was involved in the editorial process during Hezekiah's reign, but the compelling reasons for postexilic dating or even post-Solomonic dating have been generally struck down by archaeological and textual research.

The first subtitle occurs in 10:1 and signals the start of a section of proverbs that divides into two sections (10:1–15:33; 16:1–22:16). The first section is distinguished from the second by the predominance of antithetic parallelism. This collection, heterogeneous in subject matter, is homogeneous in the fact that all except one proverb (19:7, a tristich) is composed in distichs.[32]

Based upon Aramaisms in 14:34; 17:10; 18:24; 19:20, and so forth, Eissfeldt maintained that 10:1–22:16 is not preexilic material.[33] Toy, taking his cue from the absence of certain concepts and social institutions, suggested that 10:1–22:16 and chapters 25-29 received substantially their present form between 350 and 300 B.C., the second collection a little later than the first.[34] Delitzsch, on the other hand, maintained that this section originated in the time of Jehoshaphat,[35] and Harrison has more recently proposed the Solomonic era.[36]

In response to these positions, it is more generally recognized today that the presence of Aramaisms in a document does not conclusively establish its date, and certainly does not necessarily support the older scholarly opinion that Aramaisms were indicative of postexilic dating.[37] Further, there are no compelling reasons to doubt the truth of the tradition preserved in 1 Kings 4:29-34, which associates Solomon with the authorship of 3,000 proverbs and 1,005 songs, whose subject matter was taken from the flora and fauna of Palestine. Solomon may have popularized a couplet form of the proverb, but we should not assume that he adhered to that form without deviation. Scott's proposal that the title "proverbs of Solomon" (10:1; 25:1) refers to the distich or couplet[38] is unconvincing. We cannot agree, therefore, that the attribution of the major portions of

---

31. Delitzsch, 1:29.
32. James L. Crenshaw, *Old Testament Wisdom, An Introduction*, p. 73.
33. Eissfeldt, p. 474.
34. Toy, pp. xxviii-xxx.
35. Delitzsch, 1:28-29.
36. R. K. Harrison, *Introduction to the Old Testament*, p. 1017.
37. See Young's brief discussion, p. 313.
38. Scott, pp. 9, 13.

the book to Solomonic authorship is mere literary convention on the part of the editor.

Delitzsch has done an analysis of proverbs that are repeated exactly or with slight changes in comparative sections and concluded that 10:1–22:16 and chapters 25-29 were not both the product of Hezekiah's scribes. They knew the first collection but did not borrow from it because they sought to produce another book to be placed alongside it without making it superfluous.[39] In part, at least, this conclusion seems justified by the few proverbs repeated identically in both sections:

### IDENTICAL OR SIMILAR PROVERBS

| First Collection | Second Collection |
|:---:|:---:|
| *Identical* | |
| 21:9 | 25:24 |
| 18:8 | 26:22 |
| 22:3 | 27:12 |
| 20:16 | 27:13[40] |
| *Identical meaning with altered expression* | |
| 22:13 | 26:13 |
| 19:24 | 26:15 |
| 19:1 | 28:6 |
| 12:11 | 28:19 |
| 22:2 | 29:13 |
| *One line identical* | |
| 17:3 | 27:21 |
| 15:18 | 29:22[41] |

That Hezekiah's scholars worked with written sources already at hand is implied in the heading of 25:1, and that these sources were Solomonic is asserted. Although repetition of single proverbs within one section or from one section to another says something about the process of compilation, it really does not

39. Delitzsch, 1:26-27.
40. The duplication of the Hebrew text is clearer in the RSV than in the NASB.
41. Delitzsch, 1:25. For a linguistic analysis of terms common to both 10:1–22:16 and chapters 25-29, see Delitzsch, pp. 31-32.

affirm or deny Solomonic authorship. Affirmatively, however, the peaceful reign of Solomon was conducive to literary activity and the development of wisdom. And in view of the national and international fame this monarch achieved, there is no reason to disbelieve that his words and reflections were preserved in writing for posterity.

That these compositions were available to Hezekiah's scribes almost three hundred years after Solomon may be attributable to Solomon's continuing popularity in Judah and the literary activity associated with royal courts in the ancient Near East. During David's reign two scribes are mentioned, Seraiah (2 Sam. 8:17) and Sheva (2 Sam. 20:25), the latter mentioned in company with the priests and other court officials. Hezekiah's scribe, Shebnah, was a participant in the events associated with the Assyrian invasion of Judah in 701 B.C. (2 Kings 18:18), and Shaphan was Josiah's scribe when the scroll of the Law was discovered in the Temple in 621 B.C. (2 Kings 22:9). One cannot fail to see the implications of these literary figures and their maintenance under royal patronage.

It is our opinion that 1:1–29:27 is Solomonic in authorship, although some allowance may be made for editorializing in the process of compilation and final edition of the book.

The authors of 30:1-33 and 31:1-9, although known by name, are otherwise unknown. The date of their composition and the final acrostic poem in praise of the virtuous wife (31:10-31) cannot be definitely established; however, little convincing data can be presented against a preexilic date.

## CANONICITY

Sparse information on the disposition of the book of Proverbs in the canonization process is found in the Babylonian Talmud *(Shabbath* 30*b*). A question revolved around the alleged contradiction between Proverbs 26:4 and 26:5: "Do not answer a fool according to his folly. . . . Answer a fool according to his folly" (KJV; cf. the interpretative effort of NASB, "as his folly deserves"). The rabbinic resolution was to view the first as a reference to matters of the law and the second to secular affairs. The doubts about the book were dispelled early in postexilic times, and Proverbs exercised a pervasive influence upon Judaism and early Christianity.

## POETIC STRUCTURE

The book of Proverbs does not employ the one-line popular proverb (e.g., "A rolling stone gathers no moss") as the basic form but rather the two-line proverb *(distich)*, which was the basic form of *māshāl* poetry. The two-line proverb takes four basic forms, the second line being the variant element.

The first form is that of *synonymous* meaning, where the second line repeats the sense of the first line in slightly different words:

> Pride goes before destruction,
> And a haughty spirit before stumbling.
> (16:18; also 16:13, 16; 11:25)

This form follows the basic type of parallelism that was characteristic of Hebrew poetry.

The second form of the two-line proverb, which is predominant in 10:1–15:33, is that of *antithetical* meaning. The second line expresses the antithesis, or the contrary sense, of the first line:

> The merciful man does himself good,
> But the cruel man does himself harm.
> (11:17)

The third form of the two-line proverb is that of *synthetic* meaning, which extends the sense of the first line in an expanded, or amplified, form. Rather than merely reiterating or contrasting in the second line the sense of the first, the synthetic form adds to the primary idea:

> He who conceals hatred has lying lips,
> And he who spreads slander is a fool.
> (10:18)

The fourth form is that of *comparative* meaning, in which case some ethical point or practical truth is explained by an illustration from nature or experience:

> Like cold water to a weary soul,
> So is good news from a distant land.
> (25:25)

In the last form, the primary idea may occur in the first or second line.

The two-line proverb forms multiples that are based upon the structures discussed above. The four-line proverb *(tetrastich)* normally gives the variant element in the last two lines. Examples of the synonymous (e.g., 23:15-16; 24:3-4), synthetic (e.g., 30:5-6), and comparative (e.g., 25:16-17) may be cited among the four-line proverbs in the book.

The longer, more reflective proverbs sometimes take the six-line form *(hexastich)*. Frequently, the first two lines compose a prologue, and the following four lines provide the substance (e.g., 23:19-21). The eight-line *(octastich)* proverb may also be identified (e.g., 23:22-25).

The longer proverbs may be called the *māshāl ode*, or song. Many of these are incorporated in 1:7–9:18 as well as elsewhere in the book (e.g., 22:17-21; 30:7-9).

All of these are variations of *māshāl* (proverb) poetry and were probably in vogue quite early in the history of wisdom literature. To confine Solomon to the two-line proverb, as some scholars are inclined, is to commit oneself to a monolithic process of literary development from the simple to the complex, a position that is too simplistic to be credible. Further, Solomon's literary activity was evidently intensive and required the use of a variety of proverb forms. For one man to write 3,000 proverbs and never advance beyond the two-line form is in itself incredible, not to mention monotonous.

We may look briefly at the different sections of the book and observe the variety of forms that each incorporates.

### POETIC FORMS IN PROVERBS

| | |
|---|---|
| 1:7–9:18 | The predominant form is the *māshāl ode*. |
| 10:1–22:16 | All are two-line proverbs, with the greatest number antithetic in form. |
| 22:17–24:22 | Most forms occur, although the four-line proverb is preferred. |
| 24:23-34 | The two-line as well as the four-line proverb is identifiable, along with one *māshāl ode*. |
| 25:1–29:27 | These are largely two-line proverbs, with the antithetic and comparative forms predominant. |
| 30:1-33 | This section contains the two-line, four-line, and numerical (*middāh*) proverbs. |
| 31:2-9 | The two- and four-line proverbs are identifiable. |
| 31:10-31 | This is an alphabetic acrostic poem.[42] |

### HERMENEUTICAL CONSIDERATIONS ON PROVERBS

The book of Proverbs is not a theological treatise in the same sense as Job and Ecclesiastes; each of those books sets out to present a theological argument in a highly structured way. Yet Proverbs is profoundly theological. Underlying the book is a wisdom theology that seeks to bring individuals into a right relationship with God and with their neighbors.

---

42. I am indebted to Delitzsch's helpful discussion in 1:6-24 for the data in this section.

## THEOLOGICAL ASSUMPTIONS

The first hermeneutical principle is that the theological assumptions of the book are often more important than the textual context. In many cases the principles of arrangement have not as yet been determined. While a group of sayings may deal with one particular subject, as a general rule each proverb ostensibly stands on its own merits and its meaning is independent of the preceding and succeeding sayings. So context will not always be as determinative as in other biblical genres.

## NATURAL AND SOCIAL/MORAL ORDERS

Second, the underlying principle of wisdom proverbs is that there is a fundamental relationship between the natural and social/moral orders. What one observes in the natural order has implications for one's understanding of the social/moral order:

> Go to the ant, O sluggard,
> Observe her ways and be wise.
>
> (6:6)

That is, the slothful person can observe in the industry of the ant a principle that ought to inform his own behavior.

## PRINCIPLES VERSUS PROMISES

Third, it is inappropriate to treat the proverbs of this book as promises. They are theological and pragmatic principles.

> Train up a child in the way he should go,
> Even when he is old he will not depart from it.
>
> (22:6)

We are inclined to accept that as a promise, but the proverb really states a principle of education and commitment. That is, generally speaking, when a child is properly instructed in the way of wisdom from an early age, he or she will persist in that way. If, of course, other genres of Holy Scripture set forth that truth as a promise, then it is appropriate to view the proverb in that manner, while acknowledging that the promisory element does not originate with proverbs. That is not their purpose.

## COGNATE LITERATURE

Fourth, cognate literature is instructive for our understanding of Proverbs, but our book assumes its own peculiar theological posture. While sharing both literary and cognitive features with other proverbial lore of the ancient Near East, Proverbs stands in its own class. We know that Mesopotamia and Egypt were repositories of much wisdom material, very often dealing with the same subjects and reaching similar conclusions as Israelite wisdom teaching. The Edomites, for example, were famous for their wisdom, a point that Jeremiah recognized:

> Concerning Edom.
> Thus says the Lord of hosts,
> "Is there no longer any wisdom in Teman?
> Has good counsel been lost to the prudent?
> Has their wisdom decayed?"
>
> (Jer. 49:7)

We may further mention that the book of Job, which was probably Israelite in its theological origin, was most likely Edomite in its geographical provenance. This fact is not necessarily indicative of the level of Edomite wisdom, but it does suggest that the literary and spiritual climate was conducive to the development and expression of wisdom ideas and forms. And that is one of the most valuable benefits of a study of ancient non-Israelite wisdom. We learn that the same literary activity was broad, and many of the same practical approaches to life were held in common by more than one culture. Yet Israelite culture produced a superior proverbial literature. The writer of Kings paid service to the superiority of Solomonic wisdom over that of the east and Egypt: "And Solomon's wisdom surpassed the wisdom of all the sons of the east and all the wisdom of Egypt" (1 Kings 4:30). The greatest distinctive was the underlying theological foundation of Israelite wisdom with its superior ethics. Whereas Mesopotamian and Egyptian sages stressed the material advantages of heeding their counsel, the foundation stone of Hebrew wisdom was "The fear of the Lord is the beginning of wisdom" (Prov. 9:10). Wisdom was more than the good sense to follow good advice; it was a whole way of life, as this key text of Proverbs testifies.[43]

The matter of Proverbs 22:17–23:14 and its relationship to the Egyptian *Instruction of Amen-em-opet*[44] has been discussed by scholars at length. The eminent Egyptologist Adolf Erman first drew attention to the connection between these two documents.[45] The Egyptian document contains thirty "houses," or sections, addressed by an official to his son. Moreover, it shares many similar-

---

43. John Ruffle, "The Teaching of Amenemope and Its Connection with the Book of Proverbs," *Tyndale Bulletin* 28 (1977):37.

44. See James B. Pritchard, ed., ANET, pp. 421*a*-24*b*, for a translation.

45. Adolf Erman, "Eine ägyptische Quelle der 'Sprüche Salomos,' " *Sitzungsberichte der preussischen Akademie der Wissenschaften* (May 1924): 86-93. The hypothesis was further advanced by H. Gressmann, "Die neugefundene Lehre des Amenemope und die vorexilische Sprüchdichtung Israels," ZAW 42 (1924):272-96.

ities of subject matter with the Proverbs pericope, and they share one very striking metaphor ("For wealth certainly makes for itself wings,/Like an eagle that
flies toward the heavens" [Prov. 23:5]; "They make themselves wings like
geese,/And fly to heaven" [Amen. x, 5]).[46] The scholarly consensus for some
time accepted Whybray's confident claim—"it is almost certain that it was the
Israelite author who knew and made use of the Egyptian work."[47] Whereas the
similarities between Hebrew and Egyptian documents are acknowledged, John
Ruffle has raised serious questions about dependence. He points out that in some
instances the so-called parallels are complicated by large gaps in *Amen-em-
opet*.[48] He is willing to allow that an Egyptian scribe working in Solomon's
court could have recorded some proverbs from a document he remembered,[49]
but the kind of dependence on the Egyptian document often attributed to the Hebrew work has not been proved.[50]

The second document that may be non-Israelite, "the words of Agur"
(chap. 30), has been adapted to Hebrew faith, if indeed it derives from another
source. The word *massā'* in 30:1 is sometimes translated "oracle" (so NASB),
but in direct association with the phrase "son of Jakeh," it would more likely be
a gentilic noun (Massaite). An Ishmaelite people by this name lived in northern
Arabia (Gen. 25:13-14; 1 Chron. 1:30), and very likely shared common religious roots with the Hebrews. The impression of the Hebrew faith is discernible
(30:9), and nothing contradictory to Yahwistic religion is incorporated.

The third document, Proverbs 31:1-31, mentions King Lemuel, who is otherwise unknown. Unless this is some kind of symbolic name (like "King Jareb"
in Hos. 5:13 and 10:6), we likely have another non-Israelite source. Although
most scholars do not consider the entire chapter a unit and confine his words to
verses 1-9, the description of "an excellent wife" (31:10-31) may nevertheless

46. John Ruffles's trans., p. 59. See pp. 37-62 for a presentation of the alleged parallels.
47. R. N. Whybray, *The Book of Proverbs*, p. 132.
48. Ibid., pp. 60, 61, 64.
49. Ibid., p. 65.
50. Young, p. 314, contends that Amen-em-opet borrowed from Solomon. He calls attention to the
contents of 22:17–23:12, which are directly related to other parts of Proverbs. Further, Young
proposes that Amen-em-opet misunderstood "ancient landmark" (22:28; 23:10), which must be
taken over by Proverbs from Deuteronomy 19:14 and 27:17, apparently reading *'almanāh* ("or-
phan") for *'ōlām*.
        On the basis of community thought and linguistic analysis, Robert Oliver Kevin, *The Wis-
dom of Amen-em-opet and Its Possible Dependence Upon the Hebrew Book of Proverbs*, in a
convincing manner argues for the dependence of *Amen-em-opet* upon the Hebrew Scriptures.
He suggests further that, since *Amen-em-opet* is so different from the standard type of Egyptian
wisdom, the author/translator offered a moral and religious teaching of Hebrew origin that he
wanted to commend to his countrymen (p. 155). He proposes that the Egyptian author/translator
came into contact with some of the Jewish colonies that were established in Egypt after the Exile. Jeremiah mentioned four such communities (Migdol, Tahpanhes, Memphis, and Pathros
[Jer. 44:1; 46:14]). We know that the Elephantine community had possession of a copy of *Ahi-
kar*, so it is quite possible that they had other documents containing their national proverbs (pp.
156-57).

belong to the Lemuel document, particularly because this poem would tie in with the teachings of his mother very well (31:1). It contributes the Yahwistic perspective: "But a woman who fears the Lord, she shall be praised" (v. 30).

Nobody has the franchise on truth but God. If one culture has come by means of natural revelation to share certain basic ideas and ethical principles with the biblical faith (cf. Rom. 1:18-20), we are free to recognize that without diminishing the value of and need for special revelation. The necessity for the latter lies in the fact that natural revelation is indistinct in its content; in Romans Paul may have been delineating its limits as the recognition of "His eternal power and divine nature." That is, natural revelation can offer evidence for the existence of God but cannot fill in the details of His personal nature and redemptive work. Faith in Israel's God was viewed in ancient times to underlie and validate all that was good, for no other gods existed. Therefore, to stake a claim upon a piece of literature from a pagan culture and adapt it for the only true faith was not incompatible with the universal perspective of ancient Israelite wisdom.

## SECTIONED ANALYSIS OF PROVERBS

### TITLE AND PROLOGUE (1:1–9:18)[51]

*The title (1:1-6).* The title and prologue are generally thought by modern scholars to belong to the latest stage of the book's growth. However, Kitchen has shown that the Egyptian and Mesopotamian instructions (Type B) had this structure. So it may very well belong to the original edition of the book. The title sets forth the purpose of the book by the use of five infinitives: "to know," "to discern," "to receive," "to give," and "to understand." Thus the object of the book is clearly instruction, aimed at and dedicated to the youth (1:4).

*The prologue (1:7–9:18).* In this section there are wonderful reflections on wisdom. Following the methodology of form-critical scholarship, recent scholars have attempted to distinguish among the various strands of material in 1:7–9:18. Buried in this collection, they contend, are ten discourses that have been amplified and expanded by other materials, resulting finally in the present collection. Whybray, as an example of this school of thought, has identified three strands of material in chapters 1-9: (1) the first book, consisting of a general introduction followed by ten short discourses, similar to the Egyptian instruction, which set forth basic principles of conduct necessary for a happy life; (2) a supplementary strand in which "wisdom" is viewed as a basic concept and equated with the teacher's words, sometimes personified as a female figure, a teacher, and a bride; and (3) a second supplementary strand, which associated wisdom with God and made her an attribute of God.[52] In an effort to recover the

---

51. See earlier sections of this chapter, "The Book Title" and "Literary Structure and Growth," pp. 147, 153-55.
52. Whybray, pp. 14-15.

first book of ten discourses, which form-critical scholars have assumed existed, Whybray extracts the material that is particularly instructive (in the vein of the Egyptian instructions) and identifies the ten discourses as follows:

ONE FORM-CRITICAL ANALYSIS
OF THE PROLOGUE OF PROVERBS

| | |
|---|---|
| First Discourse | — 1:8-19 |
| Second Discourse | — 2:16-19 |
| Third Discourse | — 3:1-12 |
| Fourth Discourse | — 3:21-35 |
| Fifth Discourse | — 4:1-9 |
| Sixth Discourse | — 4:10-19 |
| Seventh Discourse | — 4:20-27 |
| Eighth Discourse | — 5:1-23 |
| Ninth Discourse | — 6:20-35 |
| Tenth Discourse | — 7:1-27 |

Following a different set of analytical presuppositions, older commentators on Proverbs have generally identified about fifteen discourses rather than ten. Although the form-critical school must generally be given commendation for its methods of literary analysis, some of which are helpful, their application to this collection before us presupposes that the editor(s) has slavishly followed the Egyptian model and the discourses have been enlarged by further accretions. But the search for such original documents is at best subjective. We are not convinced that the underlying strands of material were as distinct as this school of scholars has maintained.[53] We prefer to discuss the material as it has come to us rather than trying to treat it according to levels or strands.

*Motto (1:7).* In slightly different form this motto of the book stands also at the end of this division (9:10). We find the same kind of inclusion in Ecclesiastes, where the beginning and end of that book are marked by its motto "Vanity of vanities! All is vanity" (Eccles. 1:2; 12:8).

This motto serves the book as a compass. The fear of the Lord is the foundation of knowledge.[54] "Beginning" may have either the temporal ("first in order") or qualitative ("first in importance") sense. In the context of Proverbs,

53. We are ready to admit that we have different kinds of material in this collection (1:8–9:18), but the explanation for that may be altogether different from that proposed by the form-critical scholars. It is very possible that one teacher (in this case Solomon, we believe) employed different kinds of material. In light of ancient Near Eastern literature, there is no reason to presuppose that Solomon could not have been both practical and reflective, as well as engaging in the method of personification.
54. See Scott, p. 37, for the different nuances of "fear" in the Old Testament.

both nuances are possible. The author further develops the meaning of this statement in 3:5-12 (cf. Job 28:28 and Ps. 111:10).

*First Discourse (1:8-19)*. The teacher recognized peer pressure and the appeals to young people to abandon the fundamental teachings of their parents and follow the evil ways of their companions. The temptation that he warns against here is that of greed and ill-gotten gain. The substance of the enticement, consisting not only in illicit seizure of property but also in casting one's lot with those who engage in such activity, is stated in verses 11-14. After the admonition of verse 15, the teacher explains what is really involved in such activity—it leads to self-destruction. Verse 19 sums up the principle very well: violence deprives its executors of their own life.

It is characteristic of Hebrew, Egyptian, Babylonian, Assyrian, and Aramaic wisdom to address the student as "son."[55]

*Second Discourse (1:20-33)*. Here, for the first time in the book, wisdom is personified. In prophetic character, wisdom stations herself in the streets and city entrances to proclaim her message. It is indicting and reproving. The indictment is made in verses 24-25—the people have turned away wisdom as they have diverted the prophetic word. The result of their behavior is judgment (vv. 26-28, 31), executed according to the *lex talionis* (the law of retaliation in like kind, e.g., "an eye for an eye"). Wisdom warns that she will turn away from their call when distress comes suddenly upon them.

The teacher turned to the crux of the indictment, given in terms reminiscent of 1:7: "They hated knowledge, and did not choose the fear of the Lord" (v. 29). The expansion in verse 30 amplifies the meaning of their rejection of the fear of the Lord. It was tantamount to the rejection of divine counsel.

Returning to the "naive one" and "fools" of verse 22, wisdom pronounces the principle by which the world operates: abandonment to the foolish ways of the unwise is self-destruction (v. 32), but commitment to the counsel of wisdom provides peace and security (v. 33).

*Third Discourse (2:1-22)*. Wisdom is the intermediary that directs men to the Lord. The fear of the Lord is still to be the object of man's search (vv. 4-5), and wisdom is the means of arriving at that goal. The Lord is the giver of wisdom (vv. 6-8), whereas wisdom is the agent of life, the element by which one distinguishes between right and wrong (v. 9). Moreover, the outgrowth of wisdom as a dynamic force in the individual's life is protection from those who are perverse and who devise evil against their neighbors (vv. 12-15), and deliverance from adulterous temptation (vv. 16-19).

The alternative to forsaking wisdom's ways and being victimized by both the wicked and the adulteress is seeking wisdom (v. 4) and consequently dwell-

---

55. For ancient non-Hebrew wisdom texts, see Pritchard, ANET, pp. 412-25 (Egyptian); pp. 425-27 (Akkadian); and pp. 427-30 (Aramaic).

ing in the land (vv. 20-21). The discourse closes with a contrast between the end of the upright and the wicked (vv. 21-22), very much like Psalm 1:6:

> For the Lord knows the way of the righteous,
> But the way of the wicked will perish.

Some see the description of the adulteress (v. 16) as an allusion to Israel's idolatry and practice of cult prostitution. Scott makes the pedagogical observation that this chapter is "a kind of prospectus of the 'course' in wisdom which the teacher offers."[56]

*Fourth Discourse (3:1-18).* This prescriptive section capitalizes upon the motto of the book (1:7), but in a slightly different form. The formulation here is precisely that of Job 28:28: "Behold, the fear of the Lord, that is wisdom; and to depart from evil is understanding." First in this section, however, the teacher called attention to his teaching *(tôrāh)* and his commandments (v. 1), associating them with a long and peaceful life (v. 2). He concluded the discourse with the assertion that the Lord disciplines those whom He loves (vv. 11-12). One of the greatly loved verses of the King James Version is found here: "In all thy ways acknowledge him, and he shall direct thy paths" (v. 6).

In a style typical of wisdom literature, the concluding pericope of this discourse begins with "How blessed is the man" (cf. Ps. 1:1; Prov. 8:34; Matt. 5:3-11). Wisdom is depicted as a tree of life, recalling the tree in the Garden of Eden (Gen. 2:9; 3:22, 24). This association with the original creation is not coincidental. Rather it is precisely what we would expect of wisdom with its theological emphasis on creation. Just as the Exodus became a paradigm for redemption theology, the Garden of Eden was a paradigm for wisdom (3:18; 11:30; 13:12; 15:4).

To illustrate the method and results of the form-critical approach, Whybray identifies verses 13-18 with the first supplementary strand in which wisdom is considered a basic concept or is personified.[57]

*Fifth Discourse (3:19-26).* Verses 19-20 are considered by some to be a poem separate from 13-18, an opinion that is difficult to establish. In fact, the "tree of life" in verse 18 raises thoughts of creation, thus leading naturally into verses 19-20 on the role of wisdom in founding the world. The remainder of the discourse provides a description of the success and security of the life in which wisdom is dominant (vv. 21-26).

*Sixth Discourse (3:27-35).* These practical admonitions regarding the proper treatment of one's neighbor (vv. 27-29) appropriately follow the above description of the wisdom-dominated life (vv. 21-26). The concluding admonition

56. Scott, p. 42.
57. Whybray, p. 26.

cautions against admiring the man of violence (vv. 31-32). Like 2:21-22, the final verses (vv. 33-35) contrast the life of the wicked and the righteous in three different couplets.

*Seventh Discourse (4:1–5:6).* The metaphor of 4:1-9 is that of obtaining a wife, and verse 9 is a reference to the wedding when the bride placed a garland on the head of the bridegroom. The language of verse 5 ("acquire wisdom") suggests acquisition at a cost to the individual (Heb. "buy"). Although some marriage payment was often transferred (cf. Jacob and Laban, Gen. 29), the choice of the word may allude to the sacrifice that must be made to gain wisdom.

The two ways are contrasted at greater length in 4:10-19, here called "the way of wisdom" (vv. 11-13) and "the path of the wicked" (vv. 14-17). The way of wisdom occurs parallel to "upright paths" (v. 11), implying that wisdom is here equated with practical moral goodness. Concluding this pericope are two poetic couplets, which sum up the contrast of the righteous life and the wicked life respectively (vv. 18-19).

The third pericope of this discourse is constituted by 4:20-27. Introducing it is an admonition ending with the word "body" (v. 22), which becomes the point of reference for the structure of the discourse. The parts of the body are named along with their strategic functions in achieving the life of righteousness. The "heart" is the source of all behavior. In Hebrew thought the heart, rather than the head, was the center of human reason. From the heart everything else was determined. The specific functions of the mouth, eyes, and feet follow.

The fourth pericope (5:1-6) interjects the teacher's warnings a second time (cf. 2:16-19) against adultery (cf. 6:24-29; 7:25-27).

*Eighth Discourse (5:7-23).* The division of chapter 5 between verses 6 and 7 is somewhat arbitrary, particularly since the theme of adultery extends beyond verse 6. The criterion for the division, however, is the injunction "sons, listen to me" (v. 7), with which the previous discourse also opened (4:1). Other commentators would treat chapter 5 as a unit.

The address in verses 1 and 7 is to the pupil(s), who was probably not married, but the words of counsel in verses 15-20 pertain to marital fidelity, and some have assumed they were later additions. However, there is no sound reason the teacher should not offer advice that would be appropriate later, just as youths are often counseled about matters before they confront them. Observe that the discourse does not close with the usual contrast between the two ways. Rather verses 21-23 constitute a description of the way of the man who does not heed the teacher's counsel.

*Ninth Discourse (6:1-5).* The matter treated here is one of sound business practice, that of lending to a foreigner. Becoming surety for a neighbor's debt to a foreigner was a risky matter. Becoming someone else's surety was the equivalent of vouching for another's honesty. If the person making the debt defaulted, the lender could hold responsible the person offering the surety or pledge (possibly in the form of some item of collateral). Business transactions with foreigners were not handled on the same principle as those with fellow Israelites (cf. Deut. 15:2-3).

*Tenth Discourse (6:6-11)*. The object of this discourse is sloth, or laziness. The teacher referred his students to the industrious ant to learn a lesson. Citations of animal behavior as a pedagogical method were common in wisdom literature (cf. Prov. 30:19, 25-31). The writer of Kings informs us that Solomon discoursed on subjects chosen from the plant and animal kingdoms (1 Kings 4:33): "And he spoke of trees, from the cedar that is in Lebanon even to the hyssop that grows on the wall; he spoke also of animals and birds and creeping things and fish."

*Eleventh Discourse (6:12-19)*. Here occurs a statement about and a word of judgment upon the worthless person. The gestures mentioned in verse 13 were probably movements conveying contempt and enmity,[58] although they could be magical gestures.[59]

The poetic device in verse 16, the numerical proverb *(middāh)*, occurs elsewhere in the Old Testament (Prov. 30:15-31; Amos 1:3–2:8; Job 5:19-22).[60] The purpose was not only for poetic effect but for mnemonic purposes as well. The proverb names seven things that are hateful to God.

*Twelfth Discourse (6:20-35)*. Similar to 5:1-23 in theme, the introduction is rather lengthy in comparison to the others (vv. 20-23). The teacher warns against the sins of the flesh whose power is so great as to destroy those who engage in them. Adultery is described with two metaphors, playing with fire (vv. 27-29) and stealing (vv. 30-31).

*Thirteenth Discourse (7:1-27)*. This discourse is different in that the teacher related a story in parabolic form to reinforce his teaching against adultery in the preceding discourse. He followed the events from the young man's passage through the street to his seduction by the adulteress. The latter made reference to peace offerings (cf. Lev. 7:11-36), part of which was eaten by the worshiper (v. 15). She evidently invited the young man into her house to share the meal, making the sin all the more brazen. Her house, however, was no more than the vestibule to Sheol (v. 27).

*Fourteenth Discourse (8:1-36)*. The structure of this exquisite poem is essentially that of the discourses as the form critics have characterized and identified them: *introduction* (vv. 1-11), *teaching* (vv. 12-31), and *conclusion*, including the contrasting ways (vv. 32-36). That shared structure, in addition to the similarities of language (cf. 3:7/8:13; 3:15/8:11; 3:16/8:18, etc.) and the syn-

---

58. Toy, p. 126.
59. Whybray, p. 39.
60. The numerical device is used also in "The Words of Ahiqar," a sixth- or fifth-century B.C. wisdom document, Pritchard, ANET, pp. 427-30, line 92.

onymity of theme (cf. 1:20-33; 3:13-26), points in the direction of the same author for this poem as for the discourses.

Although wisdom as a divine attribute is personified for poetic effect, we would not deny that the nature of this composition points toward the ontological meaning of the Logos in the New Testament (John 1:2-3; Col. 1:15-16; Heb. 1:3). Since wisdom is more to be desired than riches (vv. 18-21), we are directed by the medium of His attribute to God Himself as the moving Desire of human existence. Just as the Lord is eternal, so are His attributes. Thus wisdom was present when He founded the world (cf. 3:19). Some scholars would render the verb in verse 22 as "create," but the sense of it is "possess."[61] The same word is used in 4:5 to admonish the teacher's students to acquire wisdom.

*Fifteenth Discourse (9:1-18).* This chapter is really composed of three sections. (1) A concluding invitation to the house of wisdom is delivered by wisdom herself. (2) Two responses to wisdom in order to highlight the way of life are offered by wisdom in the first section in contrast to the way of death offered by folly in the third section. The speaker may be wisdom (note "by me" in v. 11) who began her address in verse 4. The declaration "the fear of the Lord is the beginning of wisdom" (v. 10) suggests that we have reached a summit and recalls the motto originally stated in 1:7. (3) The final section is an invitation to the house of folly, delivered as in the first section by the lady of the house. As the language indicates, the unwary young should know "the dead are there" (v. 18), just as they should be told that wisdom's way leads to life (v. 6).

PROVERBS OF SOLOMON: FIRST GROUP (10:1–22:16)

This section is titled "Proverbs of Solomon" (omitted in Septuagint and Peshitta), a much shorter superscription than that of Section 1, "The Proverbs of Solomon the Son of David, king of Israel" (1:1). Some scholars[62] believe that the presence of identical or almost identical sayings evidences a process of compilation from different collections. Though the degree of repetition is significant, the context of the duplicates will generally indicate the purpose for the repetition.

The collection is largely composed of aphorisms stated in the form of two-line proverbs, or poetic couplets *(distichs)*, and the parallelism, especially in 10:1–15:33, is predominately antithetical.

61. Cf. W. A. Irwin, "Where Shall Wisdom Be Found?" JBL 80 (1961):142. He comments: "The full significance of this is scarcely grasped until one recognizes that for the writer, Wisdom is the total of values of the human spirit—emotional, ethical, and intellectual. He says, then, that these are ultimately a divine quality, existent in the being of God long before creation. In accord with such realities God made the world, building them, if one may so speak, into its essence and, in particular, implanting them in the being of man. It is the Hebraic answer to the question that had attracted ancient thought for ages, how it is that man is so like the beasts and yet so different." (Reprinted by permission of publisher.)
62. E.g., Scott, p. 17; Whybray, *Proverbs*, p. 57.

It cannot be said that this thesaurus of aphorisms is purely secular, for the Lord is sometimes mentioned, and the theological girders are righteousness and the fear of the Lord. The range of subjects is wide, including business ethics, personal conduct of one's life and affairs, temperance, social propriety, commonsense sayings, pedagogical advice, and familial relations.[63] William McKane, employing the form-critical approach, has proposed a system of classifying this material into three groups:

Class A: Sentences that are set in the framework of old wisdom and aimed toward educating the individual for a successful and harmonious life.

Class B: Sentences mainly composed with the benefit of the community rather than the individual in view. They frequently focus on the effects of certain types of antisocial behavior on the community.

Class C: Sentences identified by the presence of God-language or other moralizing that originates in Yahwistic poetry.[64]

McKane's view is that Class C represents a later stage in the history of Old Testament wisdom development and was intended as a reinterpretation of Class A material.[65] He has subjected each chapter to this system of classification.

One of the problems with this critical method is that we may superimpose on the material a system that is foreign to both the mentality and the intention of the compiler(s). Further, McKane's thesis assumes that the interpretive process was at work to produce the final collection. It is just as possible, however, that these different strands lay side by side in time and literary form, just as we have already contended that Proverbs need not necessarily be seen as a monolithic, evolutionary development from the simple one-sentence form to the longer instruction. It is more likely that their different forms have long overlapping histories.

There is no good reason for questioning the Solomonic connection to these proverbs. The relatively frequent mention of "king" (e.g., 16:10, 12-15; 19:12; 20:2, 8, 26, 28; 21:1) may lend support to a preexilic date and even support a Solomonic date, when the monarchy was still young and Israel still learning to live under royal leadership. Although Solomon's wisdom may not have persisted in his personal and political conduct in later years of his reign, he did begin well (1 Kings 3:6-28).

WORDS OF THE WISE: FIRST GROUP (22:17–24:22)

Some commentators and translators emend the difficult Hebrew word in 22:20 (rendered by KJV and NASB as "excellent things") to read "thirty," re-

---

63. See Scott, pp. 130-31, for a topical arrangement of the proverbs in this section.
64. William McKane, *Proverbs, A New Approach*, pp. 11, 415.
65. Ibid., p. 11.

quiring only a slight vowel change (so RSV and NIV).[66] The interpretation of the section, however, is not affected by the emendation. Since Erman recognized the affinity of this document with the Egyptian document, *Instruction of Amen-em-opet*,[67] scholars have expended much energy on the subject. However, it is generally recognized that the verbal similarities between the two compositions are largely confined to 22:17–23:14. Whichever document has priority, neither is a direct translation nor a slavish imitation of the other.[68]

The topics of this section are almost as varied as those of other sections, and their range of subjects about the same. They include proper treatment of the poor (22:22-23), disassociation with an angry person (22:24-25), prudence in making pledges (22:26-27), regulation against removing landmarks (22:28; 23:10-11), admonitions against gluttony (23:1-3, 20-21), warning against inordinate concern for obtaining wealth (23:4-5), teachings on selfishness (23:6-8), disciplining children (23:13-14), admonitions against envying sinners (23:17-19; 24:1-2, 19-20) and against intemperate drinking (23:20-21, 29-35), counsel to heed parental advice (23:22, 24-25), warning against adultery (23:27-28), commendation of wisdom (24:3-7, 13-14), and advice against glee at the fall of the wicked (24:17-18).

It is quite possible that such a collection was used as a textbook in the royal courts and other schools for the instruction of the young. It is also probable that the flurry of wisdom teaching and formulation was largely associated with royal courts, although wisdom was certainly not the exclusive possession of the courts.

That we have come to the end of the present section is signaled by the presence of a new introductory formula, "These also are sayings of the wise" (24:23). Further, the Septuagint places 24:23 after 30:14, a section that has similar material, indicating that the Greek translator considered 24:23-34 a separate unit.

The assortment of proverb literary forms in this division of the book is as manifold as the subject matter, ranging from the simple two-line proverb to the proverb ode, although the four-line proverb *(tetrastich)* is a favorite.

---

66. The Masoretic text has the difficult *šālišiōm*, which is close to the Hebrew *šilšōm*, "formerly." Already the Masoretes had recognized the difficulty and given a marginal reading as *šālišim*, "officers," a reading that the Septuagint, Vulgate, and Targum rendered "triple" or "three times." Some scholars take this to be reminiscent of what may have been the original "thirty." In view of the difficulty of the Hebrew, and in light of the "thirty houses" (chapters) of the Egyptian document known as the *Instruction of Amen-em-opet*, which has affinities with the present section, we may accept the emendation as a last resort.
67. See earlier section in this chapter, "Hermeneutical Considerations on Proverbs," pp. 161-65, for a discussion of the relationship between these two documents.
68. Whybray, p. 132.

WORDS OF THE WISE: SECOND GROUP (24:23-34)

This section contains sayings against corruption in the courts (24:23*b*), against flaunting evil as good (24:24-26), on one's domestic priorities (24:27), against false witness (24:28), against the law of retaliation (24:29), and one longer passage, which might be titled the wisdom work ethic (24:30-34). The longer passages of this type in the book of Proverbs seem to be examples of the teacher's exposition of shorter wisdom sayings. The present one may be a parable or the teacher's personal reminiscence. This theme appeared earlier in 6:6-11 where the conclusion is almost identical (cf. 6:10-11/24:33-34).

The presence of such a counterstatement to the law of retaliation in 24:29 (the law of retaliation, *lex talionis*, is contained in its classical form in Ex. 21:24 —"eye for eye, tooth for tooth, hand for hand, foot for foot") marks a milestone on the way to Jesus' own teaching in Matthew 5:38-42. Wisdom literature in some ways, as in this instance, perceived the genuine spirit of the Old Testament law and accentuated it.

PROVERBS OF SOLOMON: SECOND GROUP (25:1-29:27)

Beginning with this collection, the book of Proverbs comprises a series of three major sections headed by the names of authors: 25:1—Solomon; 30:1—Agur; 31:1—Lemuel (the "words of Lemuel" were technically those of his mother but directed to him).

Many commentators subdivide the first section into two parts. The first collection (25:1-27:27) contains miscellaneous proverbs much like 10:1-22:16, but they are generally longer. It has many comparisons and antithetic proverbs that are largely two-line in form but also assume the three-line and four-line forms. In comparison, the second collection (28:1-29:27) is more strongly reminiscent of the content and form of those proverbs in 10:1-22:16. There is really no reason, however, to assign the first collection to another author, since Solomon's literary activity was known to be diversified.

Hezekiah's instrumentality in the collection and transcription process is both interesting and enlightening. It would appear that the literary activity that characterized Solomon's court continued among the royal courts of Judah, or at least was revived by Hezekiah. We cannot determine the extent of the "transcription" activity—whether it went beyond mere transcription and included an active collecting and editing process. But the meaning of the verb in 25:1 ("transcribed," "remove from one book or roll to another")[69] implies that written records were available, most likely preserved in the royal archives. From these the scribes of Hezekiah copied our present collection (chaps. 25-29) and edited a larger instructional manual for their own pedagogical purposes.

69. Brown, Driver, Briggs, p. 801*a*.

This section opens with a brief discourse on the sagacity of kings and the proper conduct of oneself in their presence (25:2-7). The attention given to kings and rulers (25:2-7, 15; 28:15-16; 29:4, 14, 26) is certainly in alignment with a collection of proverbs attributed to a king and collected under the direction of a king. Moreover, the consideration accorded justice and law (esp. 28:1-13), as well as proper treatment of the poor and oppressed, point to the religious and judicial responsibilities of the ancient Israelite monarchs. We may submit that in light of these matters, these proverbs originiated in the earlier years of Solomon's reign, when his leadership was characterized by understanding and wisdom (1 Kings 3:6-15).

Although much of the material in this section constitutes disjunctive proverbs on miscellaneous subjects (esp. 27:1-22 and chap. 29),[70] certain units may be identified by unifying themes or ideas:

### THEMATIC UNITS IN PROVERBS

| | |
|---|---|
| 25:2-7 | The sagacity of kings and proper conduct in their presence |
| 25:8-28 | The potencies and perils of verbal communication |
| 26:1-12 | The fool and his folly |
| 26:13-16 | The sluggard |
| 26:17-28 | The busybody and the malicious person |
| 27:23-27 | The value of flocks |
| 28:1-13 | Justice and law |
| 28:15-16 | Wise leadership |

Even within some of these units, certain proverbs are only loosely imbedded. Yet, even though chapter 29 is disparate in nature, there is still a unifying factor with which Hezekiah's scribes seemed to be working. They intended to summarize in many different proverbial statements the difference between the foolish and the wise, or the wicked and the righteous. At the very heart of wisdom literature is the motive to hold up before youth these two models for life and to show how the advantages of the righteous life far outweigh those of the wicked.

THE WORDS OF AGUR (30:1-33)

The Septuagint arrangement of the last two collections diverges from the Hebrew. The following is the Greek order:

---

70. See Scott, p. 171, for his arrangement of these proverbs in subject categories.

## SEPTUAGINT REARRANGEMENT
## OF PROVERBS 22:17–31:31

22:17–24:22
30:1-14
24:23-34
30:15-33
31:1-9
25:1–29:27
31:10-31

The Septuagint translator failed to recognize any of the proper names, translating Agur as a verb ("fear") and Ithiel as "those who believe in God." Even though the rearrangement of the material in the Greek translation helps us to identify some of these sections as distinct (e.g., 24:23-34), we need not take our cue from him and conclude that the Hebrew text is in disarray. The Greek translator may have worked from a Hebrew or Greek text already disarranged or undertaken to reorder it himself. The Hebrew order is preferable.[71]

The Hebrew word in verse 1 rendered as "the oracle" (*hammassā'*) by the *New American Standard Bible* and "the prophecy" by the King James Version stands in direct association with the phrase "son of Jakeh," and may indicate a gentilic noun. There was such an Ishmaelite people of northern Arabia (Gen. 25:13-14; 1 Chron. 1:30). The rest of the verse is obscure. Some have vocalized the Hebrew (usually translated "to Ithiel, to Ithiel and Ucal") as Aramaic and read, "There is no God! There is no God, and I can . . . "[72] That leaves us, however, with an incomplete statement, which is somewhat unlikely. However, if the change is accepted, then verses 1*b*-4 become the challenge of a skeptic and verses 5-6 an answer to his challenge.

Numerical proverbs are found in verses 7-9 and 15-31.[73] The three sayings in verses 11-14 have in common the same first word, "generation" (NASB "kind"). The final two sayings (vv. 32-33) are difficult.

THE WORDS OF LEMUEL (31:1-9)

This is the only instruction in Proverbs made to a king. Such do occur, however, in Egyptian and Mesopotamian literature. Again *massā'* may be a proper name as in 30:1, but Lemuel is nowhere else mentioned in the Old Testament. He was obviously a non-Israelite king.

71. See earlier section in this chapter, "The Septuagint Order of the Text," p. 155.
72. E.g., Scott, pp. 175-76.
73. See on 6:16 above.

Other references have been made to the teaching of the mother and its importance (1:8; 6:20), and even when only the father's instruction is mentioned, the mother's may be included. Quite appropriately this passage is spoken by the king's mother, who may have exemplified the "excellent wife" described in the final section. Further, the content of this discourse is an apropos conclusion for a book largely written by a king and collected by one. It focuses, not upon the privileges of kingship, but upon the responsibilities of the office.

### IN PRAISE OF A VIRTUOUS WIFE (31:10-31)

This poem is interesting and revealing in several respects. It is an acrostic poem; each new verse begins with a different letter of the Hebrew alphabet in sequence. In 18:22 a blessing is pronounced upon him who finds a wife. That thought is developed further here. Moreover, the responsibilities this woman implemented are indicative of the important role of the woman in ancient Israelite society: she provided both clothing and food for her family and servants (vv. 13-15), managed the estate (v. 16), cared for the poor (v. 20), sold her own handwork (v. 24), and engaged in teaching (v. 26). To put the poem in context, the value and success of the "excellent wife" were determined by the same religious criterion that was applied in the beginning of the book: "A woman who fears the Lord, she shall be praised" (v. 30*b*). This extended poem on the significance of the mother and wife balances out the social spectrum of the book of Proverbs very well. And lest the male-dominated language of the book appear to excuse the women of society from religious obligations, this poem puts the joyful yoke of religious observance upon women, too.

# 6

# THE BOOK OF ECCLESIASTES

The Hebrew and Christian faiths have always provided a certain margin within which the skeptical spirit of man could be accommodated. The fact that Ecclesiastes stands within the canonical circle of Holy Scripture is a virtual witness to that truth. Although the Hebrew-Christian tradition has required faith of its adherents, it has recognized that life and faith have their high and low altitudes, and sometimes out of doubt and skepticism faith is born and nourished.

We can be grateful that the circle of the Hebrew faith was wide enough to include Job and Ecclesiastes. And in a day of skepticism we can offer the skeptic a starting point in the book of Ecclesiastes. Moreover, those who feel their case is best made when expressed in radical terms may profit from the moderate attitude of Ecclesiastes. This book rounds out the picture of biblical wisdom very well.

## Introductory Matters About Ecclesiastes

Whereas Job was a challenger of man and God, Qoheleth—the speaker in Ecclesiastes—shared Job's daring spirit, but his search was for happiness and the enduring quality rather than for personal vindication. He was no challenger and had no contempt for God or man. He, like Job, was a man of wealth, but unlike Job, he had lost nothing tangible. Yet he realized that much needed to be gained. Wealth could not soothe a heart that was troubled by the transience of human life, especially when so much else in the world caused him pain, but he did not demand that God provide an explanation, as had his spiritual brother, Job. He accepted the fact, though commending a life of charity to his wealthy students, and waited for the day of judgment. To compensate for the transience of human life, he urged the enjoyment of the present moment, recognizing it as a gift from God.

Ecclesiastes serves as an appropriate balance for the practical wisdom of Proverbs. Although Qoheleth, too, had found practical wisdom beneficial, he had come to it along a reflective path. Wisdom aphorisms for Qoheleth were not stones he had gathered along the way but jewels he had mined out of the earth. The quality of his proverbs was the result of his long, frustrating pursuit of happiness and meaning. Although he most likely wrote later than Job and Proverbs, he stood somewhere between them in philosophy and spirit. He represented, in a sense, the mediation of reflective and practical wisdom.

TITLE

The English title, *Ecclesiastes*, comes to us, as have so many other Old Testament book titles, through the medium of the Septuagint, which called this book *Ekklēsiastēs*. The Hebrew title, however, is *Qoheleth*, a feminine singular participle from the root meaning "to assemble, gather." Based upon that idea, Jerome titled the book *Concionator* (i.e., "one who gathers an assembly"). Modern English versions have generally translated the Hebrew word as "Preacher," particularly in view of Solomon's role as an assembler (1 Kings 8:1) and exhorter, or preacher (1 Kings 8:55-61). However, the choice of the *feminine* participle to designate Solomon has provoked much discussion. Generally two explanations are given: (1) the name *Qoheleth* refers to wisdom, which is feminine in gender, and is thus applied to Solomon as the exemplar of wisdom, or (2) it refers to an office, like *sofereth* ("office of scribe"?—occurs in Ezra 2:55 and Neh. 7:57 as the name of a family, but they may be called by the name of their professional office) or *pochereth* ("binder" [of the gazelles], Ezra 2:57, also a family name designating an office).[1]

The last two phrases of the title verse have historically contributed to the idea that Solomon was the author of the book, namely, "the son of David, king in Jerusalem." Although the name Solomon does not appear anywhere in the book, he was the only son of David who was also king in Jerusalem. Twice the author specifically called himself king in Jerusalem (1:1, 12), and three times he referred to his position in Jerusalem in relation to his predecessors (1:16; 2:7, 9). The implication is that he had been preceded by a relatively large group of kings, which was certainly not true of Solomon. W. F. Albright proposed that *melek* might be emended to *môlēk* or *mallōk* ("counselor"),[2] necessitating only vowel changes. This would, of course, alleviate the problem of Solomonic authorship, since it would mean that the author was possibly a descendant of David who was an official in Jerusalem but not king. Although this proposal is attractive, the textual emendation may be too easy of a solution. We will discuss the ramifications of the title later when we consider authorship.

1. See Christian D. Ginsburg, *The Song of Songs and Coheleth*, pp. 8-9, for various explanations given for the feminine gender.
2. W. F. Albright, "Some Canaanite-Phoenician Sources of Hebrew Wisdom," WIANE, p. 15, n. 2.

LITERARY STRUCTURE

One of the difficulties in determining the literary structure of Ecclesiastes is that there is no logical progression of thought by which the book is held together (except in chaps. 1-2). Eissfeldt goes so far as to say that it is "a loose collection of aphorisms."[3] That proverbs are imbedded in the text is certainly not to be denied, but it is definitely possible to identify thought segments and recurring themes. Moreover, in the absence of a unifying thought progression, these give a semblance of unity and coherence to the whole. Gordis observes that Qoheleth generally concluded a section with one of three or four ideas: (1) the weakness or transcience of man's accomplishments, (2) the uncertainty of his fate, (3) the impossibility of attaining true knowledge in this world, and (4) the need to enjoy life.[4] Using these criteria he counts nineteen sections, whereas Scott treats the book in twenty-four pericopes.[5] An attempt to identify broader sections is represented by Ginsburg, who identified four sections flanked on either side by the prologue and epilogue:

AN ANALYSIS OF
THE STRUCTURE OF ECCLESIASTES

| | |
|---|---|
| Prologue | 1:2-11 |
| Section 1 | 1:12–2:26 |
| Section 2 | 3:1–5:20 |
| Section 3 | 6:1–8:15 |
| Section 4 | 8:16–12:7 |
| Epilogue | 12:8-12.[6] |

The book begins and ends with essentially the same phrase, " 'Vanity of vanities,' says the Preacher. . . . 'All is vanity!' " (1:2; 12:8). Further, the end of each of the first three sections is signaled by a recurring formula that gives the results of the author's inquiry (2:26; 5:20; 8:15), the fourth being followed by the repetition of the opening declaration (12:8). There are obviously smaller pericopes within these broad sections, and we will recognize those in the analysis of the book.

Those scholars who have viewed the book as a collection of sayings have often seen certain recurring orthodox themes as an effort by a later editor(s) to bring the book within the circle of orthodox Judaism. Eissfeldt is a representative of that school. He views these passages as interpolations: 2:26; 3:17; 7:18b,

---

3. Otto Eissfeldt, *The Old Testament: An Introduction*, p. 499.
4. Robert Gordis, *Koheleth—The Man and His World*, p. 252.
5. R. B. Y. Scott, *Proverbs, Ecclesiastes*.
6. Ginsburg, pp. 17-21.

26*b*; 8:5, 12*b*, 13*a*; 11:9*b*; 12:7*b*; 12:12-14 (v. 12 and vv. 13-14 being by two different hands).[7] Increasingly, however, the literary unity of Ecclesiastes is being recognized by scholars.[8] The same stylistic features as well as the same pervasive philosophical tone are sustained throughout the book.

As a rule Qoheleth gave his observations on life in the first person (see 1:12; 2:1, 13, 18; 3:12, 16; 4:1, 4, 7; 5:18; 6:1; 7:15, 25, 26; 8:10, 16; 9:1, 11, 13; 10:5), although the words "says the Preacher" occur at 1:2; 7:27; and 12:8, and Qoheleth is also spoken of in the third person in 12:9-10. Some scholars see these third-person references to be the work of a later editor,[9] but there is really no sound reason for assuming that the author could not speak of himself in the third person, just as the prophets sometimes did. Particularly when we consider that Qoheleth was a literary name for the author, the awkwardness of the third person disappears, thus removing the objection. The words "says the Preacher" are just as much Qoheleth's as the "I" passages.

PURPOSE AND MEANING

The primary *purpose* of Qoheleth was didactic. He was a wisdom teacher who sought to transfer to his young pupils the conceptual and practical benefits that he had gathered over many years of thought and experience. He himself was obviously a wealthy individual and instructed upperclass youth who were potential leaders (2:24; 3:12, 22; 5:18-19; 8:1-9; 11:1-6). Aware of their potential for hoarding that wealth or enjoying it, for using it as a weapon of oppression and injustice or as a tool of beneficent brotherhood, Qoheleth sought to direct them upon the latter course. His experience and observation had taught him that. As a good teacher, therefore, he desired to give to his students an approach to life that would avoid the consequences of greed on the one hand, the dissipation of folly on the other, and would put them on the middle course where they could have the best of wealth and wisdom too. His philosophy of life was earthy, but not one that groveled in the dust. He, having become discontent with practical wisdom, had attempted to fathom the mysteries of life and the world but failed to discover them (7:23-25). At last he turned again to practical wisdom, but not to an empty pragmatism. Rather it was a practical philosophy that had been informed by his reflective approach. At points Qoheleth's advice was quantitatively no higher than that which characterizes the book of Proverbs, but qualitatively it was superior. It was that qualitative difference that he wished to transfer to his students.

The *meaning* of Qoheleth may be grasped in part by viewing three trademarks of his thought: (1) the search for happiness and enduring substance, (2)

7. Eissfeldt, p. 499.
8. See Gordis, *Koheleth—The Man and His World*, pp. 69-74.
9. E.g., George Aaron Barton, *A Critical and Exegetical Commentary on the Book of Ecclesiastes*, p. 44.

divine sovereignty and providence, and (3) the golden mean of human conduct. The book is obviously not itself the search for the meaning of life but rather the conclusions to which that search had led Qoheleth. Yet those conclusions, to be convincing, must be shown to be presupposed by valid experiments, and the author has well informed us of their details.

First, he had sought for the one *activity or principle that would give happiness and the enduring quality to life.* That is, when he set the transience of man's life over against wisdom (1:12-18) and pleasure (2:1-11), neither wisdom nor pleasure tipped the scales in its favor. The transience of human life was enough to deprive man of his happiness, to say nothing at all of his stability. It carried a leaden quality that could overbalance any of the more beneficent features of human existence. Therefore, Qoheleth had reached his skeptical conclusion, "Vanity of vanities! All is vanity!" (1:2; 12:8). This conclusion punctuates the book and lays over it a hovering haze of pessimism and despair. But we may be thankful that those who despair of life have such a cathartic resource in Holy Scripture.

The second trademark of Qoheleth's thought was his deep conviction of *the sovereignty and providence of God.* The life and destiny of man had been predetermined by God, who directs earthly affairs (2:26; 3:14; 7:13-14; 8:16–9:1; 11:5). Primary among His plans for man in the universe was the enjoyment of what He had provided. This undergirding thesis is important to the interpretation of the book. Qoheleth was not only convinced that this conclusion was verified by his personal experience, but that it was of such consequence as to merit theological status. Therefore, growing out of this conviction and supported by the harassing fact of man's fleeting life and the inevitability of death (8:16–9:3), Qoheleth urged the enjoyment of life: "There is nothing better for a man than to eat and drink and tell himself that his labor is good. This also I have seen, that it is from the hand of God" (2:24; also 3:12, 22; 5:18; 8:15; 9:7-9; 11:7-10).

The third trademark of the book is that the only model for life that Qoheleth deemed viable was *the golden mean of conduct.* This entailed avoiding certain excesses in conduct and following a path of moderation. Qoheleth had the capability of the deepest melancholy, but he was too much a patron of life to be overwhelmed by it (7:5-14). Life was a gift of God, and encumbent upon man was the responsibility to utilize it to the fullest measure. To throw it away in frivolous and immoral living was tantamount to ingratitude for the gift and could only result in bitter disappointment (9:18; 10:1-3). The ideal pair of ingredients for the full enjoyment of life were wealth and the opportunity of enjoying it. Whether greed or lack of opportunity prevented one from enjoying riches, the end was the same—it was vanity (6:1-6; 7:11).

Qoheleth manifested the moderate spirit in other perspectives of his philosophy of life. Although eager for enjoyment and pleasure, he was content with the present (7:10). Cognizant of injustice and concerned with its causes, he was nevertheless cautious about extreme measures to correct it (8:1-9; 10:8-11). He was conciliatory (10:12-14) and not given to anger or hasty action (7:8-9).

In religion, this man of mind and means was neither unduly pious nor iconoclastic (7:15-25). Again his motto was moderation. His was not the popular religion, but a fundamental faith in the sovereign God, illuminated by experience. Unlike Job, he had no strong theological tenets to prove or defend. The basic element of his religious faith was the "fear of God" (5:7; 12:13). This disposition did not obligate one to verbose prayers and profuse vows, but only to obedience (5:1-7; also 12:13). Thus Qoheleth's life and philosophy were marked by a moderation in religion as well as in politics and personal conduct. He walked a tight line between despair and arrogance, balanced only by the fear of God. Although experience was important and validating, he was never so confident of its dogmas as the book of Proverbs, even though one must live as best one could with its conclusions. Nor was his faith ever as dynamic as Job's for he was too cautious and moderate for a faith so daring and challenging.

It is too easy to lose patience with Qoheleth and Job because their spiritual perspective, though wide and deep, lacked the dimension of the New Testament revelation of God in Christ. Delitzsch is eloquent on this point:

> The Book of Koheleth is, on the one side, a proof of the power of revealed religion which has grounded faith in God, the One God, the All-wise Creator and Governor of the world, so deeply and firmly in the religious consciousness, that even the most dissonant and confused impressions of the present world are unable to shake it; and, on the other side, it is a proof of the inadequacy of revealed religion in its O.T. form, since the discontent and the grief which the monotony, the confusion, and the misery of this earth occasion, remain thus long without a counterbalance, till the facts of the history of redemption shall have disclosed and unveiled the heavens above the earth.[10]

MATTERS OF ORIGIN

*Authorship*. Even though Solomon's name is not mentioned in the book, based upon the title verse and other allusions to Qoheleth's royal status (1:12; 2:7, 9), Jewish tradition attributed Ecclesiastes to Solomon (Babylonian Talmud, *Megillah* 7a, *Shabbath* 30; Aramaic Targum; Midrash *Ecclesiastes Rabbah*). Further evidence has been alleged in support of this from reference to great wisdom (1:16) and great works (2:4-11) achieved by Qoheleth. Until the time of Luther, Solomonic authorship was generally assumed by Christian scholars. Even though Luther assumed the same in his commentary on Ecclesi-

10. Franz Delitzsch, *Commentary on the Song of Songs and Ecclesiastes*, p. 184.

astes,[11] in *Table Talk* he attributed the book to Jesus Ben Sirach.[12] Actually the strongest supports Solomonic authorship has in its favor are the title verse (1:1) and Jewish tradition. One modern proponent of Solomonic authorship, A. Cohen, contends that the alleged Greek influences were really negligible. To that we can agree. Further, states Cohen, the conditions describing Qoheleth's life were the same as those ascribed to Solomon. Moreover, the language, though akin to Mishnaic Hebrew, cannot conclusively date the book in the postexilic era because there is really insufficient Hebrew literature for comparison.[13]

On the other side of the question, reasons for rejection of Solomonic authorship include, first, that the book does not claim to be written by Solomon. Gordis remarks: "Had it been the author's intention to palm his work off as the work of Solomon, he would not have used the enigmatic name 'Koheleth,' but would have used the name 'Solomon' directly, as happened time without number in the *Pseudepigrapha*, roughly contemporaneous with our book."[14] All other writings of Solomon bear his name (e.g., Proverbs). It is not likely that a person so prominent as this king would have felt any need to choose a pen name. Even if we view the book as a satire on Solomon's reign written by him, we still are left with problems. Although injustice and oppressive politics were evident in Solomon's reign (1 Kings 12:1-4), Qoheleth, if he were Solomon, seemed impotent to do anything about the injustice (e.g., 3:16; 4:1; 5:8). As Driver remarked, "When he [Qoheleth] alludes to kings, he views them from below, as one of the people suffering from their misrule."[15]

Those who favor Solomon's authorship contend that the title verse leaves the impression that Solomon was the speaker. Any position otherwise, they hold, calls the truth of Scripture into question. We must admit, however, that the title verse is enigmatic. Although it appears to allude to Solomon, it leaves an unsolved riddle: Why would Solomon choose a pseudonym under which to write? If toward the end of his life he wished to convey the skeptical conclusions to which life had led him, their impact upon subsequent readers would have been much greater and more convincing had he written under his own name.

The phrase "king in Jerusalem" (1:1) does not occur elsewhere as a designation for Solomon. Usually he is called "king of Israel" (e.g., 2 Kings 23:13), and in Nehemiah 13:26 he is referred to both as "king of Israel" and "king over all Israel." In 1 Kings 11:42 it is said, "Solomon reigned in Jerusalem over all

---

11. Martin Luther, *Luther's Works*, ed. Jaroslav Pelikan, vol. 15. *Notes on Ecclesiastes, Lectures on the Song of Solomon, Treatise on the Last Words of David*, pp. 3-5, passim.
12. Martin Luther, *The Table-Talk of Martin Luther*, p. 13. Luther's statement is: "Ecclesiasticus is no more Solomon's work than the Book of Proverbs. They are both collections made by other people." Although he said "Ecclesiasticus" in company with Proverbs, he must have meant Ecclesiastes.
13. A. Cohen, *The Five Megilloth*, pp. 106-7.
14. Gordis, p. 40.
15. S. R. Driver, *An Introduction to the Literature of the Old Testament*, p. 470.

Israel," but that is the closest parallel to this phrase in the title verse of Ecclesiastes. Yet the phrase "son of David" certainly alludes to Solomon, and this raises the question whether the author intended to pass off the book as Solomon's. As mentioned above, Gordis has answered negatively.

We should distinguish between impersonation as literary form and literary forgery. The latter occurs when the author makes a conscious effort to conceal his own identity and write under the name of an ancient worthy in order to win an immediate hearing and esteem for his work. Impersonation as a literary form, in comparison, has no such motivation, but seeks to recapture a certain spirit represented by a historical person and to speak through his spirit. It provides a particular atmosphere for the message the author wishes to convey, one that could otherwise be provided only by laborious literary exertion. Moreover, much of the effect hoped for stands to be lost in building the necessary atmosphere. However, as in the case at hand, to reach back into the tenth century B.C. and permit the spirit of Solomon to convey the message of Qoheleth is highly effective and needs no preliminary preparation. Qoheleth provided ample clues that he was not, nor did he mean to pose as, Solomon. What he had to say, and the context from which he said it, both qualified for representation by a man of such wealth and opportunity as Solomon. It may be noted that, although my own view is to regard Job as a real person and the dialogue as a substantial record of a real interchange, some scholars have opted for dramatic impersonation. Much can be said for either position. But we would like to recognize the legitimacy of dramatic impersonation as a literary form.

Our Lord Himself seems to have recognized the validity of the form in His parables, for example, the parable of the rich man and Lazarus (Luke 16:19-31). Abraham in that parable represented the essence of the Old Testament faith and spoke in defense of the Law and the Prophets. To have the patriarch Abraham, the father of the faith, speak to the rich man called forth the full context of the covenantal privileges and responsibilities. Moreover, in this instance the form of the parable[16] itself is the clue that impersonation may be anticipated. As in the case of Ecclesiastes, however, the clues are found in the title verse (1:1), the statement "I was king over Israel in Jerusalem" (1:12, KJV, "I was" suggesting that the condition no longer prevailed), and Qoheleth's inability to correct the abuses he had observed (3:16; 4:1; 5:8), to name only three such clues.

To mention the other side of the argument, it is possible to render 1:12 as "I, the preacher, became king over Israel in Jerusalem," or "I, the Preacher, have been king over Israel in Jerusalem" (NASB), thus obviating the difficulty cited above. Yet the apparent inability of the speaker to correct the abuses he

16. The parable was a literary method of teaching a truth in the form of a typical story illustrating the truth taught. As a rule, the persons, places, and events of the parable were general enough to evoke identity in the hearers.

had observed is a more difficult objection to answer. If we assume that Solomon was merely being philosophical or that he was describing elapsed history, then we detract from the force of the book by removing the author from the situation he described. It was his firsthand observation that made the problems he treated so acute.

Generally, one of the strongest reasons against Solomonic authorship is considered to lie in a linguistic analysis of the book. Recent scholars have in general recognized the lateness of the Hebrew of Ecclesiastes, which has many affinities with Mishnaic Hebrew, incorporating Aramaic words and including two Persian loan words (*pardēs*, "park'—2:5; *pitgām*, "decree"—8:11). Delitzsch provides a list of those words that are hapax legomena and those that belong to the later period of the language.[17] So strong were his convictions about this point that he declared, "If the Book of Koheleth were of old Solomonic origin, then there is no history of the Hebrew language."[18]

On the other side of the argument, Gleason Archer disqualifies linguistic considerations as determinative, as does also A. Cohen, already mentioned. Archer proposes that the unparalleled style and language of Ecclesiastes may be explained by recourse to the original style and vocabulary of a distinct genre, which, he explains, tended to dictate the subsequent style and language of later compositions within that genre. Thus, according to this hypothesis, Ecclesiastes belongs to a genre of philosophical discourse developed in North Israel prior to the Solomonic era, and it is our only example of the style and language peculiar to that genre in Hebrew literature.[19] Although this is a bit too speculative to build upon, we may agree with Archer that linguistic analysis is not determinative. Delitzsch ironically touches upon a point too infrequently admitted, that a definitive history of the Hebrew language is still not possible from our present linguistic resources. Linguistic argument as a rule must remain tentative.

If we are not persuaded, however, that the evidence warrants the older view of Solomonic authorship, we find ourselves in company with most recent orthodox Protestant scholars. E. J. Young, for example, makes strong argument against it.[20] In that case, just who the author of Ecclesiastes was is impossible to determine. He was, to be sure, a Jew who was a wisdom teacher (12:9-10) of ample wealth and opportunity.

*Date.* If the work is Solomonic, then it probably dates from the end of his reign (late tenth century B.C.). However, if the evidence for non-Solomonic authorship presented above is accepted, we are dealing in terms of the postexilic era. Hengstenberg thought the evidence of internal corruption in Israel and de-

17. Delitzsch, pp. 190-96.
18. Ibid., p. 190.
19. Gleason L. Archer, Jr., *A Survey of Old Testament Introduction*, pp. 466-67.
20. Young, *An Introduction to the Old Testament*, pp. 347-49.

cay in the imperial power, which he believed to be Persia, pointed to the period between Cyrus and Xerxes (last quarter of the sixth and first quarter of the fifth centuries). Reinforcing this thesis, he cited certain affinities of the book with the prophecy of Malachi, proposing that both books were addressed essentially to the same period.[21] Delitzsch opted for a little later date, the time of Ezra-Nehemiah (last half of the fifth century B.C.),[22] Ginsburg for the later Persian period (c. 350-340 B.C.),[23] and Gordis for c. 250 B.C.[24] We may suggest a *terminus a quo* of the beginning of the Persian period (late sixth century B.C.) and a *terminus ad quem* of the age of Ben Sirach, since he was dependent upon Ecclesiastes (Ben Sirach wrote in about 190 B.C.).[25] The evidence is not sufficient to warrant dogmatism, but the earlier Persian period, such as Hengstenberg proposed, deserves careful consideration.

Two passages have been sometimes understood to contain historical allusions—4:13-14 and 9:14-15. The first mentions a pair of rulers, and attempts have been made to identify them with several historical persons. The second refers to a city that was besieged but saved by a poor, wise man. Efforts to identify this city have been as precarious as the identification of the persons in 4:13-14.[26] Gordis is probably correct in his view that these passages were not meant to be historical but typical.[27]

*Provenance.* Although much attention has been given to the Greek influence upon Ecclesiastes,[28] a geographical location of Palestine (probably Jerusalem) is probable,[29] particularly in view of the author's reference to the sacrificial system and the Temple (5:1-6). Plumptre and others have attempted to find traces of Stoic (3:1-9) and Epicurean (3:18-22; 5:18-20) philosophy in the book.[30] Yet these appear to be more coincidental than real.

The case made by Zimmermann[31] and Ginsberg[32] for an Aramaic original has not generally found wide support. However, it can be confidently concluded that the author was well acquainted with Aramaic, for his vocabulary and syntax

21. Ernest W. Hengstenberg, *A Commentary on Ecclesiastes with Treatise on the Song of Solomon, Job, Isaiah, Sacrifices, etc.*, pp. 10-15.
22. Delitzsch, p. 197.
23. Ginsburg, p. 255.
24. Gordis, pp. 63, 67.
25. See Barton, pp. 53-56, for Ben Sirach's dependence upon Ecclesiastes. Also see the later section in this chapter, "Qumran Fragments of Ecclesiastes," p. 205, for Muilenburg's opinion on date based upon the Qumran fragments.
26. Gordis, pp. 65-66, gives some of these identifications.
27. Ibid., p. 66.
28. See Barton, pp. 32-43; E. H. Plumptre, *Ecclesiastes; or, the Preacher*, pp. 38-50. Barton largely rejects Greek influence in both language and thought, whereas Plumptre makes a case in favor of it.
29. Gordis, p. 76.
30. Plumptre, p. 55.
31. Frank Zimmermann, *The Inner World of Qoheleth*, pp. 98-122.
32. H. L. Ginsberg, *Studies in Koheleth*, pp. 16-39.

show definite signs of Aramaic influence.[33] Yet the language of the original work seems to have been Hebrew.

CANONICITY

That Ecclesiastes was a long time achieving canonical status generally may be deduced from the attitude of two ancient apocryphal books toward it and from the controversy between the School of Shammai and the School of Hillel over its sacred status. Wright[34] and other scholars have recognized the use Ben Sirach (c. 190 B.C.) made of the book, as if it were canonical.[35] Yet another apocryphal book, the Wisdom of Solomon (c. first century B.C.), takes strong exception to Ecclesiastes, as Wright and others have demonstrated.[36] The Mishnah informs us of the controversy that the Schools of Shammai and Hillel conducted over the book. In the tractate *Eduyoth* (5:3), Shammai's rejection and Hillel's acceptance were pointed out as a noteworthy exception to Shammai's generally conservative stance on Scripture and the liberal stance of Hillel. The controversy was recognized also by Rabbi Judah in the tractate *Yadaim* (3:5). Eventually the liberal School of Hillel won out, and Ecclesiastes was accepted as part of the canon by the Council of Jamnia (c. A.D. 90).

The New Testament is not much help on the subject of canonicity, because Ecclesiastes is not quoted directly, although Plumptre insisted that traces may be detected in Romans 8:20 and James 4:14.[37]

The early church bore witness to its acceptance, however. Hermas quoted Ecclesiastes 12:13.[38] Justin Martyr alluded to 12:7,[39] and Clement of Alexandria quoted Ecclesiastes 1:16-18 and 7:13 by name.[40] Tertullian quoted Ecclesiastes 3:1 three times.[41] Origen used several quotations from the book. Therefore, though some disagreement over its canonicity existed in Jewish circles, the triumph of the School of Hillel, favorable to Ecclesiastes, was probably the development, at least in part, that paved the way for its relatively wide use in early Christian circles.

33. Gordis, pp. 59-62; also p. 363, n. 7, for Aramaic words.
34. C. H. H. Wright, *The Book of Koheleth*, pp. 41-46.
35. Wright lists some of the aphorisms of Ben Sirach (BS) that are also found in Ecclesiastes (E): BS 12:13/E 10:11; BS 13:25/E 8:1; BS 19:16/E 7:20-22; BS 22:6-7/E 3:7; BS 21:25-26/E 10:2-3; BS 27:26/E 10:8; BS 7:14/E 5:2; BS 21:12/E 1:18; BS 14:18/E 1:4; BS 16:30/E 3:20; BS 13:22-23, and 10:23/E 9:14-16.
36. Ibid., pp. 55-76.
37. Plumptre, p. 88.
38. Similitude VII (2d century)
39. *Dialogue with Trypho* 6 (2d century).
40. *Stromata* 1:13 (all 2d and early 3d centuries).
41. *Against Marcion* 5:4; *On Monogamy* 3; *On the Veiling of Virgins* 1 (late 2d and early 3d centuries).

## HERMENEUTICAL CONSIDERATIONS ON ECCLESIASTES

### COGNATE WISDOM LITERATURE

One's approach to Ecclesiastes, as with other wisdom literature, should be characterized by an awareness of the broader context in which Hebrew wisdom came into being and developed.[42] Early Egyptian wisdom literature provides examples of instructions, the literary form in which the older and experienced person instructed the younger. One such document is *The Instruction of Amen-em-het,* in which the father king advises his son, who is to succeed him.[43] From Babylonia come examples of the same spirit reflected in Ecclesiastes. We mention two. The first is called *A Pessimistic Dialogue Between Master and Servant,*[44] in which the master enjoined the servant to obedience (cf. Eccles. 8:2-5). Moreover, both the cautious attitude toward women and the need to enjoy them (cf. Par. VIII and Eccles. 7:26-28 and 9:9) are expressed, as well as an attitude of moderation in religion (cf. Par. IX and Eccles. 5:1-6). The second document, *A Dialogue About Human Misery,*[45] has been called the "Babylonian Ecclesiastes." It seems to have been spoken by a wise slave who complained about injustice and human misery (cf. Eccles. 3:16; 4:1; 5:13). Yet based upon the translated document, the slave's religious fervency seems to have exceeded Qoheleth's moderate position.

Although it is helpful to know that Hebrew wisdom was not an isolated phenomenon, it is also appropriate to recognize that we have no documents from Egypt or Mesopotamia that represent such an advanced stage of thought as do Qoheleth and Job.

### LITERAL INTERPRETIVE APPROACH

There is no reason to interpret Ecclesiastes other than literally. Some efforts have been made to allegorize it; the commentary of Jerome supplied evidence as early as the fourth century. Jerome related that the Jew interpreted 3:2-8 as referring to their past and future.[46] However, any effort to allegorize appears forced.

### IMPLICATIONS VERSUS IMPERATIVES

Another hermeneutical matter commends itself to us. Since Ecclesiastes has a place among the inspired Scriptures, should we view Qoheleth's thesis as a di-

---

42. The reader will find a lengthy survey (although Ginsburg calls it a "sketch") of exegesis in Ginsburg, pp. 27-99 (Jewish) and pp. 99-243 (Christian), with a brief update by Sheldon H. Blank (pp. xv-xxv, xxix-xxxv), which includes comments on dating and origin.
43. James B. Pritchard, ed., ANET, pp. 418-19. *Amen-em-het* probably dates between 1500 and 1100 B.C.
44. Ibid., pp. 437-38.
45. Ibid., pp. 438-40. The document is probably from the fourteenth or fifteenth century B.C.
46. Ginsburg, pp. 34-35.

vine imperative? The answer to that question may be found in the nature of wisdom literature itself. The formula for the divine word ("thus says the Lord") is infrequently found in the wisdom books. The divine imperative in wisdom literature is generally limited to the essential "Fear God," sometimes in imperative and sometimes in declarative form (Job 28:28; Prov. 1:7; 9:10; 15:33; Eccles. 3:14; 12:13). Although that presupposes the divine imperatives of the Law and the Prophets, wisdom literature itself may be viewed as revealed religion that has been lived in. It draws out the practical implications of the fear of God and draws attention to some time-tested ways of achieving that goal. Therefore, the divine imperative of Ecclesiastes is the fundamental "Fear God and keep His commandments" (12:13).

Moreover, even if some of us wanted to espouse Qoheleth's thesis, we could not, because we lack either or both of the necessary ingredients—wealth and the opportunity to enjoy it. Yet, if we need not embrace his thesis, we may nevertheless adopt his attitude. It was one that called for the enjoyment of the present, not in dissipation and foolish living, but in accepting today and its pleasures as gifts from the Lord's hand. Our Lord Himself commended to us the same attitude: "Therefore do not be anxious for tomorrow; for tomorrow will take care for itself. Each day has enough trouble of its own" (Matt. 6:34).

FUNDAMENTAL MEDIATING PREMISE

Finally, as we have already observed, Qoheleth shared the fear of God as a common element with wisdom literature, and this fundamental premise became the mediating element in his philosophy. It was the momentum that swung the pendulum to the center again, and that is where he wanted to live. He had the capacity for entertaining the extremities of human experience, moving from pleasure to the desire for nonexistence (4:2-3). We must not insist that he was a hedonist on the one hand or a nihilist on the other. He could see the advantages of both, but he had opted for a philosophy somewhere in the middle, a philosophy close enough to both so that he could never forget their disadvantages, a philosophy confirming and commending his golden mean.

Qoheleth's thought was not the kind that conquers the world, nor was it the kind that is likely to lose it. It would hardly transform society—it was too moderate for that. Yet it was realistic enough to realize when radical transformation would lead only to annihilation. When the world could not be conquered, Qoheleth would recognize that fact and surrender to the pleasures that could be derived from the status quo. He represented a realism that needs at some point to take hold of all of us lest we be broken in mind and exiled in spirit before we can fulfill our destiny. It is not, of course, a realism that should necessarily become the sum of our philosophy of life, but only one part of the whole. A world populated with Qoheleths would be a tragic place indeed so long as sin and suffering occupy it too. He lacked a sense of righteous indignation. But a world without its Qoheleths would ultimately be reduced to ashes in the fires of hatred, greed, and radical excess, or it would lie down and die of despair.

Qoheleth offers a place for the believer to rest a while and soothe his heart. This place is not a permanent home for him but can certainly provide his spirit with a lavish resort to recoup and rethink. While he is there, he can make certain mid-course corrections, learn the advantage of the moderate attitude, recapture the importance of the present moment, and regain his perspective on the transience of human life. And then he can be on his way to fulfill his divinely appointed destiny. God forbid that the spirit of Qoheleth should conquer the world! But, on the other hand, God forbid that it should die!

### EXPOSITORY ANALYSIS OF ECCLESIASTES

TITLE (1:1)

We have above taken the position that the title contains the clues that Qoheleth was not Solomon and that he sought to inform us of that by means of the enigmatic name that he chose and the unusual phrase "king in Jerusalem."[47] Nevertheless he assumed the personality of Solomon as a literary device to convey his ideas. Gordis remarks:

> The book of Koheleth is not a pseudepigraph, which the author seeks to attribute to Solomon, like "the Wisdom of Solomon." He impersonates Solomon only in the opening section because he wishes to prove that both wisdom and pleasure are worthless as goals in life (1:16-18; 2:1-12), and Solomon had the reputation of possessing both in superlative degree.[48]

The name *Qôheleth* occurs seven times in the book (1:1, 2, 12; 7:27; 12:8, 9, 10) and is used as a masculine noun except in 7:27, where the feminine verb form is used with it. Once (12:8) the article is prefixed. The usual translation of the word is "preacher" or "assembler."[49] In view of the teaching role of the speaker in the book, either meaning seems appropriate, for he has a thesis to proclaim to his students whom he has assembled for instruction.

THESIS AND PROLOGUE (1:2-11)

The message of the vanity of all earthly things makes a greater impact because it is preached through Solomon *redivivus*, a man who had both the resources and opportunity to enjoy everything life could offer. The word "vanity"

47. See earlier section in this chapter, "Authorship," pp. 183-86.
48. Gordis, p. 194.
49. See earlier section in this chapter, "Title," p. 179.

(*hevel*, "that which is unsubstantial") suggests that which does not endure (from "to breathe"). Although the word occurs many times in the book, and this exclamation occurs again in 12:8, it is not the single theme of Ecclesiastes. The idea is that both individuals and their experiences are fleeting and transient. The reason the writer declared everything useless was that nothing he did or gained provided him with enduring substance and happiness.

Hengstenberg has rightly remarked that there is no "*subjective* bitterness" in these words, for Qoheleth had both recognized and accepted as a fact the futility of earthly things. He further observed: "Negative wisdom is the condition and groundwork of positive. We cannot really see in God the highest good unless we have first of all discerned the vanity of that pretended good which is laid before us by the world."[50]

The word for "advantage" (*yitrôn*) means that which is left over, remainder, difference, thus benefit. It occurs only in this book of the Bible (2:11, 13; 3:9; 5:8, 15; 7:12; 10:10, 11), but is found frequently in later Hebrew writings. The evidence for the author's declaration came from a cyclical process in nature that he had observed—one generation displaced another; the sun rose and set and then repeated its course again; the wind followed a regular pattern; the waters flowed into the sea, never filling it, and from there they flowed again. Everything was in flux. If the beholder perceived something as new, it was only because he had not observed the phenomenon before (vv. 10-11).

### THE FIRST TEST (1:12-18)

Then the author proceeded to offer further proof of his thesis that all human efforts to satisfy the longing of man for the immortal were in vain. In a style characteristic of him, he offered his conclusions first (vv. 14-15) and then related how he set about arriving at them (vv. 16-17), finally summarizing his conclusions briefly (v. 18). He followed two lines of proof: wisdom (1:12-18) and pleasure (2:1-26).

He impersonated Solomon, using the literary name by which he introduced himself in 1:1, but not with the intention of misrepresenting the authorship of the book. The King James Version's "I the Preacher *was* king over Israel in Jerusalem" (italics added), or the *New American Standard Bible's* "I . . . *have been*" (italics added), may (but does not necessarily) imply that Solomon was no longer king at the time of speaking.[51] Our historical records do not permit such an opinion because this monarch was king until his death. The author stepped into the person of Solomon in chapters 1 and 2 and spoke through him to illustrate his thesis. But he was not deceitful about this, because he nowhere claimed to be Solomon. Rather, by the use of the literary name Qoheleth ("the Preacher"), he

---

50. Hengstenberg, p. 47.
51. See Archer, p. 469, for a discussion of this verse.

left no false impression. It was mere literary convention. Delitzsch says, "It is Solomon, resuscitated by the author of the book, who here looks back on his life as king."[52] The implication that Qoheleth had been king but was not when he spoke these words led the Aramaic Targum to resort to an old midrash that speculated that Solomon was deposed as king and wandered around the country for a time before he was restored.[53]

The assumption of the person of Solomon freed the writer of certain restraints, for a king could afford any luxury in his search for wisdom and meaning in life. Further, Solomon was the ancient exemplar of wisdom. The author sought to prove his thesis wrong but disappointingly proved it right. The mode of investigation was wisdom ("by wisdom," v. 13), and his conclusion was that the mode only intensifies the grief and pain that initiated the search in the first place (v. 18).

THE SECOND TEST (2:1-11)

Qoheleth then conducted in the person of Solomon a second experiment to test his thesis, that is, to prove that man's life was not all devoid of happiness and meaning. He turned to pleasure.

The passage (2:1-11) begins and ends with his conclusion, as is the author's manner (2:1-2, 11). The description of the experiment is found in verses 3-10.

Among the measures tried was the stimulation of wine. It was not a self-abandonment to intoxication but the intake of sufficient quantities to provide the necessary stimulus for pleasure without the loss of the rational faculties (v. 3). The second measure consisted of the enlargment of his real and personal possessions, including proliferation of slaves, entertainers, and concubines. Here was the man who had anything he wanted—"And all that my eyes desired I did not refuse them. I did not withhold my heart from any pleasure" (v. 10). Yet his conclusion was depressively negative: "behold, all is vanity and striving after wind," the same resolution he had reached in his first pursuit after wisdom and knowledge of the world (1:14, 17). Enlarging this second conclusion somewhat, the author added, "And there was no profit under the sun" (v. 11; cf. 1:3). That is, there was nothing that, when added to offset the deficits of human experience, brought about a credit balance. The debits always outweighed the credits.

That the author had impersonated Solomon may be observed in the historical accounts. Solomon's servants imported 420 talents of gold from Ophir (1 Kings 9:28), and the Queen of Sheba gave him 120 talents of gold. We are informed that in one year this monarch amassed 666 talents of gold in addition to the tribute paid by his conquered states (1 Kings 10:14-15). So profuse was sil-

52. Delitzsch, p. 226.
53. See Ginsburg's translation of the Targum, *The Song of Songs and Coheleth*, appendix 1, pp. 502-19.

ver during Solomon's reign that the author of Kings declared it was as common as stones in Jerusalem (1 Kings 10:27). The experience of the queen of Sheba reveals a bit of the emotion one might have sensed upon seeing Solomon's wealth:

> When the queen of Sheba perceived all the wisdom of Solomon, the house that he had built, the food of his table, the seating of his servants, the attendance of his waiters and their attire, his cupbearers, and his stairway by which he went up to the house of the Lord, there was no more spirit in her (1 Kings 10:4-5).

Solomon's building projects occupied much of his servant labor and absorbed much of his pecuniary possessions (1 Kings 7:1-8; 9:17-19).

In the first two chapters Qoheleth showed that both wisdom and pleasure were valueless in securing happiness (1:13-18; 2:1-11).

### WISDOM AND FOLLY COMPARED (2:12-17)

The author, through the experience of Solomon, next examined the advantage of wisdom over folly as a way of life. The comparison is introduced in verse 12. His earlier rejection of wisdom (1:12-18) was a recognition that it cannot achieve the goal of securing life and making it worth living. His investigation brought him to two conclusions: (1) wisdom has an advantage *(yitron*—this word occurs in Eccles. 1:3; 2:11, 13; 3:9; 5:9, 16; 7:12; 10:10-11) in that it increases man's understanding, yet (2) by that very truth it intensifies the depression that results from the fact that the world endures but death snaps the silver cord of life. The advantage endemic to wisdom, while it may suffice for life, is ultimately neutralized by death, the common fate of the wise and fool alike (vv. 14b-16). Qoheleth's contemplation threw him into a state of depression and led him to the same conclusion that he had reached previously, "everything is futility and striving after wind" (v. 17; cf. 1:14, 17; 2:11).

### THE ONLY VIABLE ALTERNATIVE (2:18-26)

In a depressive state of mind, Qoheleth deplored all his work, the results of which sometimes could not even be bequeathed to one's children but must be left to strangers who may be wise or foolish (vv. 18-19). After concluding that neither wisdom (1:12–2:11) nor pleasure (2:12-23) could satisfy man's yearning for the enduring, Qoheleth resolved that the existential enjoyment of the present was the only viable alternative (v. 24a). But even that was not something man could have at will—it was the gift of God (vv. 24b-26). Yet the truth must be acknowledged that even this sole alternative "too is vanity and striving after wind" (v. 26c). Nothing can assuage the deep yearning in the soul of man for that which endures. Gordis observes what this final declaration reveals: "This goal of pleasure represents for Koheleth resignation to the inevitable, rather than the cheerful contentment of a pious believer who sees God's will in his destiny."[54]

### THE TIMES AND MEANING OF LIFE (3:1-15)

Although one might find in this catalog reason to understand that man's deeds all have their appropriate time, that is not the purpose the author intended. Rather, based upon the interpretative section (vv. 9-15), he sought to say that *God* has appointed an appropriate time for everything. The endless cycle of human experience is not accidental or even dependent upon humankind. On the contrary, it is planned and executed by God Himself (v. 11). Furthermore, Qoheleth was confident that God's work and plan are all-sufficient (v. 14), and that they are so designed as to create in man a sense of awe and reverence: "for God has so worked that men should fear Him" (v. 14).

Thus, all things being immutably fixed by God, and human effort being fruitless to change them (v. 9), Qoheleth found in these facts two lessons, both introduced by "I know" (vv. 12, 14): (1) man's lot is to enjoy what God has ordered for him (v. 12; also 2:24 and 3:22), and (2) God's work is enduring and is all-sufficient (v. 14). Man can neither add to it nor take from it.

In general the pairs in verses 2-8 are opposites or near opposites. One suggests the other, if not contradicts it.

"He has also set eternity in their heart" (3:11)—some commentators argue that the word `ōlām (NASB "eternity") means "world."[55] Ginsburg argues that the word never means "world" in the Old Testament, nor does it ever denote "worldly affairs," "worldly pleasures," or "worldly wisdom," as some have held. In this book it is used of "time past" or "present, unmeasured time, eternity" (1:4; 2:16; 3:14; 9:6; 12:5). Further, it is here used in antithesis to `ēth ("time"). Thus he opts for "eternity."[56] Delitzsch has concluded:

> The author means to say that God has not only assigned to each individually his appointed place in history, thereby bringing to the consciousness of man the fact of his being conditioned, but that He has also established in man an impulse leading him beyond that which is temporal toward the eternal: it lies in his nature not to be contented with the temporal, but to break through the limits which it draws around him to escape from the bondage and the disquietude within which he is held, and amid the ceaseless changes of time to console himself by directing his thoughts to eternity.[57]

54. Gordis, p. 218.
55. E.g., Gordis, pp. 221-22.
56. Ginsburg, pp. 310-11.
57. Delitzsch, p. 261.

INJUSTICE (3:16–4:3)

Qoheleth then considered one of the obstacles that frustrates human striving toward happiness—injustice. First he entertained the solution that there will be a judgment when both the righteous and the wicked will have their day in court (v. 17). Yet he did not seem fully satisfied by that answer, for he turned immediately to consider the difference between man and beast, which is no more than man's ability to recognize that he is like the beasts. The sentence of death lay upon both human and animal life. Both man and beast were caught in that endless cycle of nature, from dust to flesh and from flesh to dust (v. 20).

Qoheleth, regardless of his despair, would not dogmatize on the matter of man's future life as compared to that of the beasts. Rather he left the question open, neither affirming nor denying. In the absence of the data to do either, however, the only formula he could offer with any degree of confidence was the enjoyment of life in the present (v. 22; also 2:24 and 3:12).

Continuing to relate his firsthand observations on human life, the author considered the inequities that had been perpetrated by those who had power. The victims of their oppression had no one to comfort them (4:1). In view of the magnitude of injustice in the world, he expressed the conviction that the dead and those yet unborn were better off than the living (4:2-3).

THE FUTILITY OF HUMAN EFFORT (4:4-16)

Qoheleth took up the alleged advantages of hard work. First, contrary to popular opinion, hard work was basically motivated by the spirit of rivalry (v. 4). Whereupon, the author likely quotes a popular proverb that encouraged hard work: "The fool folds his hands and consumes his own flesh" (v. 5), which probably carries the sense that he wastes away because he does not work and provide his own food (cf. Prov. 6:10-11; 19:15; 21:25; 24:33). The following verse likely was Qoheleth's own remonstrance to this attitude, that is, that rest was far better than work (v. 6).

We may observe that neither of these proverbs is introduced by a formula that would alert us to a direct quotation, but this is not unusual in Qoheleth or in many other books of the Old Testament.[58]

The second alleged advantage of hard work was introduced by the typical miser who had no family connections or responsibilities. Here in verse 8 is an illustration of a quotation without an introductory formula: "*and he never asked,* 'And for whom am I laboring and depriving myself of pleasure?' " The italicized words are not found in the Hebrew text but are offered by the translators for clarity. What passed off as sheer industry belied a selfish and noncommunicative attitude, just as Qoheleth had seen the deeper spirit of neighbor rivalry in

58. See Gordis, pp. 95-108, for Qoheleth's use of quotations.

work and skill (v. 4). To negate this idea, he offered four advantages of companionship: (1) much more could be accomplished by two than by one alone (v. 9), (2) if one fell, his companion would pull him up (v. 10), (3) in the cold Eastern night two warmed each other when they slept (v. 11), and (4) two or three could not easily be overpowered by robbers or marauders (v. 12).

The third reason that hard work was not to be preferred was that its achievements were too ephemeral. The illustration was that of an old foolish king whose fame, achieved as the result of arduous labor, was displaced by a young, inexperienced monarch. Yet even the latter's fame was soon forgotten by the numberless people who came after him (vv. 13-16).

### ADVICE ON RELIGIOUS MATTERS (5:1-7)

Qoheleth laid down three rules regulating religious practices. First he enjoined an attitude of obedience[59] as far more advantageous than sacrificial ritual (5:1). The second rule related to prayer. His advice was that few words were far better before God and were more reverent than verbosity (5:2-3). Ginsburg remarks: "*Fewness of words*, in the presence of our superiors, indicates a due reverence for their elevated position, and a modest acknowledgment of our inferiority."[60] The third rule concerned making vows. After having spoken of two matters related to the Temple, Qoheleth addressed himself to one's conduct outside it. Vows that bound one to a certain task or way of conduct were frequently made (Lev. 27:3-13; Deut. 23:21-23). They were not required but were purely voluntary. Thus to volunteer a vow and not fulfill it was doubly offensive.

The final injunction was the underlying principle of his religion and wisdom in general—"fear God" (v. 7). This was far more than an emotional disposition. The fear of God included the conduct of worship and ethical deportment.

### THE OPPRESSIVE POLITICAL SYSTEM (5:8-9)

Delitzsch observes that the conjunctive wisdom principle of fearing God and the king (Prov. 24:21) is evidenced here in the thought of Qoheleth.[61] The essence of verse 8 is to obviate undue anxiety over an oppressive system of government. When oppression and injustice are dispensed on the popular level of the system, the ascending order of officials and supervisors will, it is hoped, be self-corrective.

Verse 9 is difficult and has been interpreted variously. Hengstenberg understood the "king" to be God, saying the point of verses 8-9 was to direct attention away from the tyrannical government of the time to "the heavenly King,

59. Ginsburg, p. 335. Gordis, p. 237, prefers "to understand" for *lišmo'a*.
60. Ginsburg, p. 336. See similar thoughts in the Apocrypha: Ecclus. 7:14; 32:9.
61. Delitzsch, p. 291.

who in his own appointed time will bring everything again into order."[62] The idea seems to be, however, that even the top official, the king, was ultimately dependent upon the ground level of the system, which was agriculture. The Targum so understood it: "And the great advantage of cultivating the land is above all, for when the subjects of a country revolt, and the king flies from them into the country, if he has no more to eat, this very king becomes subject to a labourer in the field."[63]

### LIFE AND WEALTH (5:10–6:9)

Qoheleth countered the false premise that life without wealth was vanity with his premise that wealth without enjoyment was futile. In fact, contended Qoheleth, the acquisition of wealth was subject to the tyrannical law of diminishing returns—the more one got, the less he was satisfied (5:10). Moreover, the proliferation of pecuniary resources proportionately increased those who consumed them (v. 11). The false premise underlay the typical illustration given in verses 13-15, that of the person who hoarded wealth for its own sake. The principle stated in verse 15 was reminiscent of Job 1:21. Having exposed this false premise, Qoheleth formulated his own premise, that wealth without enjoyment was vanity (v. 18; also 2:24; 3:12, 22). The theological implications of wealth undergirded the premise: Wealth is God's gift (v. 19; also 2:24-26).

Introducing again a typical example by a formula similar to that of 5:13, Qoheleth addressed himself to the case of a man to whom God had given wealth and honor but had not permitted him to enjoy it (6:1-6). Nothing was said of this man's intended utilization of his resources, but whether wealth was compounded with the element of greed (as in 5:10-15) or with lack of opportunity to enjoy it, the end was the same—it was vanity.

Therefore, he had demonstrated that wealth had no inherent goodness or satisfaction. It was merely a means to an end, and only the end brought human contentment. To make his point more pungent, he declared the stillborn child better off than the frustrated plutocrat (vv. 3b-5). For Qoheleth, life without enjoyment was worse than never existing at all. It might be argued, however, that length of life can compensate for the lack of enjoyment. To this idea Qoheleth offered his conviction that the length of life was not self-validating, nor could it compensate for the absence of pleasure. Only the quality of life validated human existence (v. 6).

### MAN'S ILL-FATED LOT (6:10-12)

If there was a better explanation why riches fail to secure the happiness that man desires and needs, it was found in the fact that God had immutably fixed the affairs of human life so that the most attractive things of the physical world (i.e., wealth) had no inherent power to change them. Again underlying Qoheleth's philosophy of life was his undergirding view of divine sovereignty.

## MISCELLANEOUS PROVERBS: FIRST GROUP (7:1-14)

The wisdom teachers did not confine themselves to one didactic method. The reflective teacher sometimes engaged the conventional form of the proverb to teach his students. Imbedded in the reflective Job and the reflective portions of Qoheleth are proverbs of the type popularized in the book of Proverbs (cf. Prov. 10:1–22:16). Therefore, we should not be surprised to find this pericope, which is composed of conventional proverbs. Although some scholars have concluded that these verses represent a later addition to the book, based upon their conventional style and content (vv. 3-5, 7-8), the themes contained here are both conventional and unconventional. Qoheleth's theme of the inevitability of death (v. 2b; cf. 4:2), the futility of human effort (v. 6), the cyclical pattern of history (v. 10; cf. 1:9-10; 6:10a), all mark the section as Qoheleth's.

The core of this pericope is a series of seven sayings each beginning with "good" (vv. 1, 2, 3, 5, 8 [two], 11). Structurally, synonymous (vv. 1, 7, 8) and antithetic parallelism (v. 4), the use of contrasts (vv. 2, 3, 5), and the disjunctive relation between the proverbs may be identified.[64] In terms of content, verses 1-4 deduce lessons from death for the living, whereas verses 5-14 present lessons from life for the living.

*Lessons from death (7:1-4).* Since wealth could not achieve happiness, a good name was to be preferred above ointment, which was highly prized for prevention of body odors (v. 1; cf. Prov. 22:1). Qoheleth had begun this series of proverbs with reference to birth and death, just as he had begun the catalog of seasons (3:2). The preference of the house of mourning over the house of feasting (v. 2) is to be seen in the context of Qoheleth's thought that we need to be reminded of the transitoriness of life. In the same vein he commended the sad face of the suffering over empty frivolity because behind that face is the contemplative mind (v. 3). This was not contradictory to his thought that pleasure was the preferred manner of life (cf. 2:24). Rather, he seemed to speak of frivolity that was incognizant of the transience of life. Thus verse 4 amplifies the thought of verse 3.

*Lessons from life (7:5-14).* Despite Qoheleth's melancholy propensity, he never permitted the thought of life's transitoriness to cancel out the prudence of learning how life should best be lived. So he enjoined his pupils to listen to the wise, even though their words took the form of reproof, rather than to the frivolity of fools (v. 5). Expanding this injunction in verse 6, the author compared the frivolity of the fool to the crackling of thorns in a fire. They burned furiously but

---

64. See previous discussion, "Poetic Structure," in chap. 5, *Proverbs*, pp. 159-61.

quickly and did not cook the food in the pot. Verses 7 and 8 constitute a further expansion of the idea of verse 5*a*, for the wise person who did not retain proper judgment would be overcome by the perverted attraction of a bribe (cf. Ex. 23:8; Deut. 16:19). Further, the reproof of the wise, though perhaps initially hurtful, would prove to be beneficial when the matter was summed up and could be clearly evaluated. Thus the end was to be preferred to the beginning, and the only proper disposition in the process was patience rather than conceit.

The conclusion of verse 8 is expanded in verse 9 by Qoheleth's counsel to restrain the "uncontrolled bad temper."[65] Although verse 8 in one sense concludes the matter raised in verse 5, it introduces another, that of the patient spirit, which, Qoheleth contended, will manifest itself in contentment with the present (v. 10). Impatience with the present may express itself in the form of glorifying the past.

One of Qoheleth's trademarks was his assertion that wisdom and wealth form the perfect pair to produce the greatest pleasure and happiness in life (v. 11). Yet in an enhancing thought, he asserted that wisdom really had the edge of advantage over wealth (v. 12), for it "preserves the lives of its possessors."

To conclude this pericope, the author reiterated the theme of 3:14, that God's plan is immutable, so man must submit to His ways and wisdom.

TEMPERATE LIVING (7:15-25)

First Qoheleth made the observation that the conclusions of popular theology were not always validated by experience. That is, the righteous sometimes died prematurely whereas the wicked sometimes lived to old age (v. 15). From this observation he deduced the idea that one should not, therefore, give oneself to fanaticism in religion or to sinful indulgence (vv. 16-18). What he could recommend, however, was achieving the golden mean of the good life without resorting to either extreme. Showy piety may isolate others, whereas sinful indulgence may end in premature death.

Verse 19 may have been a commonly accepted proverb (cf. Prov. 21:22; 24:5), which Qoheleth countered with his own idea in verse 20. Having recognized that there is no such thing as the perfectly righteous person, he proceeded to point out that the recognition of man's weakness and failure militates against self-righteousness and hypocrisy (vv. 21-22; cf. Gal. 6:1).

Qoheleth was never truly satisfied with the benefits of practical wisdom, so he sought to fathom the mysteries of God's providence and discover the hidden meaning of life, but, like Job (Job 28), he failed. Thus he resorted to the benefits of practical wisdom again (v. 25).

65. Gordis, p. 262.

QOHELETH ON WOMEN (7:26-29)

Qoheleth's distrust of women, as Gordis observes, revealed their great attraction for him.[66] The conduct of men since Adam (Gen. 3:6, 12) in trying to exonerate themselves of guilt by transferring the culpability to woman is neither nobel nor endorsed by Scripture. It is indicative of the weakness of the male of the species rather than his innocence.

However disparaging may have been Qoheleth's opinion of woman, he concluded in verse 29 that both sexes ("men" is the generic term, "mankind") were created upright by God, but they have diverted their course from the way of the Creator.

OBEDIENCE TO KINGS (8:1-9)

There is no question that Qoheleth spoke to a class of pupils from the upper echelons of society. The emphasis upon wealth and the necessity of wisdom as its complement is evidence of this. Here also he considered a matter that would be most beneficial to the upper-class youth who might have access to the royal court. Whereupon this wisdom teacher instructed his students to render obedience to the king, particularly since they took an oath to that effect at his coronation (v. 2). Further, another reason for rendering loyal obedience to the monarch was that, even though he meted out injustice, there was a day of retribution for him (vv. 6-8). Thus patient endurance on the part of the king's subjects had its eventual vindication.

THE FUTILITY AND FATE OF ALL (8:10-9:3)

*The failure of retributive justice (8:10-15).* Although having affirmed his belief in an appointed time of retribution (8:5-8), Qoheleth could not ignore the fact that the wicked were sometimes buried and eulogized (the uncertainty of the text and the meaning of v. 10 are reflected in the commentaries). When others saw that retributive justice was not forthcoming, they too engaged in wickedness (v. 11). Yet, despite observations to the contrary—that evil was sometimes rewarded and righteousness sometimes punished—Qoheleth could not let go of the belief that righteousness had its special virtue and evil its particular retribution (vv. 12-13), even though the optical evidence may have contradicted the theoretical principle (v. 14). In the absence, however, of any better alternative to counterbalance this state of injustice in the moral government of the world, the teacher again urged his philosophy of the enjoyment of life (cf. 2:24; 3:12, 22; 5:18).

*The common fate for all (8:16-9:3).* Now Qoheleth informed his students why he had reached his philosophical position stated in 8:15. His commitment to

66. Gordis, p. 262.

discover the mysterious workings of divine providence, that is, why the moral fabric of the world so frequently broke down, proved to be futile (vv. 16-17). Man was really left to the mercy of God, not knowing whether things would go well or ill with him (9:1). But, strangely, he was left with one certainty, whether he be righteous or wicked, that death awaited him (vv. 2-3). Qoheleth had stressed this theme earlier (2:14-16; 3:18-21; 7:15; 8:8), and we have seen how it helped to shape his philosophy of life, that all should enjoy the pleasure of the present moment.

### THE CHIEF DUTY OF MAN (9:4-12)

Moving from his theme of the common fate for all men, Qoheleth returned to another major theme, that as long as man lives, he should derive all the happiness from life that he can. The climax of this pericope is verse 7, where this theme is expressed. To balance out the disparaging view of woman found earlier (7:26-28), the injunction to pleasure includes the enjoyment of the woman of one's love (v. 9). The white clothes and oil of verse 8 suggest times of festivities.

### WISDOM OBSCURED BY FOLLY (9:13–10:1)

"Also this I came to see" introduces a new section. Some have tried to identify the city under enemy siege, but Qoheleth was probably inventing a typical story to show just how temporary are the results of wisdom without concomitant wealth or power. The poor man who saved the city by his wise counsel was forgotten. Thus came the conviction set forth in 9:1, that even the deeds of wise men were in the hand of God and subject to His overpowering providence. Qoheleth closed this pericope with two proverbs that illustrate his point that folly can destroy much wisdom (9:18b; 10:1).

### MISCELLANEOUS PROVERBS: SECOND GROUP (10:2–11:6)

Even though wisdom is ignored and its benefits canceled by folly, Qoheleth still believed that it had an advantage over folly (10:2); both showed themselves in the common features of life (10:3).

In 10:4 the author put forth a principle that submission to the tyrannical ruler would prevent his committing still greater atrocities.

Qoheleth had seen many an evil despot who elevated the fool and deposed wise men (10:5-7). Yet he recognized that a vigorous attempt to dislodge the despot may endanger one's own life, just as the hunter who falls unwarily into the pit he has dug for the wild animal, or the person who is victimized by the vipers whose nest he tried to destroy in the wall of a house (10:8). The illustration continues in verse 9 to include those craftsmen who start out to do a good thing but are injured in the process. Verse 10a has been variously rendered, but the sense seems to be that to undertake a task unprepared will require the exertion of too much strength, thus illustrating further the wise counsel of verse 4.[67] Verse 11 contains the final proverb to illustrate that submission to the monarch is the most prudent way. The despot could strike quickly so that the premature efforts of the opposition would be futile.

The best course of action is conciliation (vv. 12-14), and language is one of the best conciliatory tools. The fool illustrates his folly by much talk about things the future of which he knows nothing (v. 14). His ways are as foolish as his words, and he does not even know how to find his way to the city (v. 15). That is, he does not even know the most ordinary things.[68]

Then Qoheleth showed that the policy he had just urged was not one of implicit approval of despotism. He lamented the land whose king and princes engaged in intemperate practices. Feasting and drinking in the morning were signs of dissipation (cf. Isa. 5:11; Acts 2:15). In verse 17 he phrased the opposite of the condition described in verse 16: the land "whose king is of nobility and whose princes eat at the appropriate time" (v. 17), the land "whose king is a lad and whose princes feast in the morning" (v. 16). Hengstenberg, following his proposal that the book originated in the early Persian period, referred these verses to the state of the empire and Persian royalty, understanding "lad" to connote the "boyish character" of the Persian rulers rather than age.[69] Whether or not the allusion is to Persian kings, his interpretation of "lad" is likely correct, for Qoheleth was inveighing the spirit and disposition of certain rulers of his time. In view of the general instruction offered to youth to prepare them for royal service, however, we may suggest that this is more didactic than the description on the political situation.

In verses 18 and 19, Qoheleth further exposed the meaning of verse 16. The state plagued by despotic rulers will inevitably be marked also by neglect and excessive indulgence. Then to complete the section of reflections on submission to the despot begun in verse 4, Qoheleth returned in verse 20 to the thought of prudence.

Having considered the appropriate disposition toward those above his upper-class students, next Qoheleth entertained the appropriate attitude toward those who were socially beneath the privileged class (11:1-6). It took the form of charity. Since man did not know or could not control either the future or the outcome of his own activities, he must not be overprovident but engage in deeds of charity and industry. Again he acknowledged the sovereignty of God in worldly affairs (cf. 1:13; 2:26; 3:14; 7:13-14; 8:16–9:1).

---

67. Ginsburg, p. 431.
68. Ibid., p. 439.
69. Hengstenberg, pp. 232-33.

FINAL ADVICE ON YOUTH AND AGE (11:7–12:8)

In an impassioned and eloquent appeal to youth, Qoheleth first laid upon them the responsibility of enjoying the pleasures of life while their physical and mental powers were still intact (11:7–12:1). He inculcated his theme three times (11:7-8a; 11:9a; 11:10a), and three times he offered a reason for his advice (11:8b; 11:9b; 11:10b). The reasons were that life was fleeting (8b,10b) and each would be called into judgment for the way he appropriated his opportunity to derive the most pleasure out of life (9b).

Although some scholars consider 11:9b a later gloss by a pious editor,[70] the author had at 3:17 already proposed the idea of judgment, and the book closed with the same warning (12:14). Delitzsch[71] and Ginsburg[72] both recognize in Qoheleth an undefined concept of a future judgment. This appears plausible, particularly in view of his contention that the wicked often escape punishment in this world (8:14).

In a second superb literary piece, Qoheleth put youthful opportunity over against the inevitability of old age and its debilitating effect (12:1-8). Several views on this passage have been held:

DIFFERENT INTERPRETATIONS OF ECCLESIASTES 12:1-8

1. It describes the diminishing strength and health of specific organs of the body (Babylonian Talmud, *Shabbath* 152a; Targum).
2. It describes the feebleness and debility of advancing age with the metaphor of an approaching storm (Ginsburg).[73]
3. The conditions of old age are compared to the rainy Palestinian winter (Delitzsch).[74]
4. Old age is depicted as the ruin of a wealthy estate (Gordis).[75]
5. Old age is depicted by an eclectic representation of metaphors.

The last method seems best in view of the difficulty of forcing all these metaphors into any one of the above models. In verse 2 the metaphor is that of the rainy Palestinian winter, whereas verses 3-4 may describe the declining estate.[76] Still verse 5a seems to describe literally the fears of high places and of venturing out on a stroll—fears that have developed in the old man because of his failing powers. Gordis and others, however, understand the first part of this

70. E.g., George A. Buttrick et al., eds., *The Interpreter's Bible*, vol. 5; O. S. Rankin, *The Book of Ecclesiastes*, p. 83; Scott, p. 254.
71. Delitzsch, p. 401.
72. Ginsburg, p. 454.
73. Ibid., p. 458.
74. Delitzsch, pp. 403-5.
75. Gordis, p. 329.

verse to allude to failing sexual powers.[77] Since the almond blossom is white, it may suggest the white hair of the aged.[78] The end of verse 5 is clear—old age brings man to the grave ("eternal home"). The approach of death is depicted in verse 6 by two metaphors: a golden lamp held by a silver cord is broken when the cord is severed, and the pitcher and the wheel that raises it are broken at the cistern, thus making it impossible to draw water.

Whether Qoheleth expressed a view of the afterlife is doubtful, but he knew very well that life originated in God (v. 7). We may say that his view of the afterlife was hardly more advanced than Job's. He could not embrace the idea confidently, but he did not engage in a polemic against it. Rather he operated upon the basis of what he did know and had experienced. He could not afford the luxury of heavenly contemplation to disengage himself from the pain and trouble of earthly affliction. This life, this present moment, was all he had, and he advocated draining its cup of pleasure to the dregs. Thus he ended his book as he began it (1:2)—with a solemn declaration that nothing was capable of giving man happiness and security (v. 8). He believed he had adequately demonstrated his thesis that, in view of the improbability of achieving happiness, the only sensible alternative was that which he had advocated (2:24; 3:12, 22; 5:18; 8:15; 9:7-9; 11:7-10).

EPILOGUE (12:9-14)

Although many scholars hold that the epilogue is the work of another author,[79] the style and vocabulary share common features with the book itself.[80] The concluding counsel of the book is "fear God and keep His commandments" (v. 13). This is the whole duty of man.[81] The last word issues a warning that every human deed is slated for divine judgment.

QUMRAN FRAGMENTS OF ECCLESIASTES

Among the fragments from Qumran Cave IV were three that contained brief passages from Ecclesiastes. The first fragment contained a few words from 5:13-17, substantial portions of 6:3-8, and five words from 7:7-9. Two miniature fragments contained 7:1-2 and 7:19-20. Based upon paleographical evidence, Muilenburg dated the fragments in the middle of the second century B.C.

76. Ibid., p. 333.
77. Ibid., pp. 336-37.
78. Ibid., p. 337; Scott, p. 255.
79. Gordis, p. 339, says he was likely a contemporary of Qoheleth. Scott, p. 256, suggests that an editor sympathetic with Qoheleth's views added this epilogue, gave the book the title, and inserted the words "says Qoheleth" at 1:2; 7:27; and 12:8.
80. Delitzsch, pp. 206-7, 430.
81. Gordis, p. 345, renders this phrase according to its idiomatic sense, as does KJV, which is superior at this point to NASB ("this applies to every person").

and suggested that Ecclesiastes had attained canonical status by that time. He further offered the opinion that the fragments provided no evidence of having been translated from an Aramaic original but of having been copied from a Hebrew original.[82]

82. James Muilenburg, "A Qoheleth Scroll from Qumran," BASOR 135 (1954):20-28.

# 7

# THE SONG OF SONGS

In a world where mankind has become enamored of himself and has turned sensual pleasure into the highest good, the Song of Songs provides a point of contact with the biblical faith.

Although the modern mind frequently cannot think beyond the sensual side of human sexuality, the ancient Hebrew mind saw the sensual side of man's nature and recognized it as good—not merely sensual—and as an inevasive allusion to God. That is, the creation of man as male and female constituted an important part of the divine image in man (Gen. 1:27-31). It would forever be a tangible sign of the communicative nature of God whose oneness is ultimately understood in terms of His complexity. And in man's duality God would ever seek to teach him of the divine oneness (Gen. 2:24).

Underlying the Song of Songs is the basic loyalty of woman to man (Gen. 2:23) and man to woman (Gen. 2:24), and the mutual interdependence they enjoy (Gen. 2:25). The ancient Hebrew mind could no more isolate and alienate the sexuality of man from God than he could conceive of man as a self-made creature cut loose from his divine moorings. The modern capability of mankind to conceive of himself as a biological creature whose psychosociological nature can potentially be comprehended in relation only to the phenomenal world is not evidence of his sophistication but of his spiritual poverty.

Basic, therefore, to much recent commentary on the Song of Songs is a humanism that begins with man and ends with man. It is as much or more a commentary on our own time as an exposition of the Song. Exegesis, although it can never completely throw off the element of the exegete's own contemporaneity, seeks to be aware of that factor and, to the degree that is humanly possible, minimize it so that the voice of the Holy Spirit in the text may be heard clearly. One of the basic ways of doing that is to recreate the psyche of the author and the major characters in the literature from the literature itself and from the historical and archaeological records contemporary with it. This task always carries with it an element of courageous risk, but that element inheres in the communication process in general. To communicate is to risk being misunderstood. And being misunderstood necessitates further communication. The outgrowth of this process, it is hoped, is a greater clarity in comprehending the original message.

The Song of Songs, probably as much as any other biblical book, has been the victim of this courageous risk. Sometimes the effort has been more brashly adventuresome than courageous. Fortunately we stand at this end of a long chain of interpreters who have agonized over the complexities of the Song. The observation may be made that the more difficult the book, the more bizarre the interpretations become. Yet much may be learned from these attempts that have varying degrees of success. Even the most bizarre may teach us something, if nothing more than what the Song is not.

## HERMENEUTICAL APPROACHES TO THE SONG

The history of exegesis of the Song of Songs is most fascinating, and represents not only the ability of the human mind to create, but also the deep-seated desire of the human heart to understand. Although we cannot review this history in the present study, the reader will find an excellent review by Christian D. Ginsburg in the introduction to his commentary, to which numerous commentators of the last century are indebted, and an update in the reprinted edition written by Sheldon H. Blank.[1] We will do no more than summarize the major hermeneutical methods and refer the reader to this and other secondary works.

### THE ALLEGORICAL METHOD

Allegory as a type of literature incorporates obvious symbolism intended to suggest deeper or hidden meaning. Some examples of this literary form are Judges 9:8-15; Isaiah 5:1-7; Ezekiel 16; 17:1-10; 23. In all these instances, the type of literature was consciously prescribed by the author. However, allegorizing, as distinct from allegory, may take place in the mind of the interpreter even when it was not so intended by the author. Such an example was Paul's allegorizing of Sarah and Hagar in Galatians 4:21-31. In general, the hermeneutical method applied to the Song falls within the range of allegorizing, although some interpreters would insist that the literary type is allegory.

Some scholars believe that Rabbi Akiba (martyred A.D. 135) alluded to the interpretation of the Song as allegory when he called it "the holy of holies" among the biblical books.[2] This is the earliest Jewish interpretative reference to the book known to us.

The Targum of the Song, the first full allegorical treatment that has survived, interprets it as an allegory on the history of Israel from the time of the

1. Christian D. Ginsburg, *The Song of Songs and Coheleth*, pp. ix-xliv, 1-125.
2. Herbert Danby, trans. and ed., The Mishnah. Tractate *Yadaim* 3.5.

Exodus to the coming of the Messiah and the building of the third Temple, viewing the "beloved" as the Lord and the maiden as Israel.[3] The date for this anonymous interpretation, however, seems in its present form to be no earlier than the sixth century A.D.,[4] although its origin is far more ancient. The Christians adopted this method by interpreting the "beloved" as Christ and the maiden as the church. This is evident from the fragmentary remains of Origen's commentary on the Song (third century), even though he was willing to admit the historical sense as an epithalamium on the marriage of Solomon to Pharaoh's daughter.[5] Further, the honorable champion of the Nicene faith, Athanasius (296-373), Archbishop of Alexandria, found in the Song the doctrine of the deity of Christ, commenting, for example, on 1:2 ("Let him kiss me with the kisses of his mouth," KJV) that it was the plea of ancient Israel to the Word that He become flesh.[6]

In the Middle Ages this method even received a certain impetus from philosophy. Joseph ibn Caspe (thirteenth century) maintained that the beloved was the active intellect and the loved one the receptive material intellect. Others of that era followed this philosophical trend.[7]

Closer to our own era, Matthew Henry's commentary on this book provides a good illustration of the Christian allegorist interpretation. In his introduction to the Song, he remarked that it could be viewed as an allegory depicting God and Israel in their mutual relationship. Then he added:

> It may more easily be taken in a spiritual sense by the Christian church, because the condescensions and communications of divine love appear more rich and free under the gospel than they did under the law, and the communications between heaven and earth more familiar. . . . Pursuant to this metaphor Christ and the church in general, Christ and particular believers, are here discoursing with abundance of mutual esteem and endearment.[8]

Objections to this method include the observation that Solomon was hardly a worthy candidate to represent God or Christ. The writer of Kings assessed Solomon's life and reign clearly enough: "For when Solomon was old his wives turned away his heart after other gods; and his heart was not wholly true to the Lord his God, as was the heart of David his father" (1 Kings 11:4, RSV). A further criticism has arisen from the fact that many interpreters who have followed this age-old method have done so on the presupposition that a book pre-

---

3. Hermann Gollancz, trans., "The Targum to the Song of Songs," *Translations from Hebrew and Aramaic,* pp. 15-90.
4. Ginsburg's date is A.D. 550.
5. Ginsburg, p. 61.
6. Ibid., pp. 62-63.
7. Ibid., pp. 46-58.
8. Matthew Henry, *Commentary on the Whole Bible,* 3:1053.

senting the pleasures of virtuous love is not worthy of the inspired canon of Scripture. Therefore, the author must have intended an allegory. However, underlying this presupposition may be the conviction that the sexual relationship between husband and wife belongs more to man's fallen than to his original state. But we may observe that the command to procreate was prior to the Fall (Gen. 1:28). H. H. Rowley has appropriately said: "The Church has always consecrated the union of man and woman in matrimony, and taught that marriage is a divine ordinance, and it is not unfitting that a book which expresses the spiritual and physical emotions on which matrimony rests should be given a place in the Canon of Scripture."[9]

Still further, the allegorical method has fallen into difficulty with those who believe that the main characters are three and not two, and that the object of the maiden's affections is the shepherd, not the king. Although the allegorical method has fallen on stony ground in modern times, it has been reincarnated in our own era in the form of the mythological method, which will be discussed below. Even though we may not follow the method, we cannot flaunt our own exegetical sophistication in the face of this ancient hermeneutic, which has given a peculiar kind of life and meaning to the Song for both Israel and the church through the centuries.

Admittedly the book is profuse with symbolism. The maiden is compared to a flower (2:1-2), the beloved shepherd to an apple tree (2:3), the charms and joys of love to fruit (2:3), wine (1:4; 5:1; 7:2), and a vineyard (8:12). The maiden's resistance to the advances of her lover is compared to a sealed fountain (4:12) and a high wall (8:9), and the lover's invitation to enjoy love is symbolized by a call to enjoy the vineyard (2;15), the fountain (4:15), and the garden (4:16). Such extravagant symbolism tends to push the interpreter in the direction of allegory or typology, because the richness of the symbols seems difficult to exhaust by means of a literal interpretation. Gordis expresses the richness of symbolism thus:

> When, for example, the maiden, in 2:4f., announces that she is faint with love and asks to be sustained with raisins and apples, she is calling for concrete food, to be sure, but *at the same time,* by her choice of fruits that are symbolic of love, she is indicating that only the satisfaction of her desires will bring her healing.[10]

Although Gordis does not embrace the allegorical approach, he has recognized the power of literary symbolism to demand appropriate compensation from the interpreter. Allegory or allegorizing has been the primary method of

9. H. H. Rowley, "The Interpretation of the Song of Songs," *The Servant of the Lord and Other Essays of the Old Testament,* p. 234.
10. Robert Gordis, *The Song of Songs,* p. 38.

providing that compensation, and if it has overcompensated, we may recognize it as more an error of the mind than of the heart.

Andrew Harper, quoting a late nineteenth-century scholar, has observed that the oriental mind treated sensuality and mysticism as twin moods:

> The truth is that sensuality and mysticism are twin moods of the mind, interchanging in certain natures with an inborn ease and celebrity, mysterious only to those who have confined their study of human nature to the conventional and the common-place. Hardly conscious themselves of the accepted antithesis, such carnal-spiritual minds delight to express themselves in terms of spontaneous ambiguity, for this very ambiguity lies at the root of their being.[11]

To abandon the allegorical method altogether and rule it invalid might constitute one of the many exegetical manipulations of the Western mind that superimposes our psychological and literary structures upon the ancient oriental writer. Although our attitude toward the method may legitimately be one of caution, modern biblical hermeneutics should give no place to exegetical snobbery, nor are we in a position to look down upon the absorbing and passionate love for God that has characterized the saints of Israel and the church who had fed upon the allegorical meaning of this book.

THE TYPOLOGICAL METHOD

Whereas allegory is basically a literary *type* consciously formulated by the author, typology is a *method* employed by the interpreter (as is also allegorizing). Indeed, the original author or audience may have had little or no notion of the typological significance of the historical event, person, or thing represented in the original composition. History, in fact, is one of the basic differences between allegory and typology. Allegory as a literary type may relate historical events in symbolic form, or the symbolism may be nonhistorical, whereas typology depends upon the fact of the literal presentation of history.[12] Some who have followed this method for the Song of Songs have insisted that the historical foundation of the book was Solomon's marriage to Pharaoh's daughter or some other princess, and that the marriage typically represents the union of Christ and the Gentiles.[13]

Luther, in the preface to his commentary, dismissed the thesis that it was a love song about the daughter of Pharaoh: "For we shall never agree with those who think it is a love song about the daughter of Pharaoh beloved by Solomon.

11. Walter Leaf, "Versions from Hafiz," *The Song of Solomon*, by Andrew Harper, pp. xxxvii-xxxviii.
12. For a discussion of typology and some of the differences between typology and allegory, see A. Berkeley Mickelsen, *Interpreting the Bible*, pp. 236-64.
13. Theodore of Mopsuestia (d. 429) first proposed this thesis.

Nor does it satisfy us to expound it of the union of God and the synagog, or like the tropologists, of the faithful soul."[14] He believed himself to propose a new approach by which he got the "simplest sense and the real character of this book," which he believed to be Solomon's praise to God for his divinely established and confirmed kingdom and government.[15] Yet before one is quite done reading his commentary, Luther has clearly espoused the typological interpretation. For example, of Solomon's vineyard at Baal-hamon he comments, "Solomon calls the whole church his vineyard and says that it is in Baal-hamon, that is, in an exceedingly great multitude and in a most plenteous place, since Baal means 'master,' and Hamon means 'multitude.'"[16]

No lesser modern scholar than Franz Delitzsch, denying the allegorical nature of the book, accepted the validity of the typical interpretation:

> But because Solomon is a type (*vaticinium reale*) of the spiritual David in his glory, and earthly love a shadow of the heavenly, and the Song a part of sacred history and of canonical Scripture, we will not omit here and there to indicate that the love subsisting between Christ and His church shadows itself forth in it.[17]

Yet, the Song never actually depicts the marriage of the bride and bridegroom. Further, the bride was a common keeper of the vineyard (1:6; 8:12), and the bridegroom a shepherd (1:7). And though the typological method has offered a way out of the allegorical forest, it has never achieved the popularity of the allegorical method, and to a much lesser degree does it possess that strange attraction that the allegorical method has commanded.

### THE MYTHOLOGICAL METHOD

History has many ironies, and so does exegesis. The bizarre and absurd sometimes expire at the hands of advancing knowledge and technology only to rise again in more contemporary garb. Old Testament exegesis has experienced its share of such phenomena. The mythological, or cult, theory qualifies admirably for this category. This position was strongly set forth by T. J. Meek, who proposed that the Song was a liturgy of the Tammuz-Ishtar cult.[18] It is claimed that, representationally, two people assumed the roles of the god, Tammuz, and the goddess, Ishtar, and enacted the death of Tammuz and his reemergence from

---

14. Martin Luther, *Luther's Works*, vol. 15, *Notes on Ecclesiastes, Lectures on the Song of Solomon, Treatise on the Last Words of David*, p. 194.
15. Ibid., p. 191.
16. Ibid., p. 262.
17. Franz Delitzsch, *Commentary on the Song of Songs and Ecclesiastes*, p. 6.
18. T. J. Meek, "Canticles and the Tammuz Cult," AJSL 39 (1922-23): 1-14; also Meek's article "The Song of Songs and the Fertility Cult," *The Song of Songs, A Symposium*, ed. Wilfred H. Schoff, pp. 48-69.

the netherworld through the efforts of Ishtar. Meek proposed that *dôdî* (usually translated "my beloved") was a proper noun and was none other than the god Addu, or Adad, who in Syria-Palestinian texts was called Addu and Dad, or Dadu,[19] the Syrian counterpart to the Sumero-Akkadian Tammuz. He cited 5:9 as definitely being attached to the god Dod—"Who but Dod is thy Beloved!"[20]

This position has enjoyed wide popularity in the modern era, and most recently Marvin Pope has affirmed his belief that the cultic associations provide the best context for interpreting the Song. Observing the prominence given the power of love over death in 8:6, he proposes that it may have been associated with an ancient cultic funeral feast at which life was reaffirmed in the most basic ways, involving lavish feasts and sexual orgies.[21] Pope, along with many commentators, views this profound declaration as the climax of the Song.[22] Using this as a cue, he theorizes that the cultic reaffirmation of love was made in the face of the power of death, for love is the only power that can cope with death.[23]

We are informed by Ezekiel 8:14 that the Tammuz cult had gained some popularity prior to the fall of Jerusalem in 587 B.C. We are also told that Ezekiel considered this an abomination. The possibility that any cultic associations of the Song were gradually displaced by the allegorical interpretation, thus paving the way for orthodox acceptance and canonization, is indeed remote. The process of throwing off such strong associations would have been quite difficult in the early postexilic era, especially in view of the strong anti-idolatry mood. The situation might have been eased somewhat in the later era of Hellenization, but even then the priestly and scribal guardians of Holy Scripture would possess a certain sensitivity to the matter not common among the laity.

A further observation, the idea that Tammuz returned to life from the netherworld, has been challenged. S. N. Kramer has come down on both sides of the issue, contributing to the ambiguity. In an earlier statement he stressed the absence of evidence for the resurrection of Tammuz.[24] Other scholars agreed.[25] Later, however, when the end of the Sumerian myth was discovered, he went so far as to suggest that Dumuzi's (Tammuz's) death and resurrection even left their mark on the Christ story.[26] The present ambiguity on the matter marks the data as simply too tenuous to draw hard conclusions. However, we may submit that the

---

19. Ibid., pp. 4-5.
20. Ibid., p. 5, n. 2.
21. Marvin H. Pope, *Song of Songs, A New Translation with Introduction and Commentary*, p. 229.
22. Ibid., p. 18.
23. Ibid., p. 210.
24. S. N. Kramer, "Mythology of Sumer and Akkad," *Mythologies of the Ancient World*, pp. 94-137.
25. D. J. Wiseman, "Tammuz," *The New Bible Dictionary*, ed. J. D. Douglas, p. 1238; E. M. Yamauchi, "Tammuz and the Bible," JBL 84 (1965): 283-90.
26. Kramer, "The Sacred Marriage and Solomon's Song of Songs," *The Sacred Marriage Rite: Aspects of Faith, Myth, amd Ritual in Ancient Sumer*, p. 133.

cultic hypotheses put forth in Old Testament studies generally have been over-emphasized. The Old Testament in many respects is a reaction against heathen cults, whereas the presupposition underlying modern cult theories is that the Old Testament represents an absorption of cultic elements that eventually were rendered innocuous by time and lapse of memory. Of interest also is the fact that scholars who advocate the cult view are not agreed whether the Song has been reworked to make it acceptable to the Israelite faith. Meek was of the opinion that many of the cultic associations had been forgotten and some consciously changed.[27]

The relationship of this position to the allegorical method may be seen in the contention that the Song does not celebrate human love but the marriage of a god and goddess. Further, just as the allegorical method begins with a hypothetical approach to the Song, so does the mythological, or cult, theory. The assumption is that the Jews took the allegory and engaged also in allegorizing to hide the mythical nature of the Song. The merits of this position go no further than an attempt to take seriously the religious and cultural milieu in which ancient Israel lived and developed. From that point on the hypothesis is largely extrapolation.

### THE LITERAL METHOD

If we can agree that a book that celebrates virtuous love between man and woman deserves a place in the canon of Holy Scripture, then we will have no difficulty with interpreting the Song in its literal sense. The creation of mankind as male and female and their sexual relationship were part of the original order and not a post-Fall alteration. Paul's view of marriage was that it mirrored a much higher sphere of relationships, that between Christ and the church (Eph. 5:21-33), and John described the consummation of redemption as the "marriage of the Lamb" (Rev. 19:7-9). The Scriptures elevate the love relationship between husband and wife, and we should not disparage a book that presents such ideal love, nor ought we to indict those who choose on sound exegetical grounds to interpret the Song literally and stop short of seeking a deeper meaning, even though this option may not be viable for us.

Generally, modern commentators prefer the literal method. Ginsburg traced this trend in the modern era back to Moses Mendelssohn (1729-86).[28] Ginsburg himself gave impetus to this view, and numerous others have followed. Aside from the proponents of the mythological approach, the literalists have held the field for a century. Having, therefore, settled upon the plain sense of the Song, scholarship has largely concerned itself with the literary nature of the work.

27. For other criticisms of the cultic hypothesis, see Rowley, pp. 213-32; Gordis, pp. 5-7, and n. 30.
28. Ginsburg, pp. 58-59.

In this regard, some scholars have drawn attention to the love songs of ancient Egypt and compared the Song to them. They are generally love poems that celebrate human love, much like our book. Michael V. Fox has done a thorough study of these songs and their importance for the Song of Songs, concluding that the Song is a literary unity but lacks a narrative or schematic design.[29] While its structure is loose, its unity is maintained by a coherence of thematic and verbal elements.[30] "The Song takes a single romance and turns it around and around like a gem, displaying all its facets. The reader finally sees the gem as a whole, and the order in which the facets were shown does not much matter."[31] In Fox's view, such love songs were likely sung at banquets held during the leisure time of religious holidays.[32]

## INTRODUCTORY MATTERS ABOUT THE SONG

### THE NATURE AND PURPOSE

Whereas the allegorists have generally been more interested in meaning than in literary form, those who have felt compelled to abandon the allegorical method have at the same time been constrained to inquire into the literary nature of the Song, for there is always an essential relationship between literary form and meaning of any composition. The Bible is no exception. Robert Lowth in 1787 proposed, along with others, that the Song was an epithalamium celebrating the wedding of Solomon[33] and assigned it to the category of the mystical allegory, "which, under the veil of some historical fact, conceals a meaning more sacred and sublime."[34] The form of the book called for more exact description, however, and Lowth typed it within the dramatic form but not regular drama.[35]

Delitzsch also followed the dramatic theory and called the Song a "dramatic pastoral," recognizing, as did Lowth, that it was not drama in the theatrical sense, since the theater was not a Semitic institution, but a development somewhere between lyrical poetry and drama. The "daughters of Jerusalem" suggested to him, as to Lowth, a function like that of the chorus of the Greek drama. Whereas Lowth accepted the hebdomadal division proposed by M. Bossuet, based upon the seven-day marriage festival (see Gen. 29:27; Judg. 14:12), Delitzsch divided the book into six acts of two scenes each.[36]

29. Michael V. Fox, *The Song of Songs and the Ancient Egyptian Love Songs*, p. 224. Cf. pp. 209-22 for his discussion of literary unity. See also G. Lloyd Carr, *The Song of Solomon: An Introduction and Commentary.*
30. Fox, p. 226.
31. Ibid.
32. Ibid., p. 227.
33. Robert Lowth, *Lectures on the Sacred Poetry of the Hebrews,* vol. 2, lect. 30, p. 298.
34. Ibid., lect. 31, pp. 326-27.
35. Ibid., lect. 30, p. 307.
36. Delitzsch, pp. 8-10.

The dramatic theory has been criticized because it presupposes the unity of the Song,[37] which assumption, say its critics, cannot be made. If, however, some narrative base is not presupposed, the interpreter is left with a disparate collection of love songs having an ostensibly secular disposition. It is, of course, possible that these songs assumed a religious interpretation before they achieved full canonicity.

We can easily see many reasons that such an anthology as the book of Psalms would be included in the Hebrew canon, not the least of which was the predominant praise of God, but it seems rather unlikely that a collection of love songs intended only for the praise of human love might find approval among the ancient saints and sages. This in no way pronounces the virtues of human love unworthy of the biblical canon, but rather recognizes that even the virtue and validity of human love do not stand alone but allude to a love that has religious dimensions.

Some may object that other Old Testament books, such as Ruth and Esther, have their own peculiar problems when their merits of canonicity are considered. And that we cannot deny. However, in the case of Ruth, the divine control of historical events and persons was preparatory for the birth of David and his influence and place in the divine economy. As regards Esther, a casual reading will supply the justification, for this book records the power of God to direct and save His people from the most formidable enemy.

Therefore, the bare minimum with which we can be content is that of Christian D. Ginsburg: "In its literal sense, the Song of Songs teaches a great moral lesson, worthy of Divine inspiration."[38] Thus Ginsburg concluded that the purpose of the book is not to celebrate love, even though that be worthy of canonicity, "but *to record an example of virtue*, which is still more worthy of a place in the sacred canon."[39] Our society and world can profit immensely from that message.

One of the hypotheses most appealing to modern scholars, and one that has contributed to the "collection" theory of the Song, is the "threshing board" theory set forth by J. G. Wetzstein in 1873.[40] While serving as German counsel in Damascus, Wetzstein observed Syrian weddings in which the bride and bridegroom were honored by being elevated upon the threshing sledge and designated "king" and "queen." During the festive dancing that followed the declaration that the wedding had been consummated, a song called a *wasf*, referring to the bodily perfection and beauty of the two, was sung. In the Song of Songs, 7:2-7 especially answers to this category, along with 4:1-7 and 5:10-16. Further,

37. Gordis, p. 13.
38. Ginsburg, p. xlv.
39. Ibid., p. 104.
40. Delitzsch has included some remarks by Wetzstein in an appendix to his commentary on the Song of Songs, pp. 162-76.

several times the "king" is referred to (e.g., 1:4; 3:9, 11; 7:5). Subsequent analysis of this book has been greatly influenced by Wetzstein's thesis. Gordis, for example, has praised the merits of this theory and has suggested the Song is

> a superb lyrical anthology, containing songs of love and nature, of courtship and marriage, emanating from at least five centuries of Hebrew history, from the days of Solomon to the Persian period. The *Song* thus constitutes a parallel, though of considerably smaller compass, to the *Book of Psalms*, which is a florilegium of man's yearning and love for God.[41]

Leroy Waterman, on the other hand, has criticized the "threshing board" theory because it requires too many deletions, transpositions, and modifications of the text, as well as offering analogies that are strained and cannot be traced as far back as the early Christian era.[42]

Although the unity of the book must be established upon internal grounds, there are several indicators in that direction. The "daughters of Jerusalem" are an element that may be considered to play a unifying role in the book (1:5; 2:7; 3:5; 5:8, 16; 8:4). They are likely the ladies of the court whom the maiden addresses and who also addresses her. A second unifying indicator is the recurring formula of adjuration at 2:7; 3:5; and 8:4. The third obvious element that supports unity is the leading characters. The song is of such a nature that much disagreement exists over whether there are two, the maiden (called "Shulammite" in 6:13) and Solomon (traditional view), or three, the maiden, a shepherd who is the maiden's true love, and Solomon, who attempts to redirect the maiden's devotion from her shepherd lover to himself by royal blandishments (modern view, or "shepherd hypothesis"). It would seem that the fewest difficulties are associated with the latter position, which Ginsburg has attributed to J. T. Jacobi (1771).[43] It is followed by Ginsburg,[44] Harper,[45] and Driver,[46] to name only a few representatives. Although these evidences may not be conclusive, they are at least supportive of unity.

It is extremely difficult to reconstruct the story line, if one was intended at all by the composer of the Song. It is a fair assumption that the majority of interpreters from the period of the book's canonization have provided the story line, whether or not the author intended it. The modern mind may be able to handle the idea of a collection of love songs with no religious associations, but it is very

41. Gordis, p. x.
42. Leroy Waterman, "*Dôdî* in the Song of Songs," AJSL 35 (1919):101-10, esp. p. 101.
43. Ginsburg, pp. 87-88.
44. Ibid.
45. Harper, pp. xlvi-xlvii.
46. S. R. Driver, *An Introduction to the Literature of the Old Testament*, pp. 444-46, gives a defense of this view.

doubtful that the canonical process could ever have reached completion if the book had been viewed in that way. In fact, in the final analysis we must deal with the canonical reality. The question then is whether it is appropriate to assume less than those whose understanding of the Song, and whose esteem for it, led them to consider it divinely inspired. Moreover, we should not ignore the providential work of the Holy Spirit in bringing this book within canonical bounds. I am personally convinced that the ethical demands of Scripture could not make allowance for a book that celebrated illicit love between a man and woman. In the context of a commitment toward marital fidelity between a man and woman, contemplating the marital sexual relationship has a certain legitimacy. But outside of those bounds, a purely secular collection of erotic songs stands counter to biblical propriety.

The interpreter of the Song, then, ought to begin at the point where the canonical success of the book was achieved. That, it seems to me, involved the assumption of some kind of story line with a religious meaning assumed. We must, of course, acknowlege the risk involved when we try to reconstruct the fabric of the narrative, as Delitzsch and Ginsburg, for example, have done.

In the early part of this century Leroy Waterman proposed that the Song was a satire,[47] working from the belief that the key to understanding the Song is contained in the word *dôdî*, usually translated as "my beloved." Upon examining the biblical use of *dôd*, which commonly carries the meaning of "uncle" in the biblical literature outside the Song, he concluded that the translation "my beloved" had no justification.[48] *Dôdî* was, said Waterman, a proper name, *Dôdai*.[49] He rendered 5:9 as, "What is thy Dodai in comparison with David?"[50] The reference then would be to the house of David in the person of the reigning king. Waterman further expostulated that when the literature of the Northern Kingdom fell to the responsible keeping of the Southern Kingdom after the fall of Samaria in 722 B.C., the term *dôdî* was misinterpreted and Solomon glorified by it, whereas originally he had been the villain of the story.[51]

Although I remain unconvinced of the necessity of rendering *dôdî* as a proper name, ingenious though Waterman's proposal was, I do agree with his essential conclusions on the nature and purpose of the Song: "The poem is a very definite satire upon the age and ideals of Solomon and a glorification of the northern schism, and that too without the necessary deletion of a single letter of the original."[52]

---

47. Leroy Waterman, "*Dôdî* in the Song of Songs."
48. Ibid., pp. 102-3.
49. Ibid., p. 107.
50. *Dôd* has the same consonants as *Dāvid*, and in the unpointed text the two words would look the same.
51. Ibid., pp. 105-6.
52. Ibid., p. 104.

Originating in the Northern Kingdom,[53] therefore, it may celebrate one of those rare occasions when Solomon's amorous designs were thwarted by a simple, rustic maiden whose home was located in the Plain of Esdraelon. Based upon the interpretation that follows the shepherd hypothesis (modern view), Solomon does not appear in the best light of the Song. Further, the reputation by which the writer of Kings remembered him (1 Kings 11:1-11) would not contradict the portrait of a king who believed his wealth and position could attract the country maiden and divert her love from the simple shepherd.

Furthermore, we are informed that conditions in the Northern Kingdom had deteriorated so badly during Solomon's reign due to forced labor and heavy taxation, that by the time of his death, the sentiment of the northern tribes had already turned toward secession (1 Kings 12). The satirical mood would be conveniently accommodated and bolstered by the emotional climate in the Northern Kingdom, particularly during the latter years of Solomon's reign. Thus, in addition to the king's overtures being deflected by the maiden in deference to her shepherd lover, we find the final section introduced by the same question as was Solomon's approaching cortege (3:6/8:5). Whereas the first had all the paraphernalia of royalty, the second was marked by the simplicity of the countryside. And the kind of love the maiden represented is celebrated (8:6-7) rather than the blandishments and manipulative powers of royalty.

The Song then may be viewed in its literal sense as a celebration of love between man and woman, but more than that, the elevation of a love so genuine that it cannot be purchased with royal enticements. It is, like divine love, given freely and unmeritoriously.

LITERARY STRUCTURE

To determine the literary structure of a book like the Song, we must turn to an examination of the content. Since we have direct discourse in the Song, this will both aid and complicate our efforts, for generally we are not told who is speaking, and often the content of a given speech is not decisive for identification.[54] However, some design may be detected. Three times the maiden adjures the daughters of Jerusalem (2:7; 3:5; 8:4), and 5:1 may be a concluding formula. Further, the Song as a satire on Solomon's love life may elevate the two similar but contrasting scenes introduced by the question, "Who is this coming up from the wilderness" (3:6/8:5), in order to highlight the satirical spirit. On the one hand was the king who had all the wealth and machinery to lure the object of his amorous intent, and on the other the maiden who was unaffected by the allurements and whose heart was possessed by pure, unmerited devotion.

---

53. See following section, "Authorship and Provenance," pp. 221-22.
54. To alleviate this problem, the Greek Codices Sinaiticus (fourth century B.C.) and Alexandrinus (fifth century B.C.) supplied marginal notes indicating speakers and addressees.

Delitzsch found the material to fall into six acts of two scenes each:

### A LITERARY ANALYSIS OF THE SONG OF SONGS

| | | | |
|---|---|---|---|
| Act 1 | 1:2–2:7 | Scenes: 1:2-8 | 1:9–2:7 |
| Act 2 | 2:8–3:5 | Scenes: 2:8-17 | 3:1-5 |
| Act 3 | 3:6–5:1 | Scenes: 3:6-11 | 4:1–5:1 |
| Act 4 | 5:2–6:9 | Scenes: 5:2–6:3 | 6:4-9 |
| Act 5 | 6:10–8:4 | Scenes: 6:10–7:6 | 7:7–8:4 |
| Act 6 | 8:5-14 | Scenes: 8:5-7 | 8:8-14[55] |

Ginsburg's division of the book into five sections will serve our exposition well: (1) 1:1–2:7, (2) 2:8–3:5, (3) 3:6–5:1, (4) 5:2–8:4, and (5) 8:5-14.[56]

Those scholars who believe the Song to be a collection of love songs propose varying numbers of distinct pieces. Gordis, for example, divides his translation into twenty-nine sections,[57] and Eissfeldt suggests twenty-five.[58]

### DATE

Establishing a date for the Song is no easier than deciding upon the appropriate hermeneutic. If we could be confident about the meaning of the phrase in the superscription, "le-Shelomoh" ("of/to/for Solomon"), then we would be in a better position to make a judgment. But as we have observed of the psalm superscriptions, the preposition is not always indicative of authorship, but sometimes refers to origin, or in the case at hand, possibly to dedication. Since, therefore, the superscription can hardly be accepted as a settlement of date and authorship, we must resort to other criteria. In addition to the superscription, three criteria are generally used: (1) the appearance of Solomon in the book, (2) the mention of Tirzah parallel to Jerusalem in 6:4, and (3) the language of the Song, especially the use of non-Semitic words and Aramaisms.

We may observe that Solomon's name appears in the book seven times: 1:1, 5; 3:7, 9, 11; 8:11, 12. Five of these occurrences are connected with actual appearances of Solomon in the action (3:7, 9, 11; 8:11, 12),[59] whereas 1:5 mentions the "curtains of Solomon" as a simile. Apart from the loan words that appear (see below), the superb poetry of the book certainly points to a time when the Hebrew language was in good form. The Solomonic era could well qualify.

---

55. Delitzsch, p. 10.
56. Ginsburg, pp. 7-11.
57. Gordis.
58. Otto Eissfeldt, *The Old Testament: An Introduction*, pp. 489-90.
59. Gordis, pp. 19-20, takes the position that the poem in 3:6-11 actually describes the occasion of one of Solomon's marriages, probably to an Egyptian princess. Therefore, this song became the nucleus for the tradition of attributing the entire book to Solomon.

The second criterion, the mention of Tirzah in parallelism with Jerusalem, has been cited as evidence that the composition of the Song cannot be dated earlier than the time when Tirzah was the capital of the Northern Kingdom (probably made the capital by Baasha, 1 Kings 15:21). But there is evidence that it may have been a secondary royal residence as early as Jeroboam I (1 Kings 14:17). Actually the city may have been very prominent and beautiful even before it became the capital. So this argument is rather weak.

Arguments based upon the language often have a tenuous quality about them because we still do not have sufficient data for a definitive history of the Semitic languages. At one time, for example, Aramaisms in a book were widely held to be indicative of exilic or postexilic composition because the Israelites seem to have become influenced strongly by Aramaic during and after the Babylonian Exile. Yet we now know that Aramaic influences extend all the way back to the second millennium B.C.[60] Of particular note is the occurrence of the Aramaic form of the relative pronoun in the Song (*she* rather than *asher,* the latter occurring in the superscription, *"which* is to Solomon," italics added). This element may also be found in early biblical poetry (Judg. 5:7) and prose (Judg. 6:17; 7:12; 8:26).[61] Gordis attributes the use of this element in the Song to its northern provenance.[62] Thus the argument based on Aramaisms is really not decisive for an early or a late date. Though the loan words, such as *pardēs* (Persian for "park" or "garden") in 4:13, *appiryon* (possibly related to Greek *phoreion,* "palanquin") in 3:9, as well as other terms, certainly seem to tip the scales in the direction of a late date,[63] we may very well have here evidences that the book in its continuing usage came under the influence of Persian and Greek elements during the postexilic era. The exotic items of possible Indian origin mentioned in 1:12 (nard), 4:13, 14 (nard, saffron, calamus, and aloes), and so on, could understandably be known and acquired during the Solomonic era due to the active commercial interchange of the time.

Chaim Rabin has made a strong case for the influence of the Indian culture and poetry of the Indus Valley upon Mesopotamia and neighboring cultures in the third and second millennia B.C.[64] Pope has added evidence for the interchange between the Indus and Mesopotamian valleys by calling attention to a seal impression from Southern Babylonia with an Indus design and dated in the

---

60. K. A. Kitchen, "Aram," *The New Bible Dictionary,* ed. J. D. Douglas, p. 55.
61. See Driver, p. 449, notes.
62. Gordis, p. 25.
63. Ibid., p. 24. Gordis advocates a redaction in the Persian period, not later than the fifth century B.C. Eissfeldt, p. 490, advocates a third-century date, although older material, he admits, may underlie the songs. R. K. Harrison, *Introduction to the Old Testament,* p. 1052, maintains that if the work as a whole was not Solomonic, a final redaction may well have occurred in the immediate preexilic period.
64. Chaim Rabin, "The Song of Songs and Tamil Poetry," *Studies in Religion* 3 (1973): 205-19.

twentieth century B.C.[65] Rabin's proposal is that the Song was written in the heyday of Judean trade with South Arabia and South India by one who had traveled to both places and was familiar with Tamil poetry. Assuming both thematic and stylistic features of that strain of Indian poetry, Rabin proposed that a Judean author composed the Song or put together the shorter pieces.[66] This means, of course, that the time of Solomon is a potential candidate for the composition of the Song. Pope observes, however, that one of the objections to Rabin's hypothesis is the repeated use of the verb "pasture" (*r'y*) and its participial form "pastor, shepherd," which has usually been seen to mark the Song as a pastoral idyl.[67] Rabin's solution is to see in the term a technical meaning connected with the management of camels, thus obviating the difficulty.[68]

The Song has also been assigned to the Solomonic age by M. A. Segal[69] and acknowledged to have strong Solomonic connections, although not written by Solomon himself.

In conclusion, the arguments for date possess various degrees of momentum capable of swinging the pendulum from the Solomonic era to the Persian period. In view of the observations already made, we may conclude that no substantive obstacles stand in the way of a composition date in the Solomonic era.[70] The active international trade policies of that era, the luxurious life of the court, and the exquisite Hebrew poetry all contribute momentum in that direction.

## AUTHORSHIP AND PROVENANCE

In the modern era most scholars have rejected the idea of Solomonic authorship. H. H. Rowley, for example, though not espousing Solomonic authorship, advocates a unity of authorship based upon the repetitions and the unity of theme and style.[71] Among those holding to Solomon's authorship, Gleason Archer lists among his reasons the author's knowledge of the flora and fauna (cf. 1 Kings 4:33), which includes twenty-one varieties of plant life and no less than fifteen species of animals, as well as many expensive imported items, a luxury of which Solomon was capable.[72]

Some commentators (e.g., Eissfeldt[73]) have suggested a southern provenance in or near Jerusalem, but the predominance of northern and eastern names

65. Pope, p. 27. See also B. Buchanan, "A Dated Seal Impression Connecting Babylonia and Ancient India," *Archaeology* 20 (1967): 104-7.
66. Rabin, pp. 216-17.
67. Pope, pp. 30-31.
68. Rabin, p. 214.
69. M. A. Segal, "The Song of Songs," VT 12 (1962): 470-90.
70. Ginsburg, p. 125, and Delitzsch, p. 11, to cite two other commentators, both advocate a Solomonic date.
71. Rowley, pp. 212-13.
72. Archer, p. 474.
73. Eissfeldt, p. 490.

directs us to the Northern Kingdom.[74] Admittedly we are in a speculative area, but the fact that Solomon does not appear in the best light in the Song might also point toward the northern region of the kingdom, where sentiments were directed against this monarch by the heavy burdens of taxation and forced labor that he levied upon the northern tribes.[75] We should not be surprised, therefore, to find such a satirical composition written in the north during the later years of Solomon's reign or soon thereafter. A king who had his way in the political dimensions of Israel's life may purposely be depicted by an anonymous author as one whose social designs, at least on this one occasion, were frustrated. Thus political power takes a back seat to the power and fidelity of love.

CANONICITY

We are not well informed about the vicissitudes involved in the process of canonizing the Song. Rabbi Akiba regarded the matter settled:

> No man in Israel ever disputed about the Song of Songs [that he should say] that it does not render the hands unclean, for all the ages are not worth the day on which the Song of Songs was given to Israel; for all the Writings are holy, but the Song of Songs is the Holy of Holies.[76]

This passage in the Mishnah, however, suggests that there was vacillation on the matter:

> R. Judah says: The Song of Songs renders the hands unclean, but about Ecclesiastes there is dissension. R. Jose says: Ecclesiastes does not render the hands unclean, and about the Song of Songs there is dissension.[77]

We do not know the precise nature of the dissension, but we can speculate that it had to do with the sensual nature of the Song. Undoubtedly the allegorical method helped to ameliorate the difficulties. The list of canonical books in the Talmud contains the Song.[78] But if we accept the view that the book is didactic, teaching fidelity and the virtues of pure love between man and woman, the Song deserves a place in the canon on those merits alone.

74. Northern names mentioned in the Song are: Lebanon, Hermon, Damascus, Tirzah, Sharon, Gilead, Heshbon, Mahanaim, Bethrabbim, and Shulammite.
75. See previous section in this chapter, "Nature and Purpose," beginning with par 3, p. 214.
76. The Mishnah, Tractate *Yadaim* 3.5. The phrase "renders the hands unclean" is the rabbinic way of pronouncing a book inspired, or canonical. The explanation for this is given in I. Epstein, ed., Babylonian Talmud, *Shabbath* 14a.
77. Ibid.
78. Babylonian Talmud, *Baba Bathra* 14.

EXPOSITORY ANALYSIS OF THE SONG

The following interpretative comments follow predominantly the literal method. The reader may have recourse in the commentaries to other meanings yielded by the text when examined under the allegorical, mystical, and cultic methods. Especially is Pope's commentary helpful because he has consistently brought forth these three treatments of the Song in ancient and modern writings, even though he tends to resolve many of the problems by appeal to Ugaritic mythology.

TITLE (1:1)

The title "The Song of Songs" means "the best of songs" in the same way that "Holy of Holies" means "the holiest place." As we have observed above, the second phrase, "which is of/to/for Solomon," is generally used to suggest either authorship or origin. However, here the phrase may be used in a dedicatory sense—the book is about an incident in Solomon's life but actually may not have been written by him. Pope observes that the Ugaritic texts have superscriptions consisting of *l* ("of/to/for") plus a proper name that is sometimes the god Baal or the hero Keret or Aqhat. The texts cannot, of course, have been written by those mythical figures, so a superscription need not always carry the sense of authorship but may mean that the composition deals with the hero named.[79] In view of this, the dedication is hardly in a purely honorific sense, since Solomon's designs were frustrated, but likely has a satirical nuance.[80]

SECTION ONE (1:2–2:7)

*Maiden (1:2-7).* The position we take in this study is that the characters in the Song are likely three rather than two: the maiden, King Solomon, and the shepherd who is the maiden's true love. Though some passages in the Song may be accommodated without injustice to this view or to the traditional view of two primary characters, the maiden and King Solomon, fewer difficulties seem to be associated with the modern view when applied to the book as a whole.

The maiden may be in the royal court of King Solomon, but we are not informed how she came to be there. Those who hold the traditional view understand the maiden to address King Solomon in verse 4, and those espousing the modern view hear her addressing her absent lover.

The Christian allegorists view the king as Christ and the maiden as the church. They express their esteem for each other.[81]

79. Pope, pp. 295-96.
80. Again see previous section in this chapter, "Nature and Purpose," pp. 217-18.
81. Henry, 3:1053.

The maiden's address to her absent lover is interrupted in verses 5-6 by a parenthetical explanation of her swarthy complexion.[82] Her words are directed to the court women, and we can only surmise that some disdain of her complexion on their part evoked this explanation. It is simple enough—her brothers made her the keeper of the vineyards. The reference to "my mother's sons" and the paternal responsibility the brothers were exercising would suggest that her father was dead. Delitzsch has seen some step-brotherly harshness in this passage,[83] but actually we are not apprised of the reason for the brothers' action.

The maiden resumes her apostrophe to her lover in verse 7, wishing that he might tell her where he pastures his flock.

The fact that the maiden's lover is here pictured as a shepherd would raise doubt about his identification with Solomon.

In the Christian allegorist view presented by Matthew Henry, the daughters of Jerusalem are the church in general speaking to individual churches to encourage them not to be offended at the church's suffering.[84]

*Court women (1:8).* The court women respond to the maiden's question to her absent lover, evidence that they were listening as she addressed him in absentia. That the maiden, too, was a shepherdess is implied by mention of "your kids."

*Solomon (1:9-11).* This is the first address that can be attributed to Solomon.[85] Using an affectionate term, "my darling" (or "my female friend"),[86] the king makes his first attempt to divert the maiden's love from her shepherd lover to himself. His comparison of her to a mare of Pharaoh's chariots is in no way disparaging, for horses were objects of high esteem. Yet neither his blandishments nor his offer of exquisite ornaments wins the maiden's affection. The Christian allegorical interpretation has usually been that the addressee was the church, and Christ or God the speaker.

*Maiden (1:12-14).* From the language of this passage we know the maiden is the speaker. This is obviously her reply to Solomon's overtures. She refers to the king's couch, which was probably a divan on which he reclined to eat. The meaning seems to be that as long as the king was out banqueting (if we accept the suggestion of Delitzsch) she thought of her true lover. The terms used for him are nard (a fragrant plant imported from India), myrrh (an aromatic plant whose leaves and flowers were tied in bags and worn for their fragrance),[87] and

---

82. See Pope's extended discussion on the meaning of "black" (v. 5), pp. 307-18. He leans toward the explanation that it refers to a black goddess, thus expressing his inclination for the cultic interpretation of the Song. Fox, p. 101, explains that she was black because she was forced to work outside.
83. Delitzsch, p. 27.
84. Henry, 3:1057.
85. Some commentators, e.g., Driver, p. 446, advance the opinion that the speeches of Solomon in comparison to those of the maiden's true lover are rather cold in tone.
86. This designation of the maiden by her lover occurs also in 1:15; 2:2, 10, 13; 4:1, 7; 5:2; 6:4.
87. Delitzsch, p. 37.

henna blossoms (cypress flowers)[88] in the vineyards of En-gedi (En-gedi is a place on the western side of the Dead Sea; it has a fresh-water spring).

*Shepherd (1:15).* That the speakers in verses 15 and 16 are different is indicated by the Hebrew feminine pronouns and adjectives (v. 15, pointing to either Solomon or the shepherd as the speaker), and the masculine pronouns and adjectives (v. 16, indicating the maiden's reply).

*Maiden (1:16–2:1).*The three-character scheme more easily accommodates the shepherd as the speaker of verse 15, because the maiden's response is reciprocally affectionate. The maiden recalls the rustic scenery in which their love had begun, where the cypress and cedar formed the arches of their house. Then, turning off the compliment of her lover, she describes herself as one of the ordinary flowers that grow in abundance in the valley.

The allegorist view sees Christ condescendingly declaring Himself as the "rose of Sharon" (2:1) and the church as the lily (2:2).[89]

*Shepherd (2:2).* The shepherd turns the compliment back upon the maiden in verse 2 in what Delitzsch calls "reciprocal rivalry in the praise of mutual love."[90] Using this same word, "lily," to describe her, he does not accept the idea of commonness, but converts it into extraordinariness—she is like a lily among thorns. This flower was probably a red or dark purple flower because in 5:13 the beloved's lips are compared to the lilies.

*Maiden (2:3-7).* The maiden reciprocates. Her beloved, when compared to other young men, is like an apple tree among the trees. Here the traditional view finds support, for the simple shepherd and "the banqueting house" seem to be inconsonant, unless, of course, we take the thought figuratively (so Ginsburg).[91]

Although Delitzsch suggests that the Hebrews were permitted to adjure by one other than by God (but not to swear by another), he admits that this is the only such instance in Scripture.[92] Gordis makes an attractive proposal that the lover desires to avoid mentioning God's name in this connection with the physical attractions of love, and so he substitutes for the customary oath *bē'lohei s<sup>e</sup>bhā'ōth* ("by the God of hosts") the similar sounding phrase *bis<sup>e</sup>bhā'ōth' ō b<sup>e</sup>'ay<sup>e</sup>'lōth hassādeh* ("by the gazelles or by the hinds of the field," v. 7), choosing for the substitutions animals that are symbolic of love.[93] If this is true, and the original audience knew of the practice, then the religious nature of the Song is certainly implied.

88. Ginsburg, p. 139.
89. Henry, 3:1061-62.
90. Delitzsch, p. 41.
91. Ginsburg, p. 142.
92. Delitzsch, pp. 45-46.
93. Gordis, p. 28.

SECTION TWO (2:8–3:5)

We do not have any indication that the scene has changed, but the opening line, "Listen! My beloved! Behold, he is coming," would imply a new scene in the chain of events. It may still be that of the royal court because the court ladies are present and speak. It would appear, as in the first address to the daughters of Jerusalem (1:5-6), that the purpose of the maiden's address is explanatory, possibly elucidating the circumstances that brought her to the vineyards. The closing adjuration is the same as that for the first scene and seems to be spoken to the court ladies (2:7/3:5).

*Maiden (2:8-10a).* In a reminiscent tone, the maiden recalls how her shepherd lover had approached her at the end of winter (the rainy season, v. 11) and invited her to come with him into the fields.

*Shepherd (2:10b-14).* Pope's suggestion is that the bridegroom stands outside the bride's house while she beautifies herself, and he peers through the windows coaxing her to come out, just as the Sumerian goddess kept her lover waiting until she was properly prepared.[94] He, of course, sees a cultic meaning behind the passage.

The description of spring includes the blossoming flowers, the voice of the turtledove (which spent the winter south of Palestine and returned with the first verdure of spring in early April), and the ripening of the figs (vv. 12-13). The maiden's reticence may be suggested by the image of the dove in the clefts of the rock, from which doves can hardly be coaxed when they are frightened (v. 14).

The Christian allegorist sees the bride rejoicing (2:8) in the approach of Christ (John 3:29). He comes and calls her to Himself: "Let me see your form, let me hear your voice" (2:14).[95]

*Maiden (2:15–3:5).* Though Ginsburg says the instructions of verse 15 were given by the brothers who sent the maiden away from her lover, a more likely possibility is that this is a song sung by the maiden in response to her beloved's request in verse 14 to let him hear her voice.[96] It further serves the purpose of expressing to her beloved her apprehension about circumstances or persons (we cannot tell for certain what the foxes represent, except that they are detrimental to the vineyard) that would destroy their beautiful relationship, described here with the metaphor of vineyards in blossom.

The mutual relationship between the two lovers is summed up in verse 16a, "My beloved is mine, and I am his," and repeated in 6:3. Verse 16 may be a monologue by the maiden, or an address to the court ladies, or a continuation of the song begun in verse 15. Verse 17, however, is obviously spoken to her beloved ("my beloved" is masculine), instructing him to go away until evening

94. Pope, *Song of Songs,* p. 392.
95. Henry, 3:1066-67.
96. Harper, *Song of Songs,* p. 17.

when, apparently, his visit would be less likely detected. The expression "until the day breathes" (NASB "until the cool of the day") seems to refer to evening (cf. Gen. 3:8, "at the breezy time of day," rendered by the KJV and the NASB "in the cool of the day"), as does also the clause "the shadows flee away." The description is synonymous with that of the lover in 2:9.

In the Christian allegorical view, verse 16 may be the church's profession of her relation to Christ.[97]

The faithful maiden either continues to reminisce or she relates a dream.[98] The allegorist has no special difficulty with the terms of this scene (e.g., the maiden seeking her lover in bed beside her and her search for the shepherd within the city) because he is not bound to explain the literal sense. Disappointed that her beloved did not return in the evening as she had expected, she determined to search for him. Upon entering the city or village, scarcely had she inquired of the watchmen when she found him and took him to her mother's house (v. 4). Though the meaning of the adjuration is somewhat uncertain, the sense may be that she entreats the court ladies not to solicit her love for another (v. 5).

SECTION THREE (3:6–5:1)

Solomon had entered and offered his solicitations to the maiden in 1:9-11. But he has not appeared again until now. We cannot tell where he has been, but this scene describes his retinue as it approaches, most probably, Jerusalem.

*Unidentified speaker(s) (3:6-11).* The speakers in this passage are not specified, nor can they be identified from their speech. Perhaps it is the maiden or the court women speaking in verse 6. Verses 7-11 seem to be spoken by the maiden. Someone asks who this is that is coming from the wilderness. The approaching retinue arouses attention by the "pillars of smoke," which were either dust clouds created by the members of the party or, very likely, columns of smoke from incense burned before the procession in the king's honor.

The identification and description of the cortege in verses 7-10 leave no doubt that King Solomon is the honored visitor. The king's palanquin probably resembled a couch on which the important person would sit or recline, covered with a canopy and surrounded by curtains, which kept out the sun. It would be borne by the king's attendants.[99] This one was extremely elaborate and beautifully decorated by the women of Solomon's court to show their love for him (v. 10).

The final speaker in this passage instructs the women of Jerusalem to go forth to see King Solomon, who wore a crown symbolic of his happiness. Since

---

97. Henry, 3:1066.
98. Delitzsch, p. 91, says it must be a dream because it was inconceivable as happening in real life.
99. Ginsburg, p. 152.

this maiden has not, to our knowledge, become Solomon's bride, this could not be the wedding crown unless, of course, his intentions were to marry her on that day. The latter might very well be suggested, thus heightening the suspense of the story. The maiden is very close to being married to the king against her wishes. Jewish bridegrooms and brides were customarily crowned with crowns until the war against Rome in A.D. 70 when, as a sign of mourning, this custom was adandoned.[100]

Solomon appears in the Christian allegorical view as a type of Christ. The couch (3:7) may represent His church, and some would view the chariot (3:9-10) as His human nature in which His divine nature rode.[101]

*Solomon (4:1-5).* Since Solomon's cortege has just been seen, it seems logical to identify him as the speaker here. Although the first part of verse 1 ("How beautiful . . . like doves") is identical with 1:15, which we have suggested was spoken by the shepherd lover, if our identification of this speaker is correct (i.e., Solomon), then the maiden's response to the two speeches (1:16-17 and 4:6) stands them in contrast to each other. The first was reciprocally affectionate, whereas the second was a decision for reclusion.

Solomon praises the maiden with a sevenfold description of the beauty of her body: her eyes, hair, teeth, lips and mouth, cheeks, neck, and breasts. The beauty of the maiden is overwhelming, as is the speaker's poetic imagery. Taking most of his metaphors from nature, the king is nothing but complimentary of the young woman. But the comparison of her neck to the "tower of David," though complimentary, leaves us wondering what tower he refers to. It seems to have been used as an arsenal, or else the shields were merely decorative. Ezekiel mentions such a custom in Tyre (Ezek. 27:11).

This descriptive section may be viewed allegorically as Christ's description of His espoused church. The *eyes* may be her ministers, the *hair* her comely behavior, the *teeth* her ministers again, the *lips* her praise of God, the *cheeks* her humility and modesty, the *neck* her faith, and her *breasts* the two testaments.[102]

*Maiden (4:6).* The speaker is the maiden, not Solomon. In 2:17 she had used the same words to admonish her beloved to flee away. That the purpose of her desire for reclusion may have been meditation is suggested by the imagery of myrrh and frankincense, which were used in the Temple every morning and evening (Ex. 30:34-38).[103]

*Shepherd (4:7-16b).* If we have three leading characters in the book, as the material seems to suggest, the speaker's recurring use of "bride" in reference to a maiden who had not been given to him in betrothal would be strange indeed. That Solomon would be the speaker in 4:1-5 seems natural because his cortege

100. Gordis, p. 84.
101. Henry, 3:1071.
102. Ibid., 3:1073-74.
103. Delitzsch, p. 78.

was approaching prior to that passage (3:6-11). But the use of "bride" here would point rather toward the shepherd as the speaker. In 2:17, after the maiden had used the same language as in 4:6, she went out and sought her beloved diligently, whereas here he actually appears following her statement. The fact that he reappears unannounced is part of the literary style of the author.

The shepherd lover seeks to retrieve the maiden from the mountain retreat where Solomon has taken her, a change of location of which we are totally incognizant otherwise. The verb of verse 9 may mean "to make courageous" or "to steal one's heart" (NASB "made my heart beat faster"), since the Hebrew stem (*piel*) may have either the intensive or privative sense.[104] We agree with Ginsburg that the intensive sense ("to make courageous") is more meaningful here,[105] but must admit that if Solomon is thought to be the speaker, the privative meaning ("to steal one's heart") would do as well.

The address of the maiden as "sister" is in keeping with Hebrew usage, which sometimes speaks of one's beloved with a familial term. That the wedding had not been consummated and that the kind of love treated in the Song is not promiscuous are clear from the beloved's description of his betrothed as "a garden locked" and "a spring sealed up" (v. 12). Oriental gardens and fountains were customarily enclosed to prevent intruders. Very beautifully the lover continues the metaphor of love as a garden by describing the extraordinary contents, which included a freely flowing fountain (vv. 13-15).

*Maiden (4:16c).* In the first part of this verse the fact that the speaker still refers to the maiden's love as "my garden" suggests the shepherd as the speaker. The last third of the verse, however, may be the maiden's invitation to her beloved to accept the love she offers:

> May my beloved come into his garden
> And eat its choice fruits.

The allegorical hermeneutic sometimes views 4:16 as a prayer for the Holy Spirit upon the life of the church, a prayer that was answered in the descent of the Holy Spirit on the day of Pentecost (Acts 2).[106]

*Shepherd (5:1).* Here the maiden's beloved evidently accepts his bride's offer of love. Though the verbs (come, gather, eat, drink) may be construed as past or present, if 4:16c is the maiden's offer of love, then this is appropriately read as the bridegroom's acceptance, and the verbs rendered as present tense. The call to eat and drink is made either to friends gathered for the occasion or to

---

104. Francis Brown, S. R. Driver, and Charles A. Briggs, *A Hebrew and English Lexicon of the Old Testament*, p. 525b.
105. Ginsburg, pp. 158-59.
106. Henry, 3:1078.

the bride and bridegroom. Whoever the addressees, this is a climactic point in the Song; love has been mutually offered and accepted.

### SECTION FOUR (5:2–8:4)

*Maiden (5:2-8).* The maiden has a dream in which she thinks her beloved knocks at the door. The setting seems to be prior to marriage. When the shepherd lover approaches the door, he tells her that he is drenched with the night dew (v. 2). But the maiden has retired for the night and hesitates to open the door. However, once the beloved has quit knocking, she proceeds to open the door only to find that he has gone away (vv. 5-6a). She then proceeds into the city to look for him and is taken as a suspicious woman by the watchmen. Evidently in an effort to free herself from them, she leaves her outer garment in their hands (v. 7). This passage has details very similar to 3:1-4, which may also have been a dream.

Delitzsch maintains that her search through the city rather than the fields is fatal to the shepherd hypothesis.[107] But we must remember that this was a dream, not a report of reality. Therefore, the objection hardly stands up.

Although the dream has ended in verse 8, it seems so real still that she requests the daughters of Jerusalem to tell him of her intense love if they see him.

Matthew Henry's presentation of the allegorical interpretation views this scene as one of those occasions when the church's ill behavior has caused Christ to withdraw from her.[108]

*Court women (5:9).* The daughters of Jerusalem, moved by the deep devotion of this maiden for her beloved, inquisitively ask what makes him special among men. As Ginsburg has remarked, their question shows that Solomon was not the beloved, for the question in reference to him would have been unnecessary.[109]

*Maiden (5:10-16).* In response to the women's question, the maiden describes her beloved, first by his beautiful complexion. Then, moving from his head down, she draws a word picture of his body in the most splendid of metaphors, summing up with the simile that his body is as strikingly beautiful as Lebanon, which was known for its attractive vegetation, scenery, and mountains.

*Court women (6:1).* In 5:9 the daughters of Jerusalem asked the maiden what made her beloved superior to other men; here they are again moved by her description of him, and they ask his whereabouts so that they may seek him with her.

*Maiden (6:2-3).* The maiden, probably growing suspicious of their inquisitiveness, gives an evasive answer. Her beloved, she says, has gone down into his garden, which may be a circumlocution for the field where he feeds his

---

107. Delitzsch, p. 96.
108. Henry, 3:1080.
109. Ginsburg, p. 167.

flock, for he is a shepherd. Yet in 4:12 and 5:1, a "garden" is a symbol for the maiden. She reaffirms their mutual pledge to each other, possibly in a reactionary response to the offer of the other maidens to search for him with her. The affirmation of verse 3 is a slightly altered duplication of 2:16.

By the allegorical view, those who seek Christ are directed toward Him (6:2-3). He is to be found, not in the common places (streets, etc.), but in reclusion apart from the world.[110]

*Solomon (6:4-10).* The terms of this speech suggest that Solomon is the speaker, for he mentions his queens and concubines (vv. 8-9). Just as he had interrupted at 1:9 after the maiden had inquired about her beloved's whereabouts in 1:7, so he again makes his entrance just when she has spoken of her lover. He describes her beauty in terms of two cities, Tirzah in the Northern Kingdom, and Jerusalem in the Southern. Tirzah was an important city, if not the capital, in the Northern Kingdom at the time of Jeroboam I (1 Kings 14:17). It remained the seat of the monarchy until the reign of Omri (887-876 B.C.) when he moved it to Samaria (2 Kings 16:24). The word etymologically means "beauty," and Tirzah may have already had a reputation for its beauty even during the reign of Solomon.

If we are correct in our assumption that the speaker of 4:1-5 was Solomon, then the description of the maiden used here would reinforce that contention because, with the exception of two or three words, the Hebrew text of 6:5b-6 and 4:1b-2 is a duplication. The substance of the court women's praise of this comely maiden is evidently given in verse 10.

If the text is viewed allegorically, then Christ has returned to His church, having forgiven her sinful behavior.[111]

*Maiden (6:11-12).* The maiden may now relate how she came to be in Solomon's court. She had been inspecting the plants of the garden (probably near her rural home) when she was abducted. Admittedly verse 12 is extremely difficult and has confounded expositors. Pope renders it, "Unawares I was set/In the chariot with the prince," but his interpretation appeals to Ugaritic mythology for enlightenment.[112]

*Unidentified speaker(s) (6:13-7:6).* The speaker may be the court women or Solomon. This is the first time we have had the maiden referred to as "Shulammite." This has been traditionally identified with Shunem (modern Arabic, "Sulem"), which was located in the Esdraelon plain within the tribal claim of Issachar. Abishag the Shunammite, who was brought to the failing David (1 Kings 1:3), and the Shunammite woman who befriended Elisha (2 Kings 4:8-37; 8:1-6) were probably from this town.

110. Henry, 3:1086-87.
111. Ibid., p. 1088.
112. Pope, pp. 552, 574-92.

The place Mahanaim is not, to our knowledge, associated with any kind of festival where sacred dancing was done. We do know, however, that such a festival was held at Shiloh (Judg. 21:19). The maiden appears to enact some such dance, and the description of her body is given as she performs. Harper, however, contends that the women describe her body as they help her to dress in the women's apartments. Thus the purpose would be to move the maiden to accept the king's offer of love.[113] Verse 5 would seem to support this view of their purpose, but it does appear that the maiden performs some kind of dance before the women and/or Solomon. The description begins with her feet and moves upward (cf. the description in 4:1-5, where the movement was from the head down).

*Solomon (7:7-9).* The clue that the speaker here is probably Solomon is found in verse 5, where the king is mentioned. Whether the king witnessed the maiden's dancing, we cannot tell, but the metaphors resemble those used by the king in 4:1-5 (cf. esp. 4:5 and 7:3). For the final time Solomon asks for her love. He does not appear again.

*Maiden (7:10–8:4).* The Shulammite maiden rejects the king's advances, reaffirming her loyalty to another (v. 10). We may assume that the king withdraws, for the maiden seems to engage in monologue, calling her beloved to go away with her (v. 11). Her desire was still for her beloved (7:13), who, she wishes, were like her brother so that she might show him her love without social constraint (8:1-2).

For the third and last time she adjures the maidens not to attempt to draw her affections away from her beloved (8:4; see 2:7; 5:8).

Viewed allegorically, in 7:1-9 Christ may again express His great love for His church, followed by the church's expression of delight in Him (7:10-13). Subsequently she says that her desire is for more intimate communion with Him (8:1-3), and adjures the daughters of Jerusalem not to interrupt that communion (8:4).[114]

SECTION FIVE (8:5-14)

The scene changes from the court or palace to the countryside, where the maiden and her lover now appear.

*Unidentified speaker (8:5a).* As in 3:6, we hear an unspecified voice announcing the approach of the maiden, leaning upon her beloved. She is finally rewarded for her fidelity by being united with him. At 3:6 this question announced the approaching cortege of Solomon, whereas here it calls attention to the approach of the simple maiden and her bridegroom. The Hebrew feminine forms make the maiden's identification certain. Here we sense a bit of the satirical spirit in which this book is dedicated to Solomon. The pomp and circum-

113. Harper, pp. 48-49.
114. Henry, 3:1091, 1095.

stance are absent from this occasion (cf. 3:7-11), but the intense desire of love is fulfilled.

*Maiden (8:5b-c).* The Shulammite maiden addresses the shepherd lover (the pronominal suffixes are masculine) and recounts their earlier moments of love under a certain apple tree to which they have now returned (v. 5b).

*Maiden (8:6-7).* This seems to be the climax of the Song. It is a panegyric of love, which rises to a summit, praising that genuine love that has been portrayed in the Song, a love that is as strong as death, and a most vehement flame,[115] which has its origin in God Himself. It cannot be quenched by a flood of waters, nor can it be purchased with wealth, as Solomon had tried to do (1:11). The word translated by several versions as "jealousy" in verse 6 does not have that meaning here, but rather suggests "devout affection, ardent love."[116] The idea seems to be that love, like Sheol, will not give up its object.

*Unidentified speaker (8:8-9).* The speaker may be the Shulammite maiden or one of the brothers. Harper makes the attractive suggestion that the maiden speaks and recalls the words of her harsh brothers when she was younger (cf. 1:6).[117] In this view, the brothers had planned their protective strategy before their sister was of the marriageable age.

*Maiden (8:10-12).* The bride now claims that she has proved to be an impregnable wall of virtue. The brothers had said they would bestow high honor upon her if she proved to be virtuous (v. 9).

In verses 11-12, the maiden continues to relate how Solomon had put at her disposal a highly desirable and exquisite vineyard, but she had decided to keep her own. She recites her rejection of the king's overtures and acceptance of her own humble but happy lot.

The location of Solomon's vineyard is not known for certain. The name "Baal-hammon" may have been created for effect ("master of wealth"),[118] but if so it would seem strange that the other proper names do not seem to be so created. It may have been located in the environs of Jerusalem.

*Shepherd and maiden (8:13-14).* The shepherd calls upon the maiden to sing a song, which she actually does in verse 14. In 2:14 her beloved had asked to hear her voice, and she had ended that song (2:17) with almost the exact words we have here.

The Christian allegorical view sees 8:13-14 as the temporary parting of Christ and His church, He to go to heaven ("mountains of spices") and she to remain on the earth ("the garden"). She pleads with Him to hasten His return.[119]

---

115. On this noun, which has the abbreviated form of the tetragrammaton (*yah*) in it, see Gordis, p. 26, n. 90.
116. Ginsburg, p. 188.
117. Harper, p. 59.
118. Gordis, p. 98.
119. Henry, 3:1100-1101.

# BIBLIOGRAPHY

## GENERAL WORKS

The Babylonia Talmud. Edited by I. Epstein. 35 vols. London: Soncino, 1948.

Bamberger, Bernard. "Fear and Love of God in the Old Testament." Hebrew Union College Annual 6 (1929):39-53.

Brichto, Herbert C. "Kin, Cult, Land and Afterlife—A Biblical Complex." Hebrew Union College Annual 44 (1973):1-54.

Brown, Francis; Driver, S. R.; and Briggs, Charles A. *A Hebrew and English Lexicon of the Old Testament*. 1907. Reprint. Oxford: Clarendon, 1959.

Charles, R. H. *The Apocrypha and Pseudepigrapha of the Old Testament in English*. 2 vols. 1913. Reprint. Oxford: Clarendon, 1973.

Charlesworth, James H., ed. *The Old Testament Pseudepigrapha*. 2 vols. Garden City, N.Y.: Doubleday, 1983, 1985.

Childs, Brevard S. *Old Testament Theology in a Canonical Context*. Philadelphia: Fortress, 1985.

Cohen, A., ed. *The Five Megilloth*. The Soncino Books of the Bible. London: Soncino, 1952.

Danby, Herbert, trans. and ed. *The Mishnah*. London: Oxford U., 1933.

Driver, S. R. *An Introduction to the Literature of the Old Testament*. 1897. Reprint. Cleveland: World, 1956.

Eichrodt, Walther. *Theology of the Old Testament*. Translated by J. A. Baker. 2 vols. Philadelphia: Westminster, 1967.

Eissfeldt, Otto. *The Old Testament: An Introduction*. Translated by Peter Ackroyed. New York: Harper & Row, 1965.

Erman, Adolf. *The Literature of the Ancient Egyptians*. Translated by Aylward M. Blackman. 1927. Reprint. New York: Blom, 1971.

Fohrer, Georg. *Introduction to the Old Testament*. Translated by David E. Green. Nashville: Abingdon, 1968.

Freedman, H., and Simon, Maurice, eds. *Midrash Rabbah*. 10 vols. London: Soncino, 1939.

Gelin, Albert. *The Key Concepts of the Old Testament*. Translated by George Lamb. London: Sheed and Ward, 1955.

Gordon, E. I. *Sumerian Proverbs: Glimpses of Everyday Life in Ancient Mesopotamia*. Philadelphia: University Museum, 1959.

Harrison, R. K. *Introduction to the Old Testament*. Grand Rapids: Eerdmans, 1969.

Irwin, W. A. "Where Shall Wisdom Be Found?" *Journal of Biblical Literature* 80 (1961):133-42.

Kaufmann, Yehezkel. *The Religion of Israel*. Translated by Moshe Greenberg. Chicago: U. of Chicago, 1960.

Kitchen, K. A. *Ancient Orient and Old Testament*. Chicago: InterVarsity, 1966.

_____. "Aram." In *The New Bible Dictionary*, edited by J. D. Douglas. Grand Rapids: Eerdmans, 1962.

_____. "The Basic Literary Forms and Formulations of Ancient Instructional Writings in Egypt and Western Asia." In *Separatum aus Studien zu Altaegyptischen Lebenslehren*. Edited by Erik Hornung and Othmar Keel. Orbis Biblicus et Orientalis 28. Fribourg: 1979.

_____. "Proverbs and Wisdom Books of the Ancient Near East: The Factual History of a Literary Form." *The Tyndale Bulletin* 28 (1977):69-114.

Kramer, S. N. *Mythologies of the Ancient World*. Garden City, N.Y.: Doubleday, 1961.

Lichtheim, Miriam. *Ancient Egyptian Literature: A Book of Readings*. 3 vols. Berkeley, Calif.: U. of California, 1973.

McKenzie, John L. *A Theology of the Old Testament*. Garden City, N.Y.: Doubleday, 1974.

Maimonides, Moses. *The Guide of the Perplexed*. Translated by Shlomo Pines. Chicago: U. of Chicago, 1963.

Mickelsen, A. Berkeley. *Interpreting the Bible*. Grand Rapids: Eerdmans, 1963.

Millgram, Abraham. *Jewish Worship*. Philadelphia: Jewish Pub. Soc., 1971.

Oesterley, W. O. E. *The Jewish Background of the Christian Liturgy*. 1925. Reprint. Gloucester, Mass.: Peter Smith, 1965.

Pedersen, Johannes. *Israel, Its Life and Culture*. 2 vols. London: Oxford U., 1926.

Pfeiffer, Robert H. *Introduction to the Old Testament*. New York: Harper & Row, 1948.

Pritchard, James B., ed. *Ancient Near Eastern Texts Relating to the Old Testament*. 2d ed. Princeton, N.J.: Princeton U., 1955.

————. *The Ancient Near East: Supplementary Texts and Pictures Relating to the Old Testament*. Princeton, N.J.: Princeton U., 1969.

Roth, W. M. W. *Numerical Sayings in the Old Testament, A Form-Critical Study*. Supplements to *Vetus Testamentum*, vol. 13. Leiden: Brill, 1965.

Rowley, H. H., ed. *The Old Testament and Modern Study*. Oxford: Clarendon, 1951.

Speiser, E. A. *Genesis*. The Anchor Bible. Garden City, N.Y.: Doubleday, 1964.

Von Rad, Gerhard. *Old Testament Theology*. Translated by D. M. G. Stalker. 2 vols. New York: Harper & Row, 1962, 1965.

Vriezen, C. *An Outline of Old Testament Theology*. 2d. ed., rev. and enl. Newton, Mass.: Branford, 1970.

Westermann, Claus. *Creation*. Translated by John J. Scullion. Philadelphia: Fortress, 1974.

Young, E. J. *An Introduction to the Old Testament*. Rev. ed. Grand Rapids: Eerdmans, 1960.

## HEBREW POETRY

Alter, Robert. *The Art of Biblical Poetry*. New York: Basic Books, 1985.

Budde, Karl. "Poetry (Hebrew)." In *A Dictionary of the Bible*, edited by James Hastings, 4:2-13. New York: Scribner's, 1905-11.

Craigie, P. C. "The Poetry of Ugarit and Israel." *The Tyndale Bulletin* 22 (1971): 3-31.

Gottwald, N. K. "Hebrew Poetry." In *The Interpreter's Dictionary of the Bible*, edited by George A. Buttrick, 3:829-38. Nashville: Abingdon, 1962.

Gray, George Buchanan. *The Forms of Hebrew Poetry.* Prolegomenon by David Noel Freedman. 1915. Reprint. New York: KTAV, 1972.

Harrison, R. K. "Hebrew Poetry." In *Zondervan Pictorial Encyclopedia of the Bible*, edited by Merrill C. Tenney, 3:76-87. Grand Rapids: Zondervan, 1975.

Krasovec, Joze. "Antithetic Structure in Biblical Hebrew Poetry." Supplements to *Vetus Testamentum*, vol. 34. Leiden: Brill, 1984.

Kugal, J. *The Idea of Biblical Poetry.* New Haven, Conn.: Yale U., 1981.

Lowth, Robert. *Lectures on the Sacred Poetry of the Hebrews.* Translated by G. Gregory. 2 vols. 1787. Reprint. New York: Garland, 1971.

Robinson, Theodore H. *The Poetry of the Old Testament.* London: Duckworth, 1947.

## WISDOM IN THE OLD TESTAMENT

Albright, W. F. "Some Canaanite-Phoenician Sources of Hebrew Wisdom." In *Wisdom in Israel and in the Ancient Near East*, edited by M. Noth and D. Winton Thomas, pp. 1-15. Supplements to *Vetus Testamentum*, vol. 3. Leiden: Brill, 1955.

Andrews, Elias. *Modern Humanism and Christian Theism.* Grand Rapids: Zondervan, 1939.

Barre, Michael. "'Fear of God' and the World View of Wisdom." *Biblical Theology Bulletin* 11(1981):41-43.

Barry, F. R. *The Relevance of Christianity: An Approach to Christian Ethics.* London: Nisbet, 1947.

Baumgartner, W. "The Wisdom Literature." In *The Old Testament and Modern Study*, edited by H. H. Rowley, pp. 210-37. Oxford: Clarendon, 1951.

Blank, S. H. "Wisdom." In *The Interpreter's Dictionary of the Bible*, edited by George A. Buttrick, 4:852-61. Nashville: Abingdon, 1962.

Crenshaw, James L. "Method in Determining Wisdom Influence upon Historical Literature." *Journal of Biblical Literature* 88 (1969):129-42.

_____. *Old Testament Wisdom. An Introduction.* Atlanta: John Knox, 1981.

_____. "In Search of Divine Presence (Some Remarks Preliminary to a Theology of Wisdom)." *Review and Expositor* 74 (1977):353-70.

Erman, Adolf. *The Literature of the Ancient Egyptians*. Translated by Aylward M. Blackman. 1927. Reprint. New York: Blom, 1971.

Glemser, Berend. "The Spiritual Structure of Biblical Aphoristic Wisdom." In *Studies in Ancient Israelite Wisdom*, edited by James L. Crenshaw, pp. 208-19. New York: KTAV, 1976.

Gordis, Robert. "The Social Background of Wisdom Literature." *Hebrew Union College Annual* 18 (1944):77-118.

Gunkel, Hermann. "Vergeltung." In *Die Religion in Geschichte und Gegenwart*. Tubingen: Mohr, 1927.

Hayes, John H., ed. *Old Testament Wisdom*. San Antonio, Tex.: Trinity U., 1974.

Hill, R. C. "The Dimensions of Salvation History in the Wisdom Books." *Scripture* 19 (1967):97-106.

Kidner, Derek. "Wisdom Literature of the Old Testament." In *New Perspectives on the Old Testament*, edited by J. Barton Payne, pp. 157-71. Waco, Tex.: Word, 1970.

Lambert, W. G. *Babylonian Wisdom Literature*. Oxford: Clarendon, 1960.

Lindblom, Johannes. "Wisdom in the Old Testament Prophets." In *Wisdom in Israel and in the Ancient Near East*, edited by M. Noth and D. Winton Thomas, pp. 192-204. Supplements to *Vetus Testamentum*, vol. 3. Leiden: Brill, 1955.

Malchow, Bruce V. "Social Justice in the Wisdom Literature." *Biblical Theology Bulletin* 12 (1982):120-24.

Marcus, Ralph. "On Biblical Hypostases of Wisdom." *Hebrew Union College Annual* 23, no. 1 (1950-51):157-71.

McKane, William. *Prophets and Wise Men*. Studies in Biblical Theology, no. 44. Naperville, Ill.: Allenson, 1965.

Morgan, Donn F. *Wisdom in the Old Testament Traditions*. Atlanta: John Knox, 1981.

Murphy, Roland E. "Assumptions and Problems in Old Testament Wisdom Research." *Catholic Biblical Quarterly* 29 (1967):407-18.

―――. "Form Criticism and Wisdom Literature." *Catholic Biblical Quarterly* 31 (1969):475-83.

―――. "The Interpretation of Old Testament Wisdom Literature." *Interpretation* 23 (1969):289-301.

_____. "Wisdom and Creation." *Journal of Biblical Literature* 104 (1985):3-11.

North, M., and Thomas, D. Winton, eds. *Wisdom in Israel and in the Ancient Near East*. Supplements to *Vestus Testamentum*, vol. 3. Leiden: Brill, 1955.

Paterson, John. *The Wisdom of Israel: Job and Proverbs*. New York: Abingdon, 1961.

Pederson, J. "Wisdom and Immortality." *Vetus Testamentum* 3 (1955): 238-46.

Rankin, O. S. *Israel's Wisdom Literature: Its Bearing on Theology and the History of Religion*. 1936. Reprint. Edinburgh: T. & T. Clark, 1954.

Rylaarsdam, J. Coert. *Revelation in Jewish Wisdom Literature*. Chicago: U. of Chicago, 1946.

Scott, R. B. Y. "Priesthood, Prophecy, Wisdom, and the Knowledge of God." *Journal of Biblical Literature* 80 (1961):1-15.

_____. "Solomon and the Beginnings of Wisdom in Israel." *Vetus Testamentum* 3 (1955):262-79.

Shelley, Bruce L., ed. *Call to Christian Character: Toward a Recovery of Biblical Piety*. Grand Rapids: Zondervan, 1970.

Sutcliff, Edmund F. *Providence and Suffering in the Old and New Testaments*. London: Thomas Nelson, 1953.

Terrien, Samuel. "The Play of Wisdom: Turning Point in Biblical Theology." *Horizons in Biblical Theology* 3 (1981):125-53.

Torcszyner, Harry. "The Riddle in the Bible." *Hebrew Union College Annual* 1 (1924):125-49.

Urbach, Ephraim. "Class-Status and Leadership in the World of the Palestinian Sages." *Proceedings of the Israel Academy of Sciences and Humanities* 2 (1966):1-37.

Von Rad, Gerhard. *Old Testament Theology*. Translated by D. M. G. Stalker. 1:418-59. New York: Harper & Row, 1962, 1965.

_____. *Wisdom in Israel*. Translated by James D. Martin. London: SCM, 1972.

Westermann, Claus. *What Does the Old Testament Say About God?* Atlanta: John Knox, 1979.

Wurthwein, Ernst. "Egyptian Wisdom and the Old Testament." In *Studies in Ancient Israelite Wisdom*, edited by James L. Crenshaw, pp. 113-33. New York: KTAV, 1976.

Zimmerli, Walter. "Concerning the Structure of Old Testament Wisdom." In *Studies in Ancient Israelite Wisdom*, edited by James L. Crenshaw, pp. 175-207. New York: KTAV, 1976.

————. *Old Testament Theology in Outline*. Translated by David E. Green. Atlanta: John Knox, 1978.

## WISDOM IN THE APOCRYPHA

Clarke, Ernest G. *The Wisdom of Solomon*. The Cambridge Bible Commentary on the New English Bible. Cambridge: Cambridge U., 1973.

Dentan, Robert C. *The Apocrypha, Bridge of the Testaments*. New York: Seabury, 1964.

Geyer, John. *The Wisdom of Solomon*. Torch Bible Commentaries. London: SCM, 1963.

Gregg, R. A. F. *The Wisdom of Solomon*. The Cambridge Bible for Schools and Colleges. Cambridge: Cambridge U., 1909.

Levi, Gerson B. *Gnomic Literature in Bible and Apocrypha*. Chicago: n.p., 1917.

Metzger, Bruce M. *An Introduction to the Books of the Apocrypha*. New York: Oxford U., 1957.

Oesterley, W. O. E. *An Introduction to the Books of the Apocrypha*. London: Soc. for Promoting Christ. Knowledge, 1958.

————. *The Wisdom of Jesus, the Son of Sirach, or Ecclesiasticus*. The Cambridge Bible for Schools and Colleges. Cambridge: Cambridge U., 1912.

Reider, Joseph. *The Book of Wisdom*. Dropsie College ed. Jewish Apocryphal Literature. New York: Harper, 1957.

Snaith, John G. *Ecclesiasticus or the Wisdom of Jesus Son of Sirach*. The Cambridge Bible Commentary on the New English Bible. Cambridge: Cambridge U., 1974.

## JOB

Andersen, Francis I. *Job, An Introduction and Commentary*. London: InterVarsity, 1976.

Beeby, H. D. "Elihu: Job's Mediator?" *Southeast Asia Journal of Theology* 7 (1965):33-54.

Bowker, John. *Problems of Suffering in Religions of the World*. Cambridge: Cambridge U., 1970.

Crenshaw, J. L. "Popular Questioning of the Justice of God in Ancient Israel." *Zeitschrift für die alttestamentliche Wissenschaft* 82 (1970):380-95.

Davidson, A. B. *The Book of Job*. The Cambridge Bible for Schools and Colleges. Cambridge: Cambridge U., 1895.

Delitzsch, Franz. *Biblical Commentary on the Book of Job*. Translated by Francis Bolton. Clark's Foreign Theological Library. 2 vols. Edinburgh: T. & T. Clark, 1869.

Dhorme, E. *A Commentary on the Book of Job*. London: Nelson, 1967.

Di Lella, Alexander. "An Existential Interpretation of Job." *Biblical Theology Bulletin* 15 (1985):49-55.

Driver, S. R., and Gray, G. B. *A Critical and Exegetical Commentary on the Book of Job*. The International Critical Commentary. 2 vols. New York: Scribner's, 1921.

Ellison, H. L. *From Tragedy to Triumph*. London: Paternoster, 1958.

Fine, Hillel. "The Tradition of the Patient Job." *Journal of Biblical Literature* 74 (1955):28-32.

Fitzmyer, Joseph A. "The Contribution of Qumran Aramaic to the Study of the New Testament." *New Testament Studies* 20 (1974):382-407.

_____. "Some Observations on the Targum of Job from Qumran Cave 11." *Catholic Biblical Quarterly* 36 (1974):503-24.

Freedman, D. N. "Elihu Speeches in the Book of Job." *Harvard Theological Review* 61 (1968):51-59.

Freehof, Solomon. *The Book of Job, A Commentary*. The Jewish Commentary for Bible Readers. New York: Union of Am. Heb. Congregations, 1958.

Gard, Donald H. "The Concept of the Future Life According to the Greek Translator of the Book of Job." *Journal of Biblical Literature* 73 (1954): 137-51.

Gaster, T. H. "Rahab." In *The Interpreter's Dictionary of the Bible*, edited by George A. Buttrick, 4:6. Nashville: Abingdon, 1962.

Ginsburg, H. L. "Job the Patient and Job the Impatient." *Vetus Testamentum* 17 (1968):88-111.

Godbey, A. H. "The Hebrew Mashal." *American Journal of Semitic Languages and Literature* 34 (1922-23):89-108.

Gordis, Robert. *The Book of God and Man*. Chicago: U. of Chicago, 1965.

Gray, John. "The Book of Job in the Context of Near Eastern Literature." *Zeitschrift für die alttestamentliche Wissenschaft* 82 (1970):251-69.

————. "The Massoretic Text of the Book of Job, the Targum and the Septuagint Version in the Light of the Qumran Targum." *Zeitschrift für die alttestamentliche Wissenschaft* 86 (1974):331-50.

Guillaume, A. *Studies in the Book of Job*. Supplement 2, Annual of Leeds University Oriental Society. Leiden: Brill, 1968.

Habel, Norman C. *The Book of Job*. The Cambridge Bible Commentary on the New English Bible. London: Cambridge U., 1975.

Hanson, A. T. "Job in Early Christianity and Rabbinic Judaism." *Church Quarterly* 2 (1969):147-51.

Heras, H. "Standard of Job's Immortality (Job 29:18)." *Catholic Biblical Quarterly* 11 (1949):263-79.

Irwin, W. A. "Job's Redeemer." *Journal of Biblical Literature* 81 (1962):217-29.

Kallen, Horace M. *The Book of Job as a Greek Tragedy*. New York: Hill and Wang, 1959.

Kellner, M. M. "Gersonides, Providence and the Rabbinic Tradition." *Journal of the American Academy of Religion* 43 (1974):673-85.

King, Albion Roy. *The Problem of Evil: Christian Concepts and the Book of Job*. New York: Ronald, 1952.

Kramer, S. N. "Man and His God: A Sumerian Variation on the 'Job' Motif." In *Wisdom in Israel and in the Ancient Near East*, edited by M. Noth and D. Winton Thomas, pp. 170-82. Supplements to *Vetus Testamentum*, vol. 3. Leiden: Brill, 1955.

Laks, H. F. "Enigma of Job; Maimonides and the Moderns." *Journal of Biblical Literature* 83 (1964):345-64.

LaSor, William Sanford; Hubbard, David Alan; and Bush, Frederic Wm. *Old Testament Survey: The Message, Form, and Background of the Old Testament*. Grand Rapids: Eerdmans, 1982.

Lillie, W. "Religious Significance of the Theophany in the Book of Job." *Expository Times* 68 (1957):355-58.

McKeating, H. "Central Issue of the Book of Job." *Expository Times* 82 (1971): 244-46.

McKenzie, R. A. F. "Purpose of the YHWH Speeches in the Book of Job." *Biblica* 40 (1959):435-45.

————. "The Transformation of Job." *Biblical Theology Bulletin* 9 (1979):51-57.

Meek, T. J. "Job XIX.25-27." *Vetus Testamentum* 6 (1956):100-103.

*Mikraoth Gedoloth* (The Rabbinic Bible [in Hebrew]). New York: Pardes, 1951. Not available in English.

Moore, Rick D. "The Integrity of Job." *Catholic Biblical Quarterly* 45 (1983):17-31.

Neiman, David. *The Book of Job*. Jerusalem: Massada, 1972.

Paterson, John. *The Wisdom of Israel: Job and Proverbs*. New York: Abingdon, 1961.

Pope, Marvin H. *Job*. The Anchor Bible. Garden City, N.Y.: Doubleday, 1965.

Sarna, Nahum M. "Epic Substratum in the Prose of Job." *Journal of Biblical Literature* 76 (1957):13-25.

————."Mythological Background of Job 18." *Journal of Biblical Literature* 82 (1963):315-18.

Skehan, P. W. "Job's Final Plea (Job 29-31) and the Lord's Reply (Job 38-41)." *Biblica* 45 (1964):51-62.

Smick, E. "Job." In *The Zondervan Pictorial Encyclopedia of the Bible*, edited by Merrill C. Tenney, 3:615. Grand Rapids: Zondervan, 1975.

Snaith, Norman. *The Book of Job: Its Origin and Purpose*. Studies in Biblical Theology, 2d ser. no. 11. Naperville, Ill: Allenson, 1968.

Sokoloff, Michael. *The Targum to Job from Qumran Cave XI*. Ramat Gan, Israel: Bar-Ilan U., 1974.

Tsevat, Matitiahu. "The Meaning of the Book of Job." *Hebrew Union College Annual* 37 (1966):73-106.

Westermann, Claus. *The Structure of the Book of Job: A Form-Critical Analysis*. Translated by Charles A. Muenchow. Philadelphia: 1977.

Williams, R. J. "Theodicy in the Ancient Near East." *Canadian Journal of Theology* 2 (1956):14-26.

Wilson, K. "Return to the Problems of Behemoth and Leviathan." *Vetus Testamentum* 25 (1975):1-14.

Zink, J. K. "Impatient Job: An Interpretation of Job 19:25-27." *Journal of Biblical Literature* 84 (1965):147-52.

## PSALMS

Alexander, J. A. *The Psalms.* 2 vols. New York: Baker and Scribner, 1851.

Alexander, William. *The Witness of the Psalms to Christ and Christianity.* The Bampton Lectures, 1876. 2d ed. New York: Dutton, 1877.

Barth, Christoph. *Introduction to the Psalms.* Translated by R. A. Wilson. New York: Scribner's, 1966.

Binnie, William. *The Psalms: Their History, Teachings and Use.* London: Hodder & Stoughton, 1886.

Braude, William G., trans. *The Midrash on Psalms.* 2 vols. New Haven, Conn.: Yale U., 1959.

Briggs, Charles Augustus, and Briggs, Emilie Grace. *A Critical and Exegetical Commentary on the Book of Psalms.* The International Critical Commentary. 2 vols. New York: Scribner's, 1914.

Brueggeman, Walter. *Praying the Psalms.* Winona, Minn.: St. Mary's Press, 1982.

————. "Psalms and the Life of Faith: A Suggested Typology of Function." *Journal for the Study of the Old Testament* 17 (1980):3-32.

Buttenweiser, Moses. *The Psalms, Chronologically Treated with a New Translation.* Chicago: U. of Chicago, 1938.

Buttrick, George A., ed. *The Interpreter's Bible.* 12 vols. New York: Abingdon, 1955. Vol. 4, *The Book of Psalms,* by W. Stewart McCullough and William R. Taylor.

Calvin, John. *Commentary on the Book of Psalms.* Translated by James Anderson. 5 vols. Grand Rapids: Eerdmans, 1949.

Cheyne, T. K. *The Book of Psalms.* London: Kegan, Paul, Touch, 1888.

Childs, B. S. "Psalm Titles and Midrashic Exegesis." *Journal of Semitic Studies* 16 (1971):137-50.

――――. "Reflections on the Modern Study of the Psalms." In *Magnelia Dei: The Mighty Acts of God*, edited by Frank Moore Cross et al., pp. 377-89. Garden City, N.Y.: Doubleday, 1976.

Cohen, A. *The Psalms*. Soncino Books of the Bible. London: Soncino, 1950.

Craigie, Peter C. *Psalms 1-50*. Word Biblical Commentary. Waco, Tex.: Word, 1983.

Dahood, Mitchell. *Psalms*. 3 vols. The Anchor Bible. Garden City, N.Y.: Doubleday, 1966, 1968, 1970.

Davison, W. T. *The Praises of Israel*. London: Kelly, 1902.

Delitzsch, Franz. *Biblical Commentary on the Psalms*. Translated by Francis Bolton. Clark's Foreign Theological Library. 3 vols. Edinburgh: T. & T. Clark, 1880-81.

Gruenthaner, Michael J. "The Future Life in the Psalms." *Catholic Biblical Quarterly* 2 (1948):57-63.

Gunkel, Hermann. *The Psalms, A Form-Critical Introduction*. Translated by Thomas M. Horner. Philadelphia: Fortress, 1967. This fascicle is from *Die Religion in Geschichte und Gegenwart*, vol. 1. Tubingen: Mohr, 1927.

Gunn, George S. *Singers of Israel: The Book of Psalms*. Bible Guides No. 10. Edited by William Barclay and F. F. Bruce. London: Lutterworth, 1963.

Harmon, Alan. "Paul's Use of the Psalms." *Westminster Journal of Theology* 32 (1969):1-23.

Howard, G. "Hebrews and the Old Testament Quotations." *Novum Testamentum* 10 (1968):208-16.

Johnson, A. R. "The Psalms." In *The Old Testament and Modern Study*, edited by H. H. Rowley, pp. 162-209. Oxford: Clarendon, 1951.

Keet, C. C. *A Study of the Psalms of Ascents: A Critical and Exegetical Commentary upon Psalms 120-134*. London: Mitre, 1969.

Kelley, Page H. "The Speeches of the Three Friends." *Review and Expositor* 68 (1971):479-86.

Kidner, Derek. *Psalms 1-72; Psalms 73-150*. 2 vols. Tyndale Old Testament Commentaries. Downers Grove, Ill.: InterVarsity, 1973, 1975.

Kirkpatrick, A. F. *The Book of Psalms*. The Cambridge Bible for Schools and Colleges. 1902. Reprint. Cambridge: Cambridge U., 1910.

Kissane, Edward J. *The Book of Psalms.* 2 vols. 1953-54. Reprint (2 vols. in 1). Dublin: Browne and Nolan, 1964.

Kistemaker, Simon. *The Psalm Citations in the Epistle to the Hebrews.* Amsterdam: Van Soest N.V., 1961.

Lamb, John Alexander. *The Psalms in Christian Worship.* London: Faith, 1962.

Leslie, Elmer A. *The Psalms, Translated and Interpreted in the Light of Hebrew Life and Worship.* New York: Abingdon, 1949.

Leupold, H. C. *Exposition of the Psalms.* Columbus, Ohio: Wartburg, 1959.

Lewis, C. S. *Reflections on the Psalms.* New York: Harcourt, Brace & World, 1958.

McKeating, H. "Divine Forgiveness in the Psalms." *Scottish Journal of Theology* 18 (1965):69-83.

McKenzie, J. L. "The Imprecations of the Psalter." *American Ecclesiastical Review* 111 (1944):81-96.

Martin, Chalmers. "Imprecations in the Psalms." *Princeton Theological Review* 1 (1903):537-53.

Mowinckel, Sigmund. *The Psalms in Israel's Worship.* Translated by D. R. Ap-Thomas. 2 vols. Nashville: Abingdon, 1962.

———. "Psalms and Wisdom." In *Wisdom in Israel and in the Ancient Near East,* edited by M. Noth and D. Winton Thomas, pp. 205-24. Supplements to *Vetus Testamentum,* vol. 3. Leiden: Brill, 1955.

Murphy, Roland E. "A Consideration of the Classification, 'Wisdom Psalms.'" *Vetus Testamentum* Supplements 9 (1963):156-67.

Oesterley, W. O. E. *The Psalms.* 1939. Reprint. London: Soc. for Promoting Christ. Knowledge, 1953.

Plummer, William S. *Studies in the Book of Psalms.* Philadelphia: Lippincott, 1867.

Ringgren, Helmer. *Faith of the Psalmists.* Philadelphia: Fortress, 1963.

Sanders, J. A. *The Psalms Scroll of Qumran Cave 11.* Discoveries in the Judaean Desert of Jordan. Vol. 4. Oxford: Clarendon, 1965.

Sakenfeld, K. D. *The Meaning of Hesed in the Hebrew Bible: A New Enquiry.* Harvard Semitic Monographs 17. Missoula, Mont.: Scholars Press, 1978.

Smick, Elmer B. "Ugaritic and the Theology of the Psalms." In *New Perspectives on the Old Testament*, edited by J. Barton Payne, pp. 104-16. Waco, Tex.: Word, 1970.

Tate, Marvin. "The Speeches of Elihu." *Review and Expositor* 68 (1971):487-96.

Terrien, Samuel L. "Creation, Culture and Faith in the Psalter." *Theological Education* 2 (1966):116-25.

_____. "The Yahweh Speeches and Job's Responses." *Review and Expositor* 68 (1971):497-510.

Thirtle, James William. *The Titles of the Psalms, Their Nature and Meaning Explained*. London: Frowde, 1904.

Tsevat, Matitiahu. *A Study of the Language of the Biblical Psalms*. Journal of Biblical Literature Monograph, vol. 9. Philadelphia: Soc. of Bib. Lit., 1955.

Vogels, Walter. "The Spiritual Growth of Job: A Psychological Approach." *Biblical Theology Bulletin* 11 (1981):77-80.

Weiser, Artur. *The Psalms, A Commentary*. Translated by Herbert Hartwell. Philadelphia: Westminster, 1962.

Westermann, Claus. *Praise and Lament in the Psalms*. Translated by Keith R. Crim and Richard N. Soulen. Atlanta: John Knox, 1985.

_____. *The Praise of God in the Psalms*. Translated by Keith R. Crim. Richmond: John Knox, 1965.

Wevers, John W. "A Study in the Form Criticism of Individual Complaint Psalms." *Vetus Testamentum* 6 (1956):80-96.

Williams, Donald L. "The Speeches of Job." *Review and Expositor* 68 (1971):469-78.

Wilson, R. D. "The Headings of the Psalms." *Princeton Theological Review* 24 (1926):1-37, 353-95.

Wolverton, W. I. "The Psalmists' Belief in God's Presence." *Canadian Journal of Theology* 9 (1963):82-94.

Yates, Kyle M., Jr. "Understanding the Book of Job." *Review and Expositor* 68 (1971):443-56.

## PROVERBS

Cohen, Abraham. *Proverbs*. Hindhead, Surrey: Soncino, 1945.

Crenshaw, James L. *Old Testament Wisdom, An Introduction*. Atlanta: John Knox, 1981.

Dahood, Mitchell. *Proverbs and Northwest Semitic Philology*. Rome: Pontificum Institutum Biblicum, 1963.

Delitzsch, Franz. *Commentary on the Proverbs of Solomon*. Translated by M. G. Easton. Clark's Foreign Theological Library, 1874-75. Reprint. 2 vols. Grand Rapids: Eerdmans, 1970.

Elmslie, W. A. L. *Studies in Life from Jewish Proverbs*. London: Clarke, 1917.

Erman, Adolf. "Eine ägyptische Quelle der 'Sprüche Salomos.'" *Sitzungsberichte der preussischen Akademie der Wissenschaften* (May 1924) pp. 86-93.

Fleming, James. "Some Aspects of the Religion of Proverbs." *Journal of Biblical Literature* 51 (1932):31-39.

Fritsch, Charles T. "The Book of Proverbs." In vol. 4 of *The Interpreter's Bible*, edited by George A. Buttrick. New York: Abingdon, 1955.

Gressman, H. "Die neugefundene Lehre des Amenemope und die vorexilische Spruchdichtung Esraels." *Zeitschrift für die alttestamentliche Wissenschaft* 42 (1924):272-96.

Herbert, A. S. "The Parables (*mašal*) in the Old Testament." *Scottish Journal of Theology* 7 (1954):180-96.

Kevin, Robert Oliver. *The Wisdom of Amen-em-opet and Its Possible Dependence upon the Hebrew Book of Proverbs*. Philadelphia: n.p., 1931.

Kitchen, K. A. "Proverbs and Wisdom Books of the Ancient Near East: The Factual History of a Literary Form." *The Tyndale Bulletin* 28 (1977):69-114.

Kovacs, Brian. "Is There A Class Ethic in Proverbs?" In *Essays in Old Testament Ethics*, edited by James L. Crenshaw and John T. Willis, pp. 171-89. New York: KTAV, 1974.

McKane, William. *Proverbs, A New Approach*. The Old Testament Library. Philadelphia: Westminster, 1970.

Oesterley, W. O. E. *The Book of Proverbs*. Westminster Commentaries. London: Methuen, 1929.

————. "The Teachings of Amenemope and the Old Testament." *Zeitschrift für die alttestamentliche Wissenschaft* 45 (1927):9-24.

Perowne, T. T. *The Proverbs*. The Cambridge Bible for Schools and Colleges. Cambridge: Cambridge U., 1916.

Ruffle, John. "The Teaching of Amenemope and Its Connection with the Book of Proverbs." *The Tyndale Bulletin* 28 (1977):29-68.

Scott, R. B. Y. *Proverbs, Ecclesiastes*. The Anchor Bible. Garden City, N.Y.: Doubleday, 1965.

————. "Solomon and the Beginnings of Wisdom in Israel." In *Wisdom in Israel and in the Ancient Near East*, edited by M. Noth and D. Winton Thomas, pp. 262-79. Supplements to *Vetus Testamentum*, vol. 3. Leiden: Brill, 1955.

Skehan, Patrick W. "The Seven Columns of Wisdom's House in Proverbs 109." In *Studies in Israelite Poetry and Wisdom*, pp. 9-14. Washington, D.C.: Cath. Bib. Assoc. of Am., 1971.

Stevenson, W. B. "A Mnemonic Use of Numbers in Proverbs and Ben Sira." *Transactions of the Glasgow University Oriental Society* 9 (1938-39):26-38.

Story, Cullen I. K. "The Book of Proverbs and Northwest-Semitic Literature." *Journal of Biblical Literature* 64 (1945):319-37.

Thompson, John Mark. *The Form and Function of Proverbs in Ancient Israel*. Paris: Mouton, 1974.

Toy, Crawford H. *A Critical and Exegetical Commentary on the Book of Proverbs*. The International Critical Commentary. New York: Scribner's, 1904.

Whybray, R. N. *The Book of Proverbs*. The Cambridge Bible Commentary on the New English Bible. Cambridge: Cambridge U., 1972.

————. *Wisdom in Proverbs: The Concept of Wisdom in Proverbs 1-9*. Studies in Biblical Theology, no. 45. Naperville, Ill.: Allenson, 1965.

Williams, R. J. "The Alleged Semitic Original of the Wisdom of Amenemope." *Journal of Egyptian Archaeology* 47 (1961):100-106.

## ECCLESIASTES

Archer, Gleason L., Jr. *A Survey of Old Testament Introduction*. Chicago: Moody, 1946.

Barton, George Aaron. *A Critical and Exegetical Commentary on the Book of Ecclesiastes.* The International Critical Commentary. New York: Scribner's, 1908.

Crenshaw, James L. "The Shadow of Death in Qoheleth." In *Israelite Wisdom: Theological and Literary Essays in Honor of Samuel Terrien,* pp. 205-16. Missoula, Mont.: Scholars Press, 1978.

Delitzsch, Franz. *Commentary on the Song of Songs and Ecclesiastes.* Translated by M. G. Easton. Clark's Foreign Theological Library, 1877. Reprint. Grand Rapids: Eerdmans, 1970.

Dahood, Mitchell. "The Language of Qoheleth." *Catholic Biblical Quarterly* 14 (1952):227-32.

Ginsberg, H. L. "The Structure and Contents of the Book of Koheleth." In *Wisdom in Israel and in the Ancient Near East,* edited by M. Noth and D. Winton Thomas, pp. 138-49. Supplements to Vetus Testamentum, vol. 3. Leiden: Brill, 1955.

––––––. *Studies in Koheleth.* Texts and Studies of the Jewish Theological Seminary of America. Vol. 17. New York: Jewish Theol. Sem. of Am., 1950.

Ginsburg, Christian D. *The Song of Songs and Coheleth.* 1857. Reprint. New York: KTAV, 1970.

Gordis, Robert. *Koheleth—The Man and His World.* Texts and Studies of the Jewish Theological Seminary of America. Vol. 19. 2d ed., enl. New York: Bloch, 1955.

––––––. "Was Koheleth a Phoenician?" *Journal of Biblical Literature* 74 (1955): 103-6.

Hengstenberg, Ernest W. *A Commentary on Ecclesiastes, with Treatises on the Song of Solomon, Job, Isaiah, Sacrifices, etc.* Translated by D. W. Simon. Clark's Foreign Theological Library, 3d ser. Vol. 6. Edinburgh: T. & T. Clark, 1869.

Ibn Ezra, Abraham. *Commentary on Qoheleth.* Introduction and chapter 1 translated by Christian D. Ginsburg. In *The Song of Songs and Coheleth,* pp. 47-54. Reprint. New York: KTAV, 1970.                                          •

Kidner, Derek. *A Time to Mourn, and a Time to Dance.* Downers Grove, Ill.: InterVarsity, 1976.

Knopf, C. S. "The Optimism of Koheleth." *Journal of Biblical Literature* 49 (1930):195-99.

Luther, Martin. *Luther's Works.* Edited by Jaroslav Pelikan. 34 vols. St. Louis: Concordia, 1972. Vol. 15, *Notes on Ecclesiastes, Lectures on the Song of Solomon, Treatise on the Last Words of David.*

_____. *The Table-Talk of Martin Luther.* Translated by William Hazlitt. Philadelphia: United Luth. Pub., n.d.

Muilenberg, James. "A Qoheleth Scroll from Qumran." *Bulletin of the American Society of Oriental Research* 135 (1954):20-28.

Holm-Nielsen, Svend. "The Book of Ecclesiastes and the Interpretation of It in Jewish and Christian Theology." *Annual of the Swedish Theological Institute* 10 (1976):38-96.

Plumptre, E. H. *Ecclesiastes; or, the Preacher.* The Cambridge Bible for Schools and Colleges. Cambridge U., 1907.

Rankin, O. S. "The Book of Ecclesiastes." In vol. 5 of *The Interpreter's Bible,* edited by George A. Buttrick. New York: Abingdon, 1956.

Reichert, Victor E., and Cohen, A. "Ecclesiastes." In *The Five Megilloth.* The Soncino Books of the Bible. London: Soncino, 1952.

Scott, R. B. Y. *Proverbs, Ecclesiastes.* The Anchor Bible. Garden City, N.Y.: Doubleday, 1965.

Walsh, Jerome T. "Despair as a Theological Virtue in the Spirituality of Ecclesiastes." *Biblical Theology Bulletin* 12 (1982):46-49.

Whybray, R. N. *Wisdom in Proverbs.* Studies in Biblical Theology 45. London: SCM, 1965.

Wright, Addison. "The Riddle of the Sphinx: The Structure of the Book of Qoheleth." *Catholic Biblical Quarterly* 30 (1968): 313-34.

Wright, C. H. H. *The Book of Koheleth.* London: Hodder & Stoughton, 1883.

Wright, J. Stafford. "The Interpretation of Ecclesiastes." *Evangelical Quarterly* 18 (1946):18-34.

Zimmerman, Frank. *The Inner World of Qoheleth.* New York: KTAV, 1973.

## SONG OF SONGS

Buchanan, B. "A Dated Seal Impression Connecting Babylonia and Ancient India." *Archaeology* 20 (1967):104-7.

Carr, G. Lloyd. "Is the Song of Songs a 'Sacred Marriage' Drama?" *Journal of the Evangelical Theological Society* 22 (1979):103-14.

————. "The Old Testament Love Songs and Their Use in the New Testament." *Journal of the Evangelical Theological Society* 24 (1981):97-106.

————. *The Song of Solomon.* Leicester, England: InterVarsity, 1984.

Cook, Albert. *The Root of the Thing.* Bloomington, Ind.: Indiana U., 1968.

Delitzsch, Franz. *Commentary on the Song of Songs and Ecclesiastes.* Translated by M. G. Easton. Clark's Foreign Theological Library. 1877. Reprint. Grand Rapids: Eerdmans, 1970.

Fox, Michael V. *The Song of Songs and the Ancient Egyptian Love Songs.* Madison, Wisc.: U. of Wisconsin, 1985.

Freedman, H., and Simon, Maurice, eds. *Midrash Rabbah.* 10 vols. London: Soncino, 1939. Vol. 9, *Esther, Song of Songs.* Translated by Maurice Simon.

Ginsburg, Christian D. *The Song of Songs and Coheleth.* 1857. Reprint, with prolegomenon by Sheldon H. Blank. New York: KTAV, 1970.

Godet, F. "The Interpretation of the Song of Songs." In *Studies in the Old Testament*, 9th ed., pp. 241-90. New York: Hodder & Stoughton, 1894.

Gollancz, Hermann, trans. "The Targum to the Song of Songs." In *Translations from Hebrew and Aramaic.* London: Luzac, 1908.

Gordis, Robert. *The Song of Songs.* New York: The Jewish Theol. Sem. of Am., 1954.

Harper, Andrew. *The Song of Solomon.* The Cambridge Bible for Schools and Colleges. Cambridge: Cambridge U., 1902.

Hengstenberg, Ernest W. "Prolegomena to the Song of Solomon." In *Commentary on Ecclesiastes,* translated by D. W. Simon, pp. 269-305. Edinburgh: T. & T. Clark, 1869.

Henry, Matthew. *Commentary on the Whole Bible.* 6 vols. 1710. Reprint. Vol. 3, "Job to Song of Solomon." New York: Revell, 1935.

Kramer, S. N. "The Sacred Marriage and Solomon's Song of Songs." In *The Sacred Marriage Rite: Aspects of Faith, Myth, and Ritual in Ancient Sumer,* pp. 85-106. Bloomington, Ind.: Indiana U., 1969.

Landsberger, Franz. "Poetic Units Within the Song of Songs." *Journal of Biblical Literature* 62 (1954):203-36.

Luther, Martin. *Luther's Works.* Edited by Jaroslav Pelikan. 34 vols. St. Louis: Concordia, 1972. Vol. 15, *Notes on Ecclesiastes, Lectures on the Song of Solomon, Treatise on the Last Words of David.*

Meek, T. J. "Canticles and the Tammuz Cult." *American Journal of Semitic Languages and Literature* 39 (1922-23):1-14.

_____. "The Song of Songs." In vol. 5 of *The Interpreter's Bible*, edited by George A. Buttrick. New York: Abingdon, 1956.

_____. "The Song of Songs and the Fertility Cult." In *The Song of Songs, A Symposium*, edited by Wilfred H. Schoff, pp. 48-69. Philadelphia: Commercial Museum, 1924. Facsimile ed., Ann Arbor, Mich.: U. Microfilms, 1977.

Murphy, Roland E. "History of Exegesis as a Hermeneutical Tool: The Song of Songs." *Biblical Theology Bulletin* 16 (1986):87-91.

_____. "Interpreting the Song of Songs." *Biblical Theology Bulletin* 9 (1979): 99-105.

_____. "The Song of Songs: Critical Scholarship vis-a-vis Exegetical Traditions." In *Understanding the Word: Essays in Honor of Bernard W. Anderson*, edited by J. T. Butler et al., pp. 63-69. Sheffield: JSOT Supplement 37.

_____. "Towards a Commentary on the Song of Songs." *Catholic Biblical Quarterly* 39 (1977):482-96.

_____. "The Unity of the Song of Songs." *Vetus Testamentum* 29 (1979):436-43.

Pope, Marvin H. *Song of Songs, A New Translation with Introduction and Commentary*. The Anchor Bible. Garden City, N.Y.: Doubleday, 1977.

Rabin, Chaim. "The Song of Songs and Tamil Poetry." *Studies in Religion* 3 (1973): 205-19.

Rowley, H. H. "The Interpretation of the Song of Songs." In *The Servant of the Lord and Other Essays of the Old Testament*, pp. 189-234. London: Lutterworth, 1952.

Segal, M. H. "The Song of Songs." *Vetus Testamentum* 12 (1962):470-90.

Suares, Carlo. *The Song of Songs: The Canonical Song of Solomon Deciphered According to the Original Code of the Qabala*. French ed., 1969. Berkeley: Shambala, 1972.

Waterman, Leroy. "*Dôdî* in the Song of Songs." *American Journal of Semitic Languages and Literature* 35 (1919):101-10.

White, J. B. *A Study of the Language of Love in the Song of Songs and Ancient Egyptian Poetry*. Society of Biblical Literature Dissertation Series. Chico, Calif.: Scholars Press, 1978.

Wiseman, D. J. "Tammuz." In *The New Bible Dictionary,* edited by J. D. Douglas, p. 1238. Grand Rapids: Eerdmans, 1962.

Wetzstein, J. G. "Remarks on the Song by Dr. J. G. Wetzstein." In *Commentary on the Song of Songs and Ecclesiastes,* by Franz Delitzsch, pp. 162-76. Translated by M. G. Easton. Clark's Foreign Theological Library. 1877. Reprint. Grand Rapids: Eerdmans, 1970.

Yamauchi, E. M. "Tammuz and the Bible." *Journal of Biblical Literature* 84 (1965):283-90.

# INDEX OF SUBJECTS AND PERSONS

# INDEX TO HEBREW WORDS

# INDEX OF AUTHORS

# INDEX OF SCRIPTURES

Moody Press, a ministry of the Moody Bible Institute, is designed for education, evangelization, and edification. If we may assist you in knowing more about Christ and the Christian life, please write us without obligation: Moody Press, c/o MLM, Chicago, Illinois 60610.